THE CULTURE OF
LONG TERM CARE

THE CULTURE OF LONG TERM CARE

Nursing Home Ethnography

**Edited by J. NEIL HENDERSON
and MARIA D. VESPERI**

Foreword by Philip B. Stafford

BERGIN & GARVEY
Westport, Connecticut • London

Library of Congress Cataloging-in-Publication Data

The culture of long term care : nursing home ethnography / edited by
    J. Neil Henderson and Maria D. Vesperi ; foreword by Philip B.
    Stafford.
        p.   cm.
    Includes bibliographical references and index.
    ISBN 0–89789–422–7.—ISBN 0–89789–423–5 (pbk.)
      1. Nursing homes—Anthropological aspects. 2. Nursing homes—
Sociological aspects. 3. Nursing home patients—Social conditions.
4. Aging—Social aspects—United States. I. Henderson, J. Neil.
II. Vesperi, Maria D.
RA997.C85 1995
362.1′6—dc20   94–42151

British Library Cataloguing in Publication Data is available.

Library of Congress Catalog Card Number: 94–42151
ISBN: 0–89789–422–7
    0–89789–423–5 (pbk.)

First published in 1995

Printed in the United States of America

∞™

The paper used in this book complies with the
Permanent Paper Standard issued by the National
Information Standards Organization (Z39.48–1984).

10 9 8 7 6 5 4 3 2 1

*Dedicated to those who live in nursing homes,
and those who care for them.*

Contents

Foreword

We wish that nursing homes did not exist. We wish that people could be happy and live forever. We don't, of course, and in our desperate attempts to solve the so-called problem of old age disability, we look to the medical model for answers. We reformulate human existential dilemmas as clinical problems. Perhaps nowhere is this cultural tension between medicine and morals played out more elaborately than in the American nursing home. This book, insofar as it leads us to watch that tension unfold, is a singular contribution not only to the study of gerontology, but to the increasingly urgent task of understanding American culture and its power over human lives.

Nursing home or long term care facility? We equivocate on these labels almost as much as we do about what to call old people. Are the people who live in nursing homes patients or residents? Do we place people in nursing homes or do we admit them? Is it possible for those living in nursing homes to have fun, or are they merely engaging in "therapeutic activities"?

As the ethnographers in this book teach us, euphemisms often point us to where the action is in the culture we strive to understand. Sometimes, euphemisms mask areas of life which are particularly uncomfortable for us to face. As the ethnographers also attest, language games give clues to underlying patterns of power and control. In American culture, medicine has assumed a dominant role in defining and posing solutions to everyday problems. Indeed, the ethnographic description of the use of medical metaphors to describe who lives in nursing homes and what we do for or to them could, perhaps, be the chief anthropological enterprise in this field of research. Yet, good ethnography would not simply describe *one* metaphorical practice, but, rather, seek to describe the variety of metaphorical practices which weave together to form this inter-subjective reality we call culture.

Hence, the reader of this work receives *perspective*. This book is unique in giving voice to the multiple perspectives held by those who live, work, visit, and volunteer in nursing homes. We see nursing homes through the eyes of patients, nurses, nursing assistants, volunteers, family members, housekeepers, and administrators. Moreover, most of the accounts in this collection contain an acknowledgment that the ethnographic agenda itself influences the interpretation of social life. This refers to the understanding that these "native" perspectives are filtered through yet another's perspective, that of the ethnographer—an important tenet in new ethnographies which admit to the role of the reader in textual interpretation.

Once we grant that social situations are characterized by the concatenation of multiple perspectives, we are moving along the path of a new cultural relativism. Readers will find that there are no clear "good guys" or "bad guys" in a nursing home. The actors operate on the basis of their perspectives and while we should be aware of the consequences of perspectives, those who hold them often do so for benevolent, or at least benign, reasons. Overworked, underpaid nursing assistants may snap at patients; we assume that is bad. Do we have the same evaluation of that behavior knowing that a nursing assistant has worked a mandatory double shift? Do we fault the administrator for requiring the double shift in the face of labor shortages and strict regulations regarding staff/patient ratios? Knowing where to stand in judgment when "the system" is at fault is a difficult challenge indeed.

None of us and all of us are at fault. We accede the necessity of these institutions while fervently wishing there were another way. The upshot of this is, of course, great collective guilt. Maria Vesperi, several years ago, made this very point in explaining the intermittent expose's of nursing home abuses as opportunities to assuage our guilt and rid ourselves of the bad apples in the nursing home industry.

Still, ethnography itself does not promote social action. What it does promote, when done well, is understanding, and understanding leads to respect for all the players in this human drama.

This book doesn't offer prescriptions for change. What it does offer is an authentic and contextualized rendering of nursing home life which, if valued, can lead to success in whatever changes might be called for by those who are more influential than we.

Philip B. Stafford
Bloomington Hospital
Bloomington, Indiana
1995

Acknowledgments

J. Neil Henderson would like to acknowledge the support of the Department of Community and Family Health and the Suncoast Gerontology Center of the University of South Florida. He expresses his greatest appreciation to Phillip W. Stumpff. Maria D. Vesperi would like to thank her colleagues at New College for providing an atmosphere where complex ideas can take root and develop. She would also like to thank Andrew Barnes of the *St. Petersburg Times*, whose support enabled her to remain active in the field of anthropology while working outside the university.

The editors would also like to thank Deborah McPherson and Karen Myers for their expertise and good humor in processing the many iterations of this book.

Introduction

Maria D. Vesperi and J. Neil Henderson

In the early 1970s, a handful of anthropology graduate students and recent Ph.D.s began conducting ethnographic research in nursing homes. Most of them felt as if they were inventing the wheel, working in isolation on an uncertain project with no prototype. The literature was scattered and largely non-anthropological. Academic advisors and fellow students were generally skeptical. At best, it was believed that these fieldworkers were headed down one of anthropology's narrower byways, most likely a dead end. At worst, the very nature of the work raised anxieties among colleagues and friends. "Why does a *young* person like you want to study *old* people, in *nursing homes*?" While the emphasis was often *sotto voce*, the implications were loud and clear.

Two decades later, most of these ethnographers have remained in the field of aging research, although not necessarily focused on the institutionalized aged. Since the organization of the Association for Anthropology and Gerontology as an independent professional society in 1978 and the dramatic expansion of the literature on aging that began during that period, they have come to know each other's work, and collaboration has been frequent. Acknowledgment of the anthropologist's role in aging research has increased significantly, and financial support for ethnographic fieldwork has grown accordingly.

Despite concerns to the contrary, the distinctive anthropological method of participant observation has not been overwhelmed by the quantitative approaches that were already firmly established in the multidisciplinary field of gerontology. Instead, a number of gerontologists have come to appreciate both the evocative power of qualitative methods and the critical significance of qualitative data. Jaber Gubrium, the only sociologist whose work appears in this collection, was a pioneer in this area. His discussion of the "new ethnography" speaks directly to the sociologists' use of in-depth interviews to evoke individual perspectives that may otherwise be ignored, particularly in efforts to assess such intangibles as quality of life in a nursing home.

As two of the early researchers, Neil Henderson and Maria Vesperi have watched the development of nursing home ethnography as a distinctive genre. The idea for this book was sparked by two separate but not unrelated events. In 1990, Maria Vesperi was approached by Greenwood Press to review a manuscript about nursing homes by Joel Savishinsky. While reading what was to become his award-winning book, *The Ends of Time: Life and Work in a Nursing Home* (1991), she was struck by the way Savishinsky engaged the work of other anthropologists in situating his own. His ability to draw upon a variety of field studies published in the 1970s and '80s made it clear that this was, indeed, a body of ethnographic literature. Vesperi's paper for this book, "Nursing Home Research Comes of Age," is the product of her reflections about the genre.

At the same time, Neil Henderson was beginning to formulate plans for a symposium on qualitative research in nursing homes for the annual meetings of the Gerontological Society of America. He enlisted Maria Vesperi as a co-organizer because they shared a critical perspective based on similar fieldwork experiences. Both had conducted research in nursing homes as graduate students in the 1970s. Both had since moved on to other areas of aging research but remained actively engaged in theoretical, policy, and fieldwork discussions related to nursing homes. At times, consulting for nursing homes provided another type of fieldwork experience in long term care (Henderson 1994a). Finally, both were among the very small group of anthropologists who had conducted participant-observation research by working full time as nurse aides.

"Qualitative Research in Nursing Homes" was well received at the 1992 Gerontological Society meetings. It was evident that the audience recognized and appreciated the uniquely anthropological approaches common to the presentations. Later versions of several papers delivered at that symposium are included here; the rest were solicited with respect to further developing the theme of how ethnographic methods and anthropological theories can be used to understand nursing homes as discrete field sites, as parts of the long term care system, and as deliberately constructed institutions within a larger cultural frame.

The first section of this book, "Perspective on Ethnographic Methods, Analysis, and Findings," includes articles that highlight the reflexive dimension of ethnographic research. Viewed as a collection, these articles make it clear that anthropologists who study nursing homes share historical, theoretical, and methodological concerns and that these concerns shape the ethnographic texts they produce. These articles also demonstrate how qualitative research designs can clearly distinguish between emic and etic perspectives. There is a stress on eliciting information about nursing home residents as adults with long life histories, and on how such data can be employed to develop models for predicting the likelihood of institutionalization and the degree of life satisfaction achieved by people who enter a nursing home.

Throughout the text, there is a cross-cutting theme related to the penetrance potential of qualitative inquiry. Penetrance potential is the ability of qualitative research methods to pierce the superficial layers of social dynamics and reach layers where the deeper wellsprings of basic cultural elements are found. The book explores the notion that much "on-stage" behavior is articulated with "back-stage" behavior, but often in a circuitous, oppositional, or even unconscious way. The extensive literature on dramaturgical analysis can be used to powerful effect in an institutional setting; the works of Goffman (1961) and Turner (1987, 1974) and the collections edited by Moore and Myerhoff (1977), Schechner and Appel (1990), and Schechner and Schuman (1976) are particularly useful in this context.

An example is provided by Henderson's conscious use of the term "patient" in his paper for this book. Without charting a detailed history of terms used to refer to people in institutions, the general trend has been a shift from "inmates" to "patients" to "residents." Currently, the nursing home industry, staff, policy-makers and those who study nursing home life conventionally use the term "resident." The intent is to indicate concern for the people living in nursing homes and to give voice to a more dignified way of thinking about them.

The problem is that a change of term has little impact on actual care, unless some other aspects of the behavior of institutional caregivers change, too. There is risk to those living in nursing homes that continued use of the term "resident" will not help to humanize their lives. On the contrary, the unthinking adoption of "resident" can function to obscure the reality of chronic patienthood—dependency, stigma, lack of privacy—in nursing homes. A real change in operational models, including a strong focus on psychosocial needs, is required before the spirit of the term "resident" can be accurately reflected in life experience.

Adoption of idealistic terms is equally dangerous for the social scientist. While most contributors to this text adopt the term "resident," their data reflect a highly empirical, emic perspective. Several focus quite specifically on the ethnographer's place in discerning the complex interplay among residents, staff, families, and influences from the wider society.

Overall, this volume demonstrates how qualitative research designs can be used as tools to discover and analyze relevant and otherwise hidden sociocultural data. The result is a dynamic view of nursing home life from the perspective of patients, staff and, in some cases, families. The text as a whole shows that frail, institutionalized elders possess remarkable coping strategies. It also reveals the amount of caring and concern shown by staff members, even when such efforts are subverted by the medicalized context in which they work.

Change in the nature of the American nursing home experience will be related to the degree to which the institution's inner workings are understood. Developing policy from an intellectual distance is an exercise of dubious value. Limiting the nursing home experience to "ADLs," "good appetite," and "up and around" is a form of reduction that has already been shown to dehumanize people. It is hoped that the research presented here will help to provide the details necessary to formulate caregiving improvements that can benefit the institutionalized older person on a direct, daily basis.

Part I

Perspective on Ethnographic Methods, Analysis, and Findings

1

Nursing Home Research Comes of Age: Toward an Ethnological Perspective on Long Term Care

Maria D. Vesperi

It is possible to pass through a nursing home without observing how differently life is actually lived there. Some visitors remember the experience primarily as a sensory assault, with few social details; some focus on a single person or task and develop tunnel vision with regard to the rest. For an ethnographer, however, the experience of stepping outdoors after visiting a nursing home can be as disconcerting as a certain image from one of Alfred Hitchcock's last films, *Frenzy*. Here the viewer is first utterly absorbed as the murderous protagonist attracts his victim; the outside world fades to insignificance as the pair mount the stairs to a drab apartment. Then, just as he overwhelms her, the camera backs slowly from the room, down the stairs, out to the sidewalk and across the street to a busy curbside market. As each threshold is crossed, the cries from the room recede and the lively bustle of a London neighborhood becomes more audible. The moment of true discomfiture occurs as the camera lingers on the mute facade of the apartment building, leaving viewers to ponder the proximity of chaos to the comforting, familiar routines of daily life.

Clifford Geertz (1988) has written revealingly about the effort to establish the authoritative voice that underlies a credible ethnographic text. "Ethnographers need to convince us . . . not merely that they themselves have truly 'been there,' but . . . that had we been there we should have seen what they saw, felt what they felt, concluded what they concluded" (1988:16). As Geertz and others have also noted, there is a strong relationship between credibility and distance from the ethnographic subject. The closer the setting, the less privileged an ethnographer's perspective will be. Readers who have "been there" have their own opinions; they are not so easily moved to regard the ethnographer's viewpoint as more credible than their own.

Researchers who have never conducted fieldwork in a nursing home might assume such a setting to be among the most pedestrian and familiar, hence among the least credible. As anthropologists who frequent them realize, however, nursing homes are among the most unique field sites because they combine the traditional challenges of cultural discovery and description with inescapable questions about the meaning of "otherness." Anthropologists who use nursing home residents as their informants cannot work around the perplexing issues of identity, perception, and experience that confront all fieldworkers. Philosophical rambling about who informants really are cannot be confined to the sections of ethnographies that are clearly reserved for reflexive exercise.

In "Hermes' Dilemma: The Masking of Subversion in Ethnographic Description," Crapanzano (1986) describes two paradoxes inherent in the task of creating an ethnography. The first is that all such presentations are, by nature, provisional interpretations that cannot lead to definitive renderings of the way things are. Further, he suggests, "It is even possible that the more general theories the ethnologist generates from ethnography are only refractions, distorted repetitions in another register, of the provisional interpretations that support the presentation of data" (1986:52).

I would agree with Crapanzano that many anthropologists pay lip service to this paradox but are generally resistant to acknowledging its implications. However, I will argue here that the corpus of ethnographic studies about nursing homes generated by anthropologists since the 1970s is notably candid with regard to both the provisional nature of its interpretations and the synchronic, even fleeting nature of the data upon which they are based. I also believe that the ability to take this paradox into account lends particular credence to an emerging ethnological effort in nursing home research.

The second paradox, stating the matter as plainly as possible, stems from the need to present otherness without transforming it into sameness. This paradox is central to discussion of the ethnography as text; it has been explored in slightly different language by a variety of theorists, including Clifford 1983, 1986; Marcus 1986; Geertz 1988; Lederman 1990; Bruner 1993. The ethnographer, as Crapanzano states the issue, " . . . must render the foreign familiar and preserve its very foreignness at one and the same time. The translator accomplishes this through style, the ethnographer through the coupling of a representation that asserts the foreign and an interpretation that makes it all familiar" (1986:52). Indeed, some anthropologists have come to rely so heavily on the touchstones of familiar interpretive models when holding a text up for critical inspection that the data itself begins to pale in significance.

In nursing home research, however, the task of rendering the foreign familiar is turned on its head. While the setting is indeed quite foreign, the most disconcerting aspect of nursing home informants themselves is their familiarity. [See Powers, this volume, for the contrasting perspective of an anthropologist who also has formal medical training.] Even within a single cultural or subcultural group, the populations of most total institutions are set apart as "other" by acts, influences, or events that need not touch the fieldworker, and which he or she may not fully comprehend. The nursing home is a total institution, but its population is not set apart by a crime committed, a selective disease, or a catastrophic injury.

A clear example of this distinction can be found in John Edgar Wideman's book, *Brothers and Keepers* (1985). Here Wideman, a professor of literature, sets out to trace the course of his life and that of his brother, Robby, who is serving a lengthy prison sentence for murder. The convergences are compelling, yet Wideman realizes that his brother's imprisonment, and to some extent the actions that led to his incarceration, constitute a gap that can never fully be bridged. In fact, visiting Robby and writing about him serve to reinforce rather than diminish the distance between them:

Robby was still a prisoner. . . . The book, whether it flopped or became a best-seller, would belong to the world beyond the prison walls. Ironically, it would validate the power of the walls, confirm the distance between what transpired inside and outside. Robby's story would be "out there," but he'd still be locked up. Despite my attempts to identify with my brother, to reach him and share his troubles, the fact was I remained on the outside (1985:199–200).

After so much tortured debate over what it means to identify with the other, some would abandon the effort as naive or, worse, as simply a western conceit. Others would be more likely to agree with Elliot Liebow, who confronted this issue quite directly in the preface to his study of homeless women, *Tell Them Who I Am*. "I do not mean that a man with a home and a family can see and feel the world as homeless women see and feel it," Liebow writes. "I do mean, however, that it is reasonable and useful to try to do so. Trying to put oneself in the place of the other lies at the heart of the social contract and of social life itself" (1993:xv).

Yet, differences remain. While thoughts of "there but for fortune" might well cross the ethnographer's mind, fate, inevitability, and the future are not necessarily at issue when studying prisoners, refugees and disaster victims, or the homeless. Were it otherwise, few people would find the strength to pursue such painful subjects, and few would want to read about them. Sue Estroff came close to this level of identification in her work with deinstitutionalized psychiatric clients, and she candidly acknowledges the dangers involved. In *Making It Crazy*, she cautions that "the longer one

attempts to enter the clients' world without constant, active, outside reference points, the fuzzier becomes the distinction between crazy and uncrazy,
self and other. The more time one spends amid confusion, fear, anxiety, and
unhappiness, the more it is highlighted in oneself" (1981:xvi).

In a nursing home, fate and the future are dominant, unavoidable
questions. In fact, the whole subject of aging as viewed from an anthropological perspective is highly unusual in this regard. Within the contemporary United States, many of the cultural constructions used to identify old
age deflect recognition of the shared inevitability of the aging process
(Vesperi 1985, 1994). Participant-observation researchers cannot avoid this
confrontation; instead, most embrace it fully.

An example can be found in the writings of Barbara Myerhoff, who
worked closely with a Huichol shaman-priest and his community in north-
ern Mexico and, later, with elderly Jewish retirees in Venice, California.
Myerhoff's book on Huichol cosmology, *Peyote Hunt* (1974), is an outstanding work that exemplifies the rich potential of the participant-observation
method. Her book about aging, however, is a masterpiece. "I would never
really be a Huichol Indian," Myerhoff wrote in *Number Our Days* (1978).
"But I would be a little old Jewish lady one day; thus, it was essential for
me to learn what that condition was like, in all its particulars. . . . I consider
myself very fortunate in having had, through this work, an opportunity to
anticipate, rehearse, and contemplate my own future" (1978:19).

Students are invariably moved by this book, and equally sobered to learn
that Myerhoff died at age 48. As the book's epigraph advises, *Teach us to
number our days.* Yet, while she was not to experience old age in a direct,
physical way, she did achieve a phenomenological awareness of informants' lives and, more extraordinary, she managed to communicate this in
her writing.

Close attention to the ontology of old age has consistently occupied
anthropologists who study this population, giving the anthropology of
aging a distinctive status within the field of gerontological research and
analysis. Whether or not old age is "experienced from without," as de
Beauvoir suggested (1972), an anthropological perspective would seem
particularly well-suited to the subject.

SETTING THE STAGE FOR NURSING HOME RESEARCH

Nursing homes in the United States are essentially post–World War II
phenomena; the economic and social reasons for their development are not
the direct subject of this chapter. It is important to note, however, that Social
Security, Medicare, and Medicaid have not just enabled but actually promoted the medicalization of old age. Viewed as key achievements in
national social welfare policy, these programs rest on underlying, rarely
explicit cultural constructions about the aging person. Following Piven and

Cloward (1993) in their discussion of the functions of public welfare, I would suggest that the particulars of large-scale legislation regarding the aged have less to do with what old people require to sustain their lives than with what society requires to manage them, both physically and socially. The frail elderly, like the marginally employed, are potentially disruptive. Acknowledging their needs as full citizens on an individual basis would require a fundamental shift in the direction of social life, housing patterns, employment, and the allocation of resources within the United States. Those who would question this analogy should consider that a majority of nursing home residents are supported by Medicaid, including a majority of those who enter such facilities on a private pay basis. Nursing homes, like so many programs aimed primarily at the poor and disenfranchised, meet survival needs in a way that society can comfortably accommodate, but no more.

Given the direct links between social welfare policy and the establishment of the nursing home as an alternative but widely accepted social institution, it is impossible to consider nursing home residents as research informants apart from the beliefs about old age that generate their living environment. Again, as with other aspects of aging research within one's own culture, anthropological fieldworkers are inevitably drawn to consider sameness more than otherness. Had the nursing home been widely available for study prior to the 1960s, this inevitability would likely have precluded it as a fieldwork site. The fact that contemporary anthropologists do find this a reasonable setting is largely a product of changes in the discipline of anthropology, and in the larger world system.

Contemporary anthropologists have grown accustomed to looking at themselves and their research subjects as products of very specific historical and ideological contexts. "Situated" and "embedded" are two key terms in such discussions. These words have come to connote a passive, even helpless, experience of the world, the ramifications of which are inevitably made painfully clear, but only through critical hindsight. Further, the periods under review have grown shorter in recent decades, causing ethnographers to peer nervously over their shoulders at every turn. While the much-excoriated colonial past could be kept at a comfortable if cautionary distance for most anthropologists who came of age in the 1960s, current students of anthropology find themselves questioning the shelf-life of even the most recent ideas. The margins of theoretical and political error have been radically foreshortened, to the point where would-be ethnographers are seriously daunted by books such as the Clifford and Marcus collection, *Writing Culture* (1986). As Geertz summarizes the issue, "anthropologists have had added to their 'Is it decent?' worry . . . an 'Is it possible?' one . . . with which they are even less well prepared to deal" (1988:135).

Amid the early stirrings of such contemporary worries, it is no accident that the 1970s was the decade when significant numbers of anthropology students began to undertake primary fieldwork within the United States. Some embraced new theories (Ortner 1994:383), while others employed the same methodological and theoretical models in this research that had illuminated their predecessors' understanding of other cultures. At issue in such efforts to reconfigure subject and theory was a certain hope, unarticulated at the time. In this brief, naive period before critiques of the very foundations of established thought, method, and style of presentation came into wide currency, it seemed to some that the problems of hegemony just emerging as identified sticking points (Eley 1994:321; Ortner 1994:392–93) could be circumvented by a more politically self-conscious choice of field site.

For that reason, or something like it, almost all of the students who entered my graduate school class in 1973 soon decided to conduct their early fieldwork within the United States. Trained in symbolic theory and continental philosophy, only one among us was drawn to cross-cultural research at the doctoral level. The rest studied snake handlers, Appalachian kinship, clowns, migrant construction workers and, in my case, old people in nursing homes and later in low-income, urban settings.

ASSESSING NURSING HOME ETHNOGRAPHY

There are marked differences in focus and scale between contemporary ethnographic works and the ethnographies produced by earlier generations of anthropologists. According to Johnson and Johnson:

Prior to 1960 a significant number of ethnographies were broad-ranging and holistic in their descriptions, with remarkably similar tables of contents, listing geography, history, language, physical type, economy, social organization, politics, religion and world view, and, often, a chapter on recent cultural change. Now, virtually the only form in which such comprehensive accounts are still published is the abbreviated case study for teaching purposes. The typical new-style ethnography may have a "setting" chapter in which the ethnography of the community is summarized in a few pages, but the remainder of the work is devoted to some focal issue. . . . (1990:173).

Most nursing home studies fit this contemporary description quite closely. Even researchers who explore the setting as a total institutional "community" do not make the mistake of presenting it as a self-contained world or a cultural whole. They recognize that the nursing home is not a microcosm of aging in the larger world, an effort to replicate social identity on a tiny scale. It is a product of radical differentiation within a social system, as significant as the shift from home apprenticeship to public schooling and as dependent on the larger society for its character, its content, and its very existence. The nursing home, like the public classroom, cannot be considered apart from the social and economic context that furnishes and animates it.

As Marcus (1986) and others have noted, negotiating and explicating the relationship with a larger system is a complex task that has traditionally been sidestepped. Until recently, Marcus states, "The descriptive space of ethnographies itself has not seemed an appropriate context for working through conceptual problems of this larger order. The world of larger systems and events has thus often been seen as externally impinging on and bounding little worlds, but not as integral to them" (1986:166).

Aware from the outset that their fieldwork settings are deliberate constructions of a larger system, nursing home ethnographers recognize that their "descriptive space" cannot exclude elements of that system's social, political, and economic processes. Not only is the interpretation of meaning in a nursing home self-consciously critical; the description of structure and function is critically grounded as well. We cannot say, for instance, that family care conferences are designed to improve communication between relatives and staff without acknowledging the presence of competing, contested values. While the ethnographer tries not to take sides in such struggles, he or she cannot observe and interpret what takes place without reference to evaluative subsets regarding kinship, the resident's "best interest," and the institution as a workplace.

Speaking to the relationship between literary theories and the texts they purport to interpret, Henry Louis Gates advises that "the concern of the Third World critic should properly be to understand the ideological subtext that any critical theory reflects and embodies and the relation this subtext bears to the production of meaning. No critical theory . . . escapes the specificity of value and ideology, no matter how mediated it may be" (1994:264–265). Increasingly, anthropologists have come to heed the same caution. In the context of nursing home research, they are working with multiple ideological subtexts. These range beyond identified anthropological theories, with their obvious impact on the interpretation of meaning, to include multidisciplinary perspectives and closely examined but unabashed beliefs about the value of the aged person in American society.

Can this be the makings of reliable ethnography? Following James Clifford (1983), Roger Sanjek (1990) has provided a useful set of criteria for considering the validity of ethnographic reports. He first clears up a common confusion between reliability and validity, linking the first with laboratory science and the second with anthropological field science. "Reliability is extremely important in laboratory work. . . . We want to be certain that other investigators performing the same experiment or test get the same results" (1990:394). In contrast, "In ethnography, 'reliability' verges on affectation. We cannot expect and do not hope that another investigator will repeat the fieldwork and confirm the results before they are published" (1990:394).

Instead, ethnography's strong suit is validity, Sanjek asserts. Quoting Pelto and Pelto (1978:33), he defines validity as "the degree to which scientific observations actually measure or record what they purport to measure" (1990:395). Identifying ethnography as "a potentially validity-rich method," he develops three criteria for evaluating individual texts. One measure is the degree to which the ethnographer makes theoretical decisions and other influences explicit to the reader. Another concerns the network of informants, the "ethnographer's path." Sanjek values ethnographic texts that reveal such networks, providing the reader with a multidimensional view of how the fieldwork was actually conducted by an individual person moving in time and space among other individuals. He notes, however, that there is a distinction between this element of an ethnographic text and a journal; his example of the latter is Paul Rabinow's 1977 account, *Reflections on Fieldwork in Morocco*. Sanjek's third measure is the degree to which the anthropologist makes the relationship between the finished ethnography and the fieldnotes clear (Sanjek 1990:395–404).

Influences, Theoretical and Otherwise

Already self-conscious about their choice of fieldsite, anthropologists who study nursing homes are rarely bashful about Sanjek's first measure, the degree to which their work reveals their preconceptions and concerns about these facilities as social institutions [see Gubrium, this volume]. For instance, my own interest in the subject was originally sparked by a series of newspaper articles about Bernard Bergman, a New York nursing home owner who was widely criticized for neglecting residents. Setting out in the summer of 1974 to do participant-observation research, I visited one facility after another, explaining that I would like to conduct a study for my master's thesis while working full-time as a nurse aide. I was turned down flat by eight administrators before finding two who accepted my proposal; the experience certainly confirmed my preconception that nursing homes had something to hide.

The resulting thesis was a comparative study of symbolic interactions between staff and residents at a traditional nursing home and at a nursing facility attached to a denominational "life care" complex, although that term was not in use at the time. As a text, my work upset people. My advisor, who treated most fieldwork revelations with equanimity, remarked that mine was the only thesis he ever had to read with a drink in his hand. Another faculty member confided that reading my work had forced an emotional rethinking of whether or not to place a parent in a nursing home.

An article I extracted from the section about the traditional nursing home and published under the title "The Reluctant Consumer: Nursing Home Residents in the Post-Bergman Era" continues to disturb readers (Vesperi 1987). Students, in particular, ask whether "conditions" in nursing homes have changed much since the 1970s, and if I believe that the underlying issues attached to being old and institutionalized have become less painful. Thinking through my respective answers, "yes" and "no," I have considered the relationship between the individual, synchronic studies of nursing homes conducted during this period and the significant policy changes that have brought about markedly improved physical conditions for residents and career status improvements for nursing home personnel. Taken as a whole, the literature provides a comparative record of these changes. It is easier to trace change in the nursing home than in many other ethnographic contexts because of the way the data is presented and analyzed.

Returning for a moment to Crapanzano's discussion of how heavily most ethnographers are invested in the definitive nature of their findings about other cultures, it is clear that nursing home ethnography poses a different challenge, and a different set of temptations. Nursing home culture is not "original," or "authentic"; the researcher can have nothing invested in "discovering" or preserving it. Unlike the ethnographer who stakes a claim to the beliefs and practices of "his" village, anthropologists working in American nursing homes might well prefer *not* to lay claim to what they find. There is no choice, however; as participants in the same cultural system, they are obliged to "own"—or at least own up to—a shared set of underlying constructions.

The works that anthropologists often cite as inspiration for nursing home research incorporate certain features of a familiar belief system, one that is best summed up in Jules Henry's 1963 title, *Culture Against Man*. The implication, also reflected directly in more recent titles, such as Sharon Kaufman's *The Ageless Self* (1986), is that late adult life is marked by efforts to defend and maintain a core identity in the face of repeated challenges. This idea of a core self that matures and then remains essentially fixed—and by implication, defendable—is admittedly an ethnocentric concept. Its implications for field research have increasingly come under scrutiny, particularly with regard to the ethnographer's concept of a "gendered" self. At the end of a brief but generally positive commentary on *Self, Sex and Gender*, a 1986 collection about field research edited by Tony Whitehead and Mary Ellen Conaway, Diane Bell notes critically that "the preoccupation is with a 'self' that reflects the American training of the contributors" (Bell, 1993:10). This endemic "preoccupation" cannot go unremarked; it has profound implications for all types of ethnographic encounters.

In *Aging and Its Discontents*, another title that speaks directly to this issue, Kathleen Woodward explores Freud's assumptions about the self in old age and their impact on psychoanalytic theory and on representations of aging in 20th century Western literature. She notes that "Freud found aging more threatening than death itself. The emphasis on death, which we commonly find represented as an *event*, conceals a denial of aging, a *process* that usually stretches out over many years" (1991:38). Woodward finds significance in the fact that psychoanalytic theory is event-oriented, and that the events Freud marked as critical for identity formation are concentrated in the early years of life. Further in the same paragraph, she states: "In old age, in contrast, *nothing dramatic happens* for a long period of time, although of course we will commonly speak of a person as having aged suddenly or overnight."

I would argue that such assumptions are central to how residents of the United States explain and legitimize the existence of nursing homes. With the exception of life care facilities, which are specifically designed to bridge this transition, the move to a nursing home is a brutally abrupt event. It is accepted, or at least not strenuously challenged, because it is perceived as the logical consequence of a trauma in the life of the individual. Something irreversible has "happened," be it a stroke or fall or, in the case of persons with dementia, a last-straw escalation of stressful behaviors. In some cases, the event is external; a vital caregiver might die, or government budget cuts might result in the loss of community-based services for a frail older person.

Whatever the precipitating circumstances, it is clear that society antici-pates no further development of the self among those aged people for whom the average nursing home environment is designed. The ethnogra-pher, who cannot avoid recognition of eager, familiar "selves" among nursing home informants, experiences a painful dissonance. Literature that assumes the existence of a core identity reinforces the ethnographer's perspective, particularly with regard to withdrawn residents who are treated, quite literally, "as if they weren't there."

A different but not necessarily contradictory model draws on Erikson's life cycle approach. While this model suggests that personality continues to evolve throughout the life course, it shares the notion that the ontological awareness of aging is a process that interacts with external cultural con-structions in ways that can be judged more or less satisfactory for each individual.

The insistent focus on the self among many anthropologists who study nursing homes can be understood in this context. The challenges to adult identity that invite systematic analysis by those who conduct field research among the aged in community settings become the core issues for re-searchers in nursing homes. In the world at large, older people face issues of engagement with the full range of social institutions. Suitably, ethno-graphic descriptions of their lives tend to focus on family life, cultural conceptions of wellness and disease, economic engagement, mobility within a bounded environment (Rowles 1978; Rubinstein, Kilbride, and Nagy 1992), and the status bargaining chips of specialized knowledge. Fieldwork within planned communities for the well elderly mirrors these concerns through comparisons of new social institutions with the ones that individuals have left behind. The measure of satisfaction among informants in such settings is often an assessment of how well the elements of their new environment substitute for familiar structures in the wider society. Similarly, significant innovations are often gauged by their effectiveness in assisting the older person to explore or develop aspects of the self that were de-emphasized during the working, child-bearing years.

By their very presence in an institutional setting, nursing home residents have transcended such concerns. For some, of course, engagement with family continues to be significant. Beyond their role as emotional links to the world beyond the institution, kin can have a direct, if debated, impact on the quality of life within the nursing home [see Foner, this volume]. However, even those who enjoy the most regular visits from kin cannot, with rare exception, expect to live with them again. In subtle ways, the act of receiving visitors reinforces the separation from them in daily life. Drawing on Henri Bergson's (1911) understanding of the difference between time and duration, we might say that *visits* to an institution exist in bounded, measurable units, while *life* in the institution is an enduring experience that cannot be adequately described in the same terms.

Issues of wellness and disease, subsistence activities, mobility, and status knowledge are likewise moot with regard to the larger society. Although wellness is defined by sets of culturally and personally relative criteria, nursing home residents share the label "unwell." Economically, long term residence in a nursing home is also a powerful leveler. While elders of means can conserve their achievements for the next generation, a majority of those who enter nursing homes eventually exhaust their resources and must turn to welfare, as discussed above. By every standard of traditional engagement in social and economic life, nursing home residents have accepted or been forced to accept the belief that they are no longer viable as functioning adults [see Groger, this volume].

Again, it becomes obvious why locating and measuring the sense of self are so central to nursing home research. It is a fairly safe bet that May Sarton's *As We Are Now* (1973) and Carobeth Laird's *Limbo: A Memoir about Life in a Nursing Home by a Survivor* (1979) can be found on the shelf of almost any anthropologist who has seriously considered a nursing home as a site for fieldwork. While Sarton is a novelist and Laird is an anthropologist relating an autobiographical experience, these two powerful narratives resonate with the same cultural themes. Both recount, in journal form, a series of assaults on the sense of self and the individual's efforts to defend identity by literally capturing it on paper. An example from Sarton is revealing:

I am forcing myself to get everything clear in my mind by writing it down so I know where I am at. There is no reality now except that I can sustain inside me. My memory is failing. I have to hang on to every scrap of information I have to keep my sanity, and it is for that purpose that I am keeping a journal.

By the time I finish it I shall be dead. I want to be ready, to have gathered everything together and sorted it out, as if I were preparing for a great final journey.

I intend to make myself whole here in this Hell. It is the thing that is set before me to do. So, in a way, this path inward and back into the past is like a map, the map of my world. If I can draw it accurately, I shall know where I am (1973:4).

Asylums (1961), Erving Goffman's landmark study of total institutions, is another powerful early influence on those who study nursing homes. Of particular relevance to this discussion is his emphasis on the self as seen in conflict with the demands of the institution. Phrases such as "mortification of the self," "curtailment of the self," and "territories of the self" are used to describe the process of incorporation into institutional life. Goffman's discussion of the self as possessing a "territory" that is susceptible to physical as well as psychic violation resonates not only with the realities of life in a nursing home, but also with the larger, disputed question of the relationship between the aged self and the aged body.

Woodward puts it succinctly: "We say that our real selves—that is, our youthful selves—are hidden inside our bodies. Our bodies are old, we are not. Old age is thus understood as a state in which the body is in opposition to the self" (1991:62).

The Path Not Taken

Sanjek states that "readers would be in a much better position to assess ethnographic validity if they had a road map of the ethnographer's path" (1990:399). Making the relationship between ethnographer and informant explicit has been, and remains, an outstanding feature of book-length nursing home ethnographies and of many articles as well. This is not unique to the genre, however; anthropological fieldwork conducted in other formal institutional settings is equally explicit. The clarity of the ethnographer's path varies from text to text in community-based studies, partly because it is often classed as an issue of method, not content. In contrast, ethnographies based on anthropological research in institutions are at least partially "about" informants' positions within clearly defined organizational hierarchies.

In an article entitled "Gender Bias and Sex Bias: Removing Our Blinders in the Field" (1986:275–288), Elizabeth Faithorn discusses the anthropologist's ability to emphasize and de-emphasize a variety of roles in a constant play between one's own and the host culture's assumptions about sex, gender, and kinship. Working in a New Guinea Highlands village, Faithorn found that she could "be Ayalunta," her fictive kin name, when it suited her. At other times she was "more comfortable being Lisa," an outsider, particularly when she felt herself reacting against perceived restrictions on female behavior. Faithorn's path was marked by ongoing shifts and discoveries; it led variously among several groups of informants, depending in part on which role was emphasized.

In his work with heroin addicts, Michael Agar (1980) found that his path among informants was heavily influenced by their perceptions of the institutions that supported his research. In San Francisco, where he was affiliated with a trusted grass roots organization, "This is Mike. He's working on something with the clinic," was enough of an introduction to set potential informants at ease (1980:28). In New York City, where he worked for a government agency that addicts disliked and distrusted, "Often, people would discover that they had other things to do, and I would be left talking to a mailbox" (1980:56). Emphasizing his role as an independent social scientist, while remaining honest about who paid his bills, provided the balance he needed to conduct effective street-level fieldwork.

Free-ranging participant observers are much less common in full institutional settings. In most cases, the anthropologist gains entré as a volunteer, an academic researcher with an administratively sanctioned agenda or, occasionally, as a staff member. Such roles are not transmutable. For instance, a staff member cannot fall back on an outsider role when ordered to perform a stressful task. In turn, volunteers cannot directly experience the physical and emotional challenges of staff routine, nor can they easily draw the line when nursing home residents ask for personal favors or intervention with staff and family [see Henderson, Savishinsky, this volume]. Cast as high status, potentially powerful outsiders, academic researchers may have difficulty gaining staff trust [see Mason, McLean, this volume]. In each case, the ethnographer's place in the institutional hierarchy structure is a primary, well-identified influence on the direction of his or her path among informants.

Fieldnotes: An Open Book?

How, when, and where to take notes are often among the ethnographer's most strategic field decisions. At best, the practice must be explained and justified to informants; at worst, note taking can feel secretive, mystical, or even unethical. In a nursing home, however, taking notes is an acceptable—even predictable—activity. Residents know that nurses' notes and care plans provide a working script for daily life in the facility. While such documents are explicitly *not* shared with residents and family visitors, notes are developed, revised, and openly consulted in their presence.

The nursing home ethnographer benefits from this established practice in at least three ways. The most obvious advantage is that most residents have already accepted the tradition of note taking, or at least become resigned to it. If note taking behavior was limited to staff members with clipboards, ethnographers who do not seek to be identified with staff might have trouble convincing residents of their free-lance status. However, in addition to the familiar image of the nurse with a clipboard, residents can observe note taking behavior among volunteers, patient-rights advocates, and their own relatives and visitors.

A second, less obvious benefit is that the ethnographer's note taking behavior is often in accord with residents' desires. The opportunity to articulate a viewpoint or memory and fix it in tangible, permanent form is rarely taken for granted by people who live in nursing homes. For those with vision or manual dexterity problems, or who can no longer trust their recall and their ability to keep track of time, "writing it down" or recording a statement on audio tape can be deeply satisfying. For some, speaking to an ethnographer is truly an act of the imagination, like placing a note in a bottle and setting it afloat. Only once have I met a nursing home resident who expected to read the book or article for which she was interviewed. For most, it is enough to entertain the idea that a bit of themselves might be carried beyond the nursing home walls, to rejoin the conversation taking place in the outside world.

Finally, the direct impact of nurses' notes on residents' lives underscores the power inherent in taking notes and the responsibility to "get things right." Significant differences in perspective and interpretation between a fieldworker and the staff, as evidenced by contrasts in how they record the same event, are continually apparent to anthropologists working in this setting. Of course, these differences are also evident to staff members, who may be anxious about fieldworkers' note taking as a challenge to their authority or because they regard the anthropologist as a potential spy [see Henderson, Mason, McLean and Perkinson, this volume].

TOWARD AN ETHNOLOGICAL PERSPECTIVE

In his chapter for this book, "Perspective and Story in Nursing Home Ethnography," Jaber Gubrium argues for methodological approaches that explore the multiple perspectives and evaluations which various members of a nursing home population might bring to the same setting. Further, he calls for an approach to policy making that reflects the needs of individuals.

Gubrium echoes the danger identified by Crapanzano in "Hermes' Dilemma," namely, that ethnographers are wont to preface their elaborately interpreted descriptions with *the* rather than *a*. "In traditional ethnography the ethnographer's encounter with the people he has studied is rarely described. Often . . . even the activity that is described and interpreted—a cockfight, a carnival, a test of prowess, or, for that matter, the weaving of a basket or the preparation of a meal—is not presented in its particularity as a single, and in some ways unique, performance. We are usually given a general picture" (1986:75).

In her chapter on the dynamics between residents' families and staff, Nancy Foner observes that in-depth fieldwork can capture the complexities of daily life in nursing homes. Indeed, for most nursing home residents, daily life is all there is. Stepping from their accustomed routine into a nursing home, and bringing with them a linear, future-oriented concept of time, most visitors too readily equate a cyclical pattern of events with rote predictability. A researcher who set out to describe *the* routine, *the* mealtime ritual, or *the* resident-staff relationship would generate a static picture, not unlike early anthropologists' descriptions of life in non-western societies— and for much the same reasons.

In contrast, the ethnographic literature on nursing homes reveals that uncertainty and change are inherent elements of the necessarily intimate and personalized interactions that take place between staff and residents, and among residents themselves. The ethnographies that best reflect this are insistently synchronic, focused on direct interactions between closely described individuals. "Probably one must write a book about his society in order to really understand what change is, in society and in one's self," Jules Henry wrote in his preface to *Culture Against Man* (1963:vii). More than three decades have passed since Henry turned an anthropologist's eye on three American nursing homes. Viewed as aggregate and as informed by overtly identified theories and field methods, the literature that has emerged since that time provides a unique set of data for furthering our understanding of cultural change.

2

Perspective and Story in Nursing Home Ethnography

Jaber F. Gubrium

Twenty years ago, I completed fieldwork that led to the publication of *Living and Dying at Murray Manor*, an ethnography of a nursing home (Gubrium 1975). It was my first research foray into the many-versioned world of everyday life. As in the classic Japanese film *Rashomon*, in this world the real is filtered through participants' perspectives. I have since come to think of this world as "storied," that is, articulated and animated through its storytellers' diverse narratives, leading to the view that the nursing home experience is something subjectively meaningful, told about and conditioned by processes and circumstances of telling. I take this opportunity to trace this line of thinking, from its origins in the Murray Manor fieldwork to its most recent manifestation in research on the narrative linkages and horizons of meaning for the quality of care in nursing homes.

STORY AND NEW ETHNOGRAPHY

That everyday life is versioned and articulated through participants' stories reflects an important turn in the descriptive aims of ethnography. In both anthropology and sociology, ethnography was once viewed as the systematic observation of a social setting, the discovery of patterns of meaning and interaction, and the description of a related way of life. Fieldwork combined looking, listening, asking questions, taking notes, and managing social relations in a wide variety of settings, including nonliterate societies, urban communities, formal organizations, gangs, and social movements (Bogdan and Taylor 1975; Filstead 1970; Glaser and Strauss 1967; McCall and Simmons 1969; Schwartz and Jacobs 1979; Shaffir, Stebbins, and Turowetz 1980; Spradley 1979; Wax 1971). Writing was a matter of putting on record the details of the setting studied, as true to life as possible. There was little sense that participants within a setting might have authoritative stories of their own to tell, or that participants' accounts and descriptions constituted, rather than just reflected, the realities of their worlds. There was relatively minor interest in how participants' stories accorded with each other or what discrepancies among them might mean. Questions concerning the relationship between participants' stories and the ethnographer's account were not seriously considered.

Ethnography has come a long way. We no longer limit our analytic concerns to issues dealing with the objective or naturalistic representation of social life. Indeed, much of the so-called "new ethnography" centers on the question of how to deal with participants' own representations or versions of their worlds, objectivity being only one of several related issues (Atkinson 1990; Clifford and Marcus 1986; Clough 1992; Geertz 1988; Marcus and Fischer 1986; Spencer 1989; Strathern 1987; Van Maanen 1988). Where the older ethnography cast its subjects as mere components of social worlds, new ethnography treats them as active participants who construct their realities through talk and interaction, stories, and narrative (see, e.g., Burgos-Debray 1984). What is "new" about this is the sense that participants are themselves ethnographers in practice—storytellers of their own worlds.

Methodologically, the emphasis now is as much on documenting the interpretive practices through which the realities of social settings are assembled as on observing and describing their social life in detail (Emerson 1983; Heritage 1984; Holstein and Gubrium 1994b; Silverman 1993). Recent empirical studies have shown how the taken-for-granted world of everyday life is interactionally accomplished. The studies demonstrate how realities such as family (Gubrium 1988; Gubrium and Holstein 1990, 1992; Holstein and Gubrium 1994a), community (Hazan 1990), and mental illness (Holstein 1993) are constructed through the social organization of talk and telling.

New ethnography can shed light on the social construction of individual lives, such as those of nursing home residents. My collaborators and I have referred to this as *biographical work* to underscore participants' activeness in the process, without overemphasizing it (Gubrium, Holstein, and Buckholdt 1994). Whether it is the personal past, the present quality of life, the future, or a combination of these, participants work at characterizing their lives in relation to the interpretive horizons of social settings. For example, the nursing home resident who speaks of life in an interview and, in the process, produces a sense of its quality, takes account of the conditions of nursing home living in relation to his or her sense of life as a whole

(Gubrium 1993). The legal and mental health agents who participate in involuntary mental hospitalization hearings consider a candidate patient's dangerousness or so-called grave disability in terms of professional and organizational interests and agendas (Holstein 1993). While lives are narratively constructed by participants in such settings, the lives are not constructed arbitrarily. Biographical work reflects local relevancies so that what is constructed, while distinctively crafted, is assembled from the pertinent categories and vocabularies of the settings. Participants construct their lives, but not completely on their own terms.

MURRAY MANOR PERSPECTIVES

Before I began the fieldwork at Murray Manor that eventually centered on perspective and story, I had developed a quite uniformly negative sense of what nursing home life was like, informing me that living, dying, and working in such facilities were cut out of the same set of meanings and categories. In frequent exposés, the media communicated the generally poor quality of long term care. I could hardly mention my research interest without being told things such as "Those awful places you read about," "I would never put mother in one of them," and "That's the end of the road."

I had never been in a nursing home, and I knew no one who lived or worked in such a setting. At the time, the research literature on the social organization of nursing homes was scant. Anthropologist Jules Henry (1963) provided a comparative view of a hospital and two nursing homes. He called one of the nursing homes "Hell's Vestibule" because it offered residents filth and neglect. A few articles by sociologists were forthcoming, such as Elizabeth Gustafson's (1972) paper on the moral career of the nursing home patient and Charles Stannard's (1973) on the social conditions for patient abuse in a nursing home. *As We Are Now*, May Sarton's (1973) fictional account of elderly protagonist Caro Spencer's experience as a resident in a rural nursing home called Twin Elms, was yet to be published.

This suggested that I take a look for myself, to get a firsthand view. I contacted seven facilities and arranged to speak with administrators about my research plans, especially the need to spend time in a few homes to get a sense of the rhythms of everyday life and caregiving. Each administrator expressed interest in the study, but some were understandably wary of my intentions because of what one called the "bad press" nursing homes were getting. One administrator, whose name I fictionalized as Mr. Filstead in *Living and Dying at Murray Manor*, showed the kind of interest that I later realized was an ethnographer's dream. Filstead prided himself on being research-oriented, and he aimed to improve the living conditions of nursing homes. He admired my desire to get a firsthand view of things. I recall him explaining that things can't be "just labeled as all bad or all good and leave it at that, like you read in the papers." I had mentioned how I felt about the need to understand the complexities of nursing home life. I appreciated Filstead's commitment to the welfare of residents and his decided preference for seeing "all sides."

Inviting me to "take a look" at Murray Manor, Filstead eased my way into various units, introducing me to the floor staff and some of the residents. Interacting with the staff and the residents, I began to think that their daily lives offered quite different perspectives on the meaning of care and caregiving. It occurred to me that a single nursing home might, from the points of view of its participants, be several quite different organizations in practice. I used the term "worlds" to convey the differences because it suggested something separate and distinct, yet equally compelling. What the administrative staff saw as good and efficient caregiving, floor staff could consider "just getting the job done." What a resident felt was time well spent chatting with a friendly aide could, from the aide's point of view, be time away from other duties.

These separate worlds prompted diverse stories to be told about what, ostensibly, was the same event. I draw on a Murray Manor "incident," described in my book, *The Mosaic of Care* (Gubrium 1991), to illustrate how the concept of worlds, and especially the concept of story, came to organize the ethnographic material gathered in the facility. The protagonists were Phoebe and John, aged 80 and 82 years, respectively, and both residents of the facility since it opened for business. What actually happened during the incident, how its events were represented, and recommended courses of action all depended on whose point of view was taken. Staff members oriented to the incident in terms aligned with organizational and professional concerns, while John and Phoebe, although at odds with each other, interpreted things differently.

According to Phoebe and her visible clique of women friends on the residential floor, John had "absolutely lost all his marbles." What's more, he was the vilest man alive. The women complained that John was repeatedly using "their" bathing room, which was located at "their" end of the hallway. It was felt that John could just as easily use the bathing room at his end of the hall or use the toilet in his own room. While the residential floor's two bathing rooms were available for use by anyone living on the floor, residents whose rooms were located in the vicinity of a particular bathing room tended to claim it as their own. As clique members loudly mused, "Why anyone would want to come over here to take a bath or 'do his business' when he could use the bathroom at the other end is beyond me."

An allegedly outrageous incident brought the matter to a head. From clique members' point of view, it proved John was demented. One of the women, Lillian, had been using "their" bathing room, and the women had agreed to post a sign on the door saying that it was occupied to "prevent the likes of John from walking in and setting his dirty eyes on everything and everyone."

While none of the women admittedly saw what actually happened, the incident nonetheless was vividly recalled, as if all had been there. It was reported that things had been quiet that eventful morning, that is, until the women put "two and two together," as several noted. Bella, for one, believed she had seen John walking along with his cane, but initially dismissed it as John being "up to his usual," which was "gadding about" at their end of the hallway where he "really has no business." Since it was the women's habit to keep to themselves in their rooms after breakfast, Bella thought little of John possibly taking a morning constitutional.

Another woman thought she had heard someone say, "Get out," but guessed the voice to be coming from one of the several, barely audible television sets in nearby rooms.

The incident began when several women heard what was described as a chilling scream, "like someone being murdered in cold blood." Each explained how she felt frozen in place. Phoebe, the vocal leader of the clique, reported that she stuck her head out the doorway of her room to see what was happening. Then, as allegedly chilling as before, Phoebe heard, "Get out of here, John! Get out!"

Phoebe immediately recognized it as her friend Lillian's voice and claimed to have heard John unmistakably shout back, "Shut up, you old bag! This room isn't your property! I can come in here any time I want. You old bags think you own the place!"

As clique members related, after what seemed to be an eternity, John walked out of the bathing room waving his cane, caught it in the handrail, and stumbled. According to the women, this was to be expected when the devil was at work and, what's more, served John right. They felt that if the stumble incapacitated John, he would be transferred to one of the patient floors where care requirements were higher and the staff was better equipped to handle the demented.

The story of the incident was repeated and embellished by each of the women according to the part she construed herself as playing. Phoebe's version was the most widely circulated, and it was conveyed to Miss Hanson, the Manor's social worker. As Phoebe explained, all the women on the floor knew John was "*non compos mentis* and really, really rude, dirty-minded, and foul-mouthed on top of it." As self-appointed representative of the women, Phoebe demanded that Hanson "do something about it and do it quick!"

Speaking with floor staff, Hanson pieced together a different account. She already knew that the sniping between John and his friends and Phoebe and her clique had become serious. To floor staff, what happened that morning was part of a history of mutual resentment and competition for status. Still, as one staffer noted, there was "good" and "bad" in both groups. Phoebe's clique could be considerate and gracious, showering staff and others with small favors. They also could be cruel to those they resented, especially John.

John and his friends, too, had their good and bad sides. John was the floor's most ribald storyteller. Staff were regularly amused by his good humor, quick wit, and intriguing tales, sharing many among themselves. Yet, John was no respecter of social airs and, in that regard, was deeply offensive to Phoebe and her friends.

Floor staff's version of the incident was sprinkled with mockery. In one telling, John became the proverbial sly fox with an eye for the women. Lillian took the role of the demure lady. Phoebe was the protective witch. In this version, the incident was a parody on the confrontation of purity and danger, in which all played appropriate and recognizable parts. Residents were seen more as characters toying with appearances than as clashing personalities. Embarrassment was something to laugh about as much as it was a lesson about the invasion of privacy. Anger was as much amusing as a cause of sympathetic resentment. One staff member remarked that he would have given anything to see the expressions on each of their faces, or "what *must* have gone through their minds," when Lillian screamed at John. The question of whether John actually "peeked" at Lillian or if Lillian actually saw John in the bathing room did not spoil the thoroughly enjoyable drama about "things that happen in a place like this."

John and his friends, like Phoebe and her circle, told less impartial stories. According to John, what happened that fateful morning was not an incident but a coup. The unfortunate thing about it, as one of John's friends mentioned, was that John got a bit "roughed up" in the process.

The friends routinely referred to the "old bags" down the hall and talked at length about what should be done about their bossiness and claims on "everything in the place." One time, Sadie, one of the friends, joked about how the men had decided to give Phoebe's clique "the old hiss-hiss routine," which entailed hissing loudly as clique members passed by.

But, as John told it, "The straw that broke the camel's back was when I walked into that bathroom and pretended that I didn't know where I was." John explained that he knew "just about when they liked to take a bath in there." On the morning of the incident, he guessed that he'd just stroll down the hall to see what was happening.

Sadie interjected jovially, "Yeah and we all knew what you were up to, John. Don't give us that innocent act."

John chuckled. The telling seemed to be as much fun as the events reported. John added, however, "I'll never know why that girl [the LPN] made such a big stink about that little slip of mine, making an [incident] report and all that stuff."

When Hanson compared this version of what happened with what Phoebe reported, she wondered whether she was even hearing the same things described. Hanson soon received related complaints from a few families. Phoebe's son, for one, had spoken to the administrator about the lack of privacy in the facility, and the administrator conveyed this to Hanson. Other staff members reported that they had been told by family members that it was their understanding that the first floor of the facility was reserved for those only in need of personal care, not the confused or demented. What Hanson heard from complaining family members supported the view that John was mentally unfit to be in the residential unit.

The alleged incident was discussed by staff members in a patient care conference, which I attended. Hanson attempted to convey each side of the story. She indicated that while she was trying to be fair to all sides, the home also had to respond to the complaints. To make matters worse, Phoebe's son had warned the administrator that several families would "pull" their private pay residents out of the home and "give it a bad name" if the incident were overlooked.

Hanson concluded, "It's not a very pretty picture. Whatever we do will be unfair to someone."

The associate director of nursing responded, "Welcome to the real world!"

It is evident that this so-called real world—the world of everyday life—is as much a configuration of stories, differentially constructed by those concerned, as it is a concrete set of events. Yes, something seemed to have happened in the bathing room that fateful morning. Those at the actual scene of events, John and Lillian, had either observed with their own eyes or heard with their own ears that they were occupying a room not meant for their common presence. But what was seen or heard by John, Lillian, and the others came in strikingly different versions, the communication of which had both serious and not-so-serious consequences for those concerned. Indeed, the stories took on a life of their own, so much so that it was difficult to distinguish them from what they allegedly were about.

Sometime later, Hanson and I discussed the incident, and she told me that she had done all she could about it. Things had not changed much between John, Phoebe, and their respective friends. Hanson remarked that she expected another such occurrence any day now, not necessarily involving the same residents. There would be complaints, stories, and versions. She added, "Such is life." As if to suggest that Murray Manor, as a social setting, is ultimately a diverse world of stories, Hanson wondered, "Maybe what you have to do in the end is just say what you have to, to whoever."

LIFELONG EXPERIENCES AND NARRATIVE LINKAGES

Now, thinking back on the Murray Manor fieldwork twenty years later, I would say that my approach to perspective and story was rather present-oriented. If the role of fieldworker as participant observer lent itself to the storied representation of life, deliberate attention to setting and ongoing interaction favored stories about current, daily events, although the past was not ignored. At Murray Manor, my observations centered on what was inferred from, done, and said about the interactions of staff members and residents, not on the subjective meaning of conditions and events in the context of lifelong experiences. I was not as much concerned, for example, with how the nursing aide's personal history, especially her family, class, or ethnic background, related to what I called the "bed and body" work for which she was responsible. I approached the aide's story as a narrative of current social relations with co-workers, employers, residents, and family members. Residents' stories were heard, likewise, as narratives about living and dying at Murray Manor.

I take the role of the in-depth, ethnographic interviewer in my most recent research foray into the nursing home, which is focused on the links between residents' lifelong experiences and personal accounts of the qualities of care and of life in their facilities (Gubrium 1993). This research has raised two important questions. What can be learned about the meaning of the resident's nursing home experience when it is examined in connection with his or her life story? How does a life story inform interpretations of these qualities? The questions lead to an alternative sense of story, one less centered on the present—nursing home living—than broadened to make meaning in relation to life as a whole.

Residents do bring life experiences with them to the facilities in which they live. They don't cease being the persons they were after checking in. They are not just more or less sick, alert, oriented, and ambulatory, but in their own words:

"As well as can be expected for a man who's been ill much of my life."

"Not as confused as most of them are here."

"Feeling more at home than ever before."

Or, "Crying my eyes out because it's come to this."

Such expressions communicate what life was in relation to what it has become. It is these narrative linkages that now concern me.

Following psychologist Jerome Bruner's (1986) procedure, I began open-ended interviews in 1988 with residents from six comparable nursing homes by asking them to tell their life stories, even if it seemed difficult to do in a relatively short time. They were encouraged to begin wherever and however they wished. During the interviews—which dealt with commonplace matters of everyday life in nursing homes, including the quality of care—each resident was invited to address the matters in relation to lifelong as well as current experiences.

Trial interviews had shown that beginning with the life story, however brief, set two narrative precedents. It served to inform residents that I was interested in whether and, if so, how their lives as a whole related to their immediate circumstances. Some residents had warned me that their lives weren't very interesting or claimed that there was little to tell. The life story served to assure them that I would listen to whatever linkages they cared to make between the present and the past. This also offered an empirical basis for me to suggest possible linkages among the past, the future, and the present, which I told them they were free to ignore or recast in their own terms. The interviews were more active than conventionally conceived, being a kind of narrative collaboration between the interviewer and the resident (Holstein and Gubrium 1995).

Findings from the study show evidence of respondents' biographical activeness. One finding indicates that life can be separated from experience. The separation is significant for understanding what is being voiced in studies of experience because it alerts us to the possibility that while respondents may speak in detail about daily living, they may not be describing their lives. It suggests that we, as researchers, should be especially careful in designating to what our findings will be attributed.

Take the following case in point. Eighty-six-year-old resident Ida Stone's remarks about the quality of life in her facility first alerted me to the possibility that life could be separated from experience. In a conversation about the meaning of home, Ida linked home with family, trust, and love, as many other residents did. She spoke at length of growing up in poverty on a farm some distance from the nearest town and explained that "even if we was poor, we didn't know it." She described how her mother made them all feel wanted and "rich" in the important things of life. Ida then traced the warm and loving atmosphere of her early life through to the home she eventually made for her own husband and children. Theirs, too, was not a materially prosperous life, but it was loving and, as she emphasized, their modest abode was a home.

We gradually turned to life in the nursing home. Ida spoke at length about other residents, the staff, the so-called atmosphere, families, the food, and other services. Having just discussed the meaning of home, she compared what was offered in the facility with her understanding of a proper household. While the food in the facility was not bad, she said, she added that it was not like home. The staff, particularly two "very sweet aides," were nice to her and treated her like a mother. While Ida complained that the staff sometimes could be flip and uncaring, she understood that "the girls," meaning the nursing staff, had jobs requiring them to be more than just friendly to residents. Evaluating the facility's atmosphere, Ida remarked that "they" (the staff) try to make it as much like home as possible. She had been in worse places. Ida explained that there were very sick people in the facility and it was difficult to think of the place as a home; in that regard, it was more like a hospital. Still, Ida lived there and, to the extent "they" tried, it was home-like. We spent much time discussing this.

Attempting to clarify what I assumed to be the current experiential connections of her life, Ida remarked several times, "It doesn't matter anyway." At first, I took this as a shorthand way of not being too harsh in judging the facility, unfairly singling it out for what characterized nursing homes in general. I had typified Ida as the kind of person who does not ask life to be perfect, only acceptable and livable, as she repeatedly reminded me her poverty had taught her. But Ida persisted. No, the food was not that bad, but it didn't matter anyway. Yes, the staff didn't spend as much time as they might with residents, but it really did not matter. Yes, by and large, she was satisfied under the circumstances, but what did it matter? I eventually addressed this, asking her why it didn't matter. She answered, "Because my life's over."

In retrospect, I cannot say that this answer itself caused me to begin contemplating that life could be separated from experience, that Ida, in effect, was telling me that while she was giving voice to experience, it was not about her life. Rather, a theoretical interest in the relation between voice, context, and experience was alerting me to the need to listen for the subjective bounds and meaningful backgrounds of what the aged or others say about elderly lives. The combination led me to consider the possibility that life was not just something lived, but might be a thing, like a cherished heirloom or a bad dream, that one could look upon, inspect, think back on, look ahead to, close off, and open up to experience. It occurred to me that when Ida and other residents spoke about daily living, they were not necessarily telling me anything about a life—their lives—even while they could describe and evaluate current living conditions. I considered that when I asked Ida how satisfied she was with her life now, she was telling me more about *now* than she was speaking about her life. Indeed, I have come to wonder whether what we, as gerontologists, know about life satisfaction "in general" is a conglomeration of life and "just living." Perhaps we have overlooked that nursing home residents distinguish what they once were from what they now withstand.

The findings also speak to narrative diversity, especially in relation to quality of care and quality of life. The effect of public alarm over the high cost of care and the aim of offering the best care for the fewest dollars has made quality assurance a leading goal of health care delivery. One result has been the development of systems of quality management to assess quality on several fronts, from the quality of care provided to the resulting quality of life for care receivers. This is increasingly evident in long term care. A quality assurance industry has emerged to design assessment instruments, offer data management services, and monitor results and compliance activity. Yet, for all the alarm and rationalization, few are asking what the subjective meaning of quality of care and quality of life are for those whose lives are affected. In contrast to the relatively short stays of hospital patients, nursing home residents are typically "long stayers" and, for better or worse, are likely to encounter the nursing facility as a final household. Matters of home, family, interpersonal ties, life history, self-worth, dependence, disappointment, and destiny confront residents in ways irrelevant to hospital patients or other short-stay care receivers. The matters significantly mediate interpretations of quality of care and quality of life.

The subjective meaning of the nursing home's quality of care and quality of life was an important focus of the life narrative study. The members of my sample, 58 residents in six nursing homes recognized as comparable in the quality of the care they offered, were given the opportunity to tell their stories—to speak of life and to convey in their own terms the meaning of the qualities in their facilities in relation to such significant matters of long stays as the loss of home, family, and the interpersonal ties just mentioned. No attempt was made to confine residents' narratives and judgments to the present. Taken together, the subjective meanings I will selectively illustrate here reveal how a nursing home's life and care qualities narratively figure into lives as a whole. It is a bottom-up rather than top-down look, and it shows how what may be administratively deemed qualities of care and life do not necessarily reflect what the qualities mean to care receivers.

The study's key concepts were *horizons of meaning* and *narrative linkages.* Horizons arise from the pattern of narrative linkages each resident makes with experiences in and out of the nursing home. In referring to meaning as having horizons, I take it that what residents say about matters such as the quality of care needs to be understood in relation to the pattern of linkages made with other experiences. It is the pattern that gives the qualities subjective meaning.

Interview responses indicate that residents convey the meaning of the quality of care and the quality of life against horizons of narrative linkages they make with lifelong experience. One example is provided by Lula Burton, a 74-year-old African American. In her interview, Lula identified repeated linkages with the special circumstance of having grown up and grown old alongside her twin sister, Lily, who now shares a room with her in a nursing home. Against this lifelong horizon of meaning, Burton's orientation to the qualities of care and life contrasts with others who lack close and continuing relationships, or whose relationships have been troublesome.

In other instances, making a new home forms a horizon of meaning. Residents Martha Gilbert and Jane Nesbit, whose life stories, as they put it, convey little or no home life "to speak of," talk of the quality of their facilities in terms of *new* meanings of home.

The following two cases illustrate the application of the concepts in greater detail. Some residents speak of being enduringly wary of infringements on their personal space. An example is provided by Bea Lindstrom, a 90-year-old widow whose narrative horizon centers on vigilance. For such vigilant residents, it matters that people keep their places and mind their manners. Their narratives attest to "taking no lip," as Lindstrom repeats in her interview, especially from disrespectful aides or other residents.

It is the opinion of the vigilant that residents believed to know better, but who persist in bothering others, being verbally abusive, or otherwise acting inconsiderate to a roommate, should be physically removed from the premises. The resident who knowingly wanders into someone else's room, disturbs belongings, or pilfers cannot be tolerated. Those who don't know better should be kept under surveillance. Public spaces such as hallways, lounges, and the dining room are to be used with concern for others' privileges.

From the perspective of the vigilant, nurses and aides should do their jobs with the utmost respect for those served, being kind and considerate in the process. The staff should promptly attend to bodily cares, see to personal requests, and keep the premises clean and odor-free. The aide who perfunctorily cleans a resident following a bout of incontinence, ignoring the resident's right to privacy, should not be working with frail, elderly people. Vigilant residents don't expect to be treated royally by staff members, even though some are perceived to desire that, but they clearly and forcefully request decency. At times, such residents wonder why they are judged "demanding."

Vigilance is a narrative horizon girded by lifelong independence and linked to an ethic of distributive justice. A firm standard of fair treatment prevails, which residents also apply to themselves. They can be excruciatingly circumspect about their conduct, lest it carelessly overstep its own bounds. From the vigilant, we hear repeated, emphatic mention of how *they* scrupulously keep to themselves, how *they* would never do thus-and-so to someone else, and what *they* would not themselves say under any circumstance.

Vigilance and ethic combine to narratively highlight the quality of care. Against the horizon of vigilance, the quality of care in the nursing home becomes an all-consuming matter. At times, quality of care is so narratively foregrounded that the overall quality of life for these residents centers on uncooperative roommates, administrative indifference, impertinent aides, even plastic bedsheets. For some, like Lindstrom, this is directed outward and angrily or sarcastically conveyed. For others, it is aimed inward and is an admitted source of agitation.

Compare this horizon with that of Jake Bellows, a 76-year-old, widowed male who has had a left-leg amputation and is afflicted by what he calls a "vascular condition" and other health problems. Like a few others, mostly men, Bellows was an itinerant traveler. He was in show business, and to paraphrase him, he did a "lot of livin'" on the road and has many stories to tell about it. The special circumstance narratively mediates the subjective meaning of the quality of nursing home life for Bellows.

For these men, for most of their lives, home represented time out from the usual and customary. These men *went home* for vacation; they didn't leave it. They accept the nursing home as a place offering care, security, and shelter for the weary, who might not otherwise be able to carry on. It isn't home, but under the circumstances, the next best thing to it. Indeed, care apparatus and sickness aside, the nursing home is a kind of hotel, having both the best and the worse features of such establishments. As they see it, residents more or less get fed, have a bed to sleep in, and have their cares addressed, but understandably not to everyone's satisfaction.

The fate of having come to reside in a nursing home is not particularly puzzling or decried. Fate is something that one accepts and follows, like life on the road. These residents' narratives are sprinkled with phrases like "*c'est la vie,*" "things just happen," "goin' where the road takes you," "so be it," "easy come, easy go," which not only signal equanimity, but narratively link with where the road of life has led them. While these residents colorfully describe the many paths their lives took, the so-called ups and downs of the years and the good and poor choices they made at various turns, they recognize that such matters are part of the grand design of living. They don't lament fate, as some other residents do; it is just there, the essential "road" ahead.

These men take pride in the quality of their lives and what they have accomplished, none of which is defined by their present circumstances. While it wouldn't be correct to describe them as awed by fate, they appreciate what fate has brought, both the easy triumphs that have come "down the road" and the hard lessons they have learned along the way. As Bellows and others repeatedly remind us in their narratives, "such is life."

One mark of a nursing facility that would seem to affect the quality of life is the extent that it is "homelike." From a bureaucratic perspective, this commonly means amenities such as an atmosphere of soft, noninstitutional lighting, warm colors on the walls, and being surrounded by personal possessions. For travelers like Bellows, a different horizon signals home. Home is a kind of vacation, such as a hotel might accommodate or a long weekend might offer. Accordingly, for these residents, the quality of life of a nursing facility is not figured chiefly in terms of care provision or homeyness, but in relation to another place along the road of life that fate has led them.

Taken together, the residents' narratives have clear implications for quality assessment. First, as far as knowledge of care and life quality is concerned, the narratives show that assessment systems provide a very narrow view of quality, albeit a significant and useful one. When residents are asked to tell their stories and speak of the quality of care and life in relation to lifelong experiences, quality is revealed to be diverse, linked with, and given meaning in relation to, lifelong experiences. One lesson of the narratives is that we need to begin to understand the qualities of care and life for nursing home residents in terms of the variable experiential contexts in which meanings are conveyed, which extend well into the past lives of their subjects.

Second, and equally important, is the implication for intervention. We cannot simply design intervention to improve the lot of *the* nursing home resident. To do so would be to formulate expensive and time-consuming window-dressing meaningfully reflective of few residents' experiences, even while standard quality assessment does inform us of the "objective" conditions of nursing facilities. That there are horizons of meaning for nursing home residents does not suggest that standardized quality assessment is irrelevant. Such assessment is useful for helping to maintain minimum levels of care. However, we need to remind ourselves that residents live as much in subjective worlds as in relation to objective conditions. The intervention into lives that quality of life and quality of care assessment might recommend needs to be most inclusive and take heed of both objective conditions and subjective meaning.

CONCLUSION

By foregrounding perspective, story, and the biographically active subject, new ethnography takes us in directions virtually absent in older ethnography. In the case of the nursing home, it opens to view the possibility that the everyday realities of such settings, including their ubiquitous "incidents" and qualities, are constitutively diverse. The many versions of events offer quite distinct understandings of important matters such as privacy, mental competence, and the quality of care.

Methodologically, new ethnography orients researchers to the ethnographic behavior of participants themselves. In the case of long term care, this points to the many-versioned world of the nursing home. New ethnography orients us to subjects in a new way, prompting researchers to "listen in order to see" how subjects construct their world and its realities (Gubrium and Holstein 1990). The overall lesson is that what we know of living, dying, and being in the nursing home must appropriate the accounts of its storytellers.

3

The Culture of Care in a Nursing Home: Effects of a Medicalized Model of Long Term Care

J. Neil Henderson

INTRODUCTION

The pervasive influence of medicine on contemporary American society has led to the concept of "medicalization" of many aspects of life which, in earlier times, were not at all considered germane to medicine (Illich 1975; Ory and Ables 1989). For example, fundamental religious values have been subject to medicalization in the definition of life and death. Also, medicalization has permeated the concept of aging (Estes and Binney 1989; Lyman 1989). At the 1993 Gerontological Society of America (GSA) meetings, a poster of a vigorous-looking elderly woman who is juggling several body organs, including a brain, heart, and kidney, over her head was commissioned and circulated by the GSA. Notably, this icon of "elderhood" did *not* show her juggling dollars, grandchildren, houses, or churches, since they are not a fitting part of the medicalized view of aging, although they are critical to the late life experience.

In this paper, I will show how qualitative research methods can reveal the more subtle aspects of medicalized aging in the context of institutionalized care (cf. Light, Jr. 1983). The notion that a nursing home is where health-impaired elders live and would "naturally" be a place of medicalized caregiving neglects the fact that most placements are made due to lack of adequate community resources, not actual need for constantly supervised medical care. Actually, a nursing home is the singular place for elders in which it should be incumbent upon the facility to provide the best of humanizing, psychosocial care (Bowker 1982).

This research was a thirteen-month-long ethnographic community study of a 90-bed skilled care nursing home (Henderson 1979, 1981, 1987, 1994b). The principle research question was: "What is the nature of long term institutional care at the interface of the patient[1] and certified nursing assistant (CNA)?" I used the ethnomedical model as a guiding principle of inquiry so that I could be most sensitive to the emic dynamics of long term care (Hughes 1978; Fabrega 1974). For example, there is a detailed policy and procedures manual in all nursing homes which purports to establish and govern the work to be done. However, rather than assuming adherence to written rules for behavior, the ethnomedical model delves beyond these superficial caregiving rules to the analysis of actual behavior and concepts of care.

Three aspects of routine nursing home operation are examined below. All are products of a medicalized concept of institutional long term care of elders that devalues humanizing psychosocial care. First, the rapid, task-oriented nature of CNA work is shown to be derived from medical values of time conservation and care focused on physical tasks. Next, delivery of direct psychosocial care is found in its purest form to come not from the CNAs or activity coordinators, who would be considered the natural providers of such care, but from the housekeeping staff. Last, the lack of staff awareness regarding patients' real experience of nursing home life is reflected in patients' daily need to engage in food procurement strategies to get their meal when it is appropriately hot or cold.

Collectively, these findings are the product of long term fieldwork, using a qualitative data collection and analysis design. Without such lengthy and penetrating inquiry, the detailed, emic delineation of the staff and patient experience would remain inaccessible.

Overall, the administration and staff placed a great emphasis on the quality of care for the patients of Pecan Grove Manor. The emphasis on caring for the patients was sincere, as many personal gestures of true care and concern were shown to most patients, both publicly and behind the scenes. There was, however, a failure to see the larger picture of patient life through the eyes of the patients. "Basic (i.e., physical) care" was the gold standard for measuring quality of life. Still, there were regulations that mandated psychosocial care in the form of "activities." Consequently, activities were undertaken, but they were of the simplest kind and were accompanied by the attitude that a mere charade was sufficient. It was in the psychosocial care domain that there was the greatest staff blindness to what quality of life in long term care should and could be.

The product of this organizational culture was that patients with chronic, incurable disease lived their remaining days in a system based on acute care hospital models. Psychosocial care was a footnote grudgingly delivered in muted forms. Although the patients' mood and spirit were amenable to nurturing and improvement, the physical care model was master. Daily operation of the facility was one of conducting basic care by the rapid execution of bed and body tasks with a thin overlay of effort to provide patients a comprehensive quality of life. The unstated rule was "As long as staff does basic care reasonably well and patients are in a protected environment with sufficient food, then our job is done." Such a veterinary approach leaves the real qualities of the *human* condition virtually untouched.

THE SETTING

Pecan Grove Manor, a pseudonym (as are the names of all individuals), was a 90-bed, skilled nursing home located in a southern midwestern state. Its design was a one-story "T" shape in which the lobby and dining areas were located at the T's apex. Its exterior was a decorative dark gray brick up to the window level, above which was white block with dark gray trim around the roof. It was nestled amidst a grove of pecan trees alongside a meandering creek.

The interior was well lit and boasted truly gleaming tile floors. Odors from incontinence were very slight and confined to the "heavy care" wing where the most debilitated patients lived. The other two wings were also designated in accordance with their purposes. The "ambulatory care" wing was the location for those with the greatest level of functional ability. The remaining wing was for those needing "intermediate care." Each of the three wings was lined with the usual rails to assist with ambulation.

The largest nursing station faced the main lobby. It was a single counter with an ornamental wood shingle roof above. Licensed nurses in white did charting there, patient chart racks were clumped together, and medical instruments, such as stethoscopes, blood pressure cuffs, and an autoclave, were kept there as well. This nurses' station was the main visual element seen from the vantage point of the building's entryway.

Patients' rooms were semi-private, with some toilets positioned for joint use between two rooms. The interior wall surfaces were concrete block, painted in pastels. Each patient had been encouraged to bring furnishings and decorative items from home. However, with patients' room location based on functional status, each wing had its own "look" related to the predominant cognitive levels of the patients placed there. The result was a descending scale in the amount of personal items per room from the ambulatory care wing to the heavy care wing, where some rooms were truly stark. Those with the most severe cases of dementia were typically housed in the stark rooms.

The facility had occasional space devoted to activities, typically singing, reminiscing, and playing bingo. Major holidays were public spectacles, with upwards of a thousand dollars spent for local entertainment, food, and decorations. Yet, the activity most appreciated by patients was the rare outing that took them into the real community. A small lobby area at the end of the "T" was the place of most activities. One time, however, a room usually reserved for patients was empty prior to a quality of care inspection by the state. Overnight, this room was redecorated so that it appeared to be the headquarters for a very vigorous activities program. Three weeks after the inspection, the room was used to house two new patients.

METHODS

I used participant observation extensively, but also conducted confidential, structured interviews with a sub-sample of 30 high functioning patients, anonymous questionnaires with each staff group, and an anonymous mailed questionnaire for family members. In addition, I collected some basic epidemiologic information from patient charts, such as disease prevalence, functional status, and medication usage (cf. Brewer and Hunter 1989; Fielding and Fielding 1986). Only one patient was unwilling to have information recorded, although it was a single family member who made the actual refusal by proxy.

Entering the field and beginning the data-collection process was done with much forethought (cf. Morse 1994). I explained my purpose as wanting to understand how nursing homes worked. While this is correct, my research agenda had numerous specific questions to pursue. The primary purpose at the outset was to understand the nature of long term care at the interface of the Certified Nursing Assistant (CNA) and the patient. I worked as a paid CNA for thirteen months to pursue this question. I also would go to the facility on "off duty" time to question, observe, and write more notes. For the first three months, I did not take any notes publicly. I felt this would be too obtrusive to staff and would retard the process of developing rapport. After three months, I used small pocket-sized notebooks, which were inconspicuous. I would later elaborate these "raw notes" into detailed, typewritten notes. Later, coding and retrieval by code category assisted in analysis. By the eighth month, I could take notes with little concern about being obtrusive.

The note writing process was clearly a phased-in strategy. The first time I took notes publicly, I contrived a situation in which I was very conspicuous. I chose a spot in the middle of the lobby under three spot lights and used a large three-ring binder with blank paper in it. I fully intended to be seen, "apprehended," and have my notes examined, either casually or with a little more than normal curiosity.

Within a few minutes, the assistant administrator and the Director of Nursing (DON) walked across the lobby, passing me by inches, but without acknowledging my presence. In a few more minutes, they were in my area of the lobby talking loudly with the few patients there and being overly solicitous to the "sweet" patients. I occasionally wrote innocuous notes about who was present, that the television was on with two people watching, and how many chairs of what type were in the lobby. Finally, the assistant administrator and the DON came directly to me and asked, "What are you writing?" I leaned back from the notebook and handed them the notes, stating that at this point I didn't know whether the items noted would be of any use or not but that it was a way to start. I suspect that the entries were so boring that they went away puzzled about why it would take so many years of education to do what they just saw.

Nursing homes have been the targets of numerous muck-raking exposés over the years and have become very sensitive to those who evoke the specter of "inspectors." Fieldworkers with notebooks in hand, rapidly jotting notes as they nose into every nuance of activity, can be perceived by the administration and staff as a real risk, and this was my experience. However, I found that the patients were not sensitive about this [see Vesperi, this volume].

The effect of participant observation as a method itself cannot be under-estimated in this study. My time was split between working as a CNA and observing CNA work. The two experiences were very different. The work experience not only conveyed the energy expenditures required but also put me in a position of real responsibility for the care of the patients. The emotive sense of responsibility for a patient's welfare at times transcended my intellectual curiosities, which otherwise fueled the study. However, when I observed CNA work without being "on the clock," I felt distinctly less burdened by not being, for example, the one at risk of mishandling the transfer of a heavy patient from bed to chair. Such common CNA work could result in a patient falling, possibly breaking a hip, requiring surgery, and literally leading in a deteriorating cascade to the person's death.

Moreover, I came to be accepted as not just a part of the work setting landscape but, at least at times, simply as a co-worker. The co-worker perception was a mix of being defined just like any other CNA and the special status I had as a curious researcher (cf. "marginal native" Freilich 1970). Many times, work demands were so heavy that my researcher role was not explicitly present. During such times, I would purposely suspend the constant mental tracking of events, language, and the complex social dynamics just to get the necessary tasks done. Yet, there were many other times when I was able to be vigilantly alert to the social dynamics that could provide answers to my research questions.

Using a variable mix of participant observation over time (cf. Gold 1969), I was able to emotively experience and be intellectually active in investigating long term care at the interface of the CNA and the patient. The result is less a sterile view of CNA work, and more a psychologically connected analysis of CNA work (cf. Stein 1991; Holstein and Gubrium 1994b). Of course, issues of transference and countertransference must be understood and controlled. This research method led to the insight that part of nursing home care is a series of hollow rituals intended to fabricate a facsimile of meaningfully transacted life.

RITUALS OF FABRICATED LIFE

Time and Task

There would seem to be only a slight connection between the work cultures of biomedical practitioners and CNAs in nursing homes. However, there is a surprisingly strong link with the occupational culture of medicine regarding "time." In medical culture, time is not just a tracking tool, it is a commodity that can be wasted, conserved, or correctly used. The value placed on time is so strong that it becomes a virtually sacred commodity (Stein 1991). There is an acquisition path for the valuing of time that reaches CNAs via medical culture's shaping of the nursing profession. In turn, nursing homes have licensed nurses who exert strong influences on the paraprofessional staff and transmit the medical "cult of time" to the CNAs.

The cult of time is interdigitated with another medical culture precept. The biomedical focus is on physical health, disease, and cure. For example, issues of psychosocial illness may occupy the majority of physician visits, yet the "worthy" patient is one who presents with only physical complaints and without a substrate of neurosis. In contrast, the circumstances of institutional long term care include not only incurable chronic disease, but also life in an environment of ill health, suboptimal function, and patient stays measured in years, all of which are psychosocial concerns. Yet, the biomedical model, so useful in many ways, inappropriately intrudes into this very different type of health care environment.

The cult of time is also related to the large amount of tasks to do in the situation of understaffing. While nursing homes must meet minimum staffing numbers, the perception of many researchers and staff alike is that there are simply not enough staff to do much beyond "basic care." Stated otherwise, enough staff to do basic care is enough staff. Basic care is essentially what has been referred to as "bed and body" care (Gubrium 1975) or the "domestic service pattern" (Freidson 1973). The attention to basic care is also driven by requirements demanded by inspection surveys, which evaluate the quality of care given by nursing homes. These inspections are fundamentally tied to the medical model, as evidenced by their minimal evaluation of psychosocial issues. This devaluing of psychosocial care can be seen by constructing a potential contrast. If psychosocial issues were truly considered crucial care, the bulk of inspections would be comprised of an intensive examination of psychosocial care programs and activities, rather than pouring over the written record via chart care plans or spending hours documenting medication usage in charts. Care plans and medication usage are very important but, in long term care, putting psychosocial care into actual practice could be equally or more important (Bowker 1982).

The net effect of the cult of time and task in nursing homes is suboptimal psychosocial care. This outcome is apparently acceptable due to an occupationally derived perception of time, in which time exists only in insufficient quantities and is not to be wasted by non-medical complaints so that physical care tasks can be done. Moreover, this perception of time is reinforced by the CNA experience of having to rush through an eight-hour shift in order to complete the basic care tasks.

The cult of time and task is further revealed in the nature of daily CNA work (cf. Diamond 1986). As I began the first day of my work as a CNA, I discovered I was constrained from simply distributing breakfast trays to those who ate in their rooms. For example, before taking the tray to Mr. Smith, I was told to remove the knife and fork because he hid them to use as weapons later. Also, his juice and milk glasses should be placed on the opposite corner of the tray from where the kitchen staff always placed it. This positioning was so that he could use his "good arm" that had not been impaired by a cerebrovascular stroke. Additionally, I needed to place him in his wheelchair next to the sink top, facing toward the door so he could rest his good arm on the sink top when needed.

The most telling incompetence of mine as a novice CNA was related to the knowledge that Mr. Smith's medication capsule needed to be pulled apart and the contents emptied onto his oatmeal and stirred in. These instructions came to me rapid-fire in the midst of four other CNAs grabbing trays and quickly making the necessary adjustments to meet individual patient needs and peccadillos. I tried to mentally note all that was told me as I was bringing the tray back to the cart, from which I had too hastily taken it. I made the corrections and then entered Mr. Smith's room. I made the appropriate congenial greeting and leaned forward to place the tray on his stand, having taken time to position him correctly. While I was leaning over the tray, I recalled the need to open his medication and mix it into his food. Within a second of starting to stir the bright purple powder into the gray oatmeal, a resounding crack of wood-on-bone resonated throughout the room. As I slowly returned to cognitive clarity, I realized that Mr. Smith had taken his cane from the back of his wheelchair and delivered a corrective blow to the skull of the bastard who was trying to poison him. As the senior CNA to whom I was assigned came to inquire about the strange noise, she quickly ascertained the scenario. Only then was I informed of the little detail regarding Mr. Smith's flagrant paranoia and his conviction that the staff was always trying to kill him by poisoning him.

I had been a CNA for about seven minutes. This seemingly simple job had proven to be replete with large amounts of patient-specific knowledge that only weeks of experience could transfer to me. On this unit alone, there were thirty patients. Yet, over time, I also became expert in the detailed needs and preferences of the patients.

This knowledge bank held by the CNAs functioned in the context of both desire to provide quality care and ways to make the job tasks easier. Most CNAs aspired to meet patient needs in a courteous manner. However, the "time-task" factor pushed the CNAs along in a fast gallop toward the end of a grueling eight-hour shift. For example, after all the food trays were distributed to the rooms, I came back out to the food tray cart and found myself alone in the corridor. Moments before, there had been hustling, white-uniformed CNAs everywhere. Now, they had vanished. I located the senior CNA in a patient's room and was told to go feed Mr. Johnson, whom I had earlier observed to be extremely debilitated. It was then that I realized that I had been the day's loser in a silent race to get to the patients who were easiest to feed.

Mr. Johnson was severely physically and mentally impaired. With the head of the bed raised, his torso, head, and neck were so inflexible that unless he was perfectly balanced, he slid rapidly toward one side of the bed or the other. Since the bed rails needed to be left up while feeding him, I had to lean over with my ribs on the rails so that I could direct a spoon of food straight into his mouth because he couldn't turn his head well. Also, he had a pureed diet, which meant lots of very fluid food. Maybe it was just me, but the distance from the food tray beside the bed, over the rails to his mouth, resulted in a great deal of spillage no matter how slowly I went or cautious I was. I finally finished feeding Mr. Johnson and felt virtually exhausted from my awkward efforts. At lunch, I "got stuck" with Mr. Lynn, who constantly choked.

Typical CNA work is shown in the following sample from fieldnotes. In this case, I was present on a day off, which meant that I could assist if needed, observe behavior, record conversation, and be more flexible in seeking data than when I was there on a paid day. Flexibility allowed for going on different units, circulating through staff lunch areas, selecting certain people to talk to in the pursuit of specific information, and the ability to leave public areas to write crucial fieldnotes.

The pressure of time and task produces a fairly superficial type of social interaction with patients. In the interactions between CNAs and patients below, the rapid discharge of tasks is clear (Henderson 1981:302).

6:21 A.M.	CNAs Miller and Foster in Mrs. White's and Mrs. Palmer's room. CNA Foster leaves room. CNA Foster in and out of Mrs. Morgan's and Mrs. Taylor's room.
6:23	CNA Price in Mrs. Sprague's and Mrs. Jones's room. Gives washcloths.
6:24	CNA Price out. CNAs Price and Miller in Mr. Horne's room.

6:25   CNA Foster out of Mrs. White's and Palmer's room saying, "Oh, my stars. I dread these three," in reference to her next patients.

         CNAs Price and Miller out of Mr. Horne's room.

         CNA Foster: "Where is Mrs. Rogers?"

         CNA Price: "She's home with her son. Don't you remember in report?"

         CNA Foster: "No, I didn't hear it."

         CNA Foster: "Here's the heavyweight" in reference to Mrs. Dunn.

         CNA Miller in Mrs. Cobb's room. Mr. Richard's door closed, skipped by, CNAs don't knock, light showing under door.

6:29   CNA Miller out of Mrs. Cobb's room to get help from CNA Price. Work with Mrs. Cobb continues. Mrs. Dunn left on toilet.

6:30   CNA Miller asks CNA Foster for help getting Mrs. Dunn into wheelchair. Both CNAs make comments about effort to lift Mrs. Dunn.

6:31   CNA Foster in Mrs. Polk's room. There have been two CNAs helping with Mrs. Cobb on a rotating basis.

6:32   Patient call light comes on in Mrs. Perkins's and Mrs. Starn's room. Buzzer not on yet.

6:33   CNA Foster leaves Mrs. Polk's room (19 seconds total time to respond to call light).

6:34   Mrs. Cobb work finishes.

In response to my explicit question to the Director of Nursing about CNA communication style as superficial, she referred to the minimal staffing levels. "All of them [CNAs] are needed for basic care, so that the emotional side . . . is kind of left [undone]. . . . It is hard to just sit down and have eye-to-eye contact and really feel close to the patient when you are giving them daily care. . . . if [patients] are going to do any talking or visiting, it has got to be done quickly while they have got the [CNAs], so a lot of things are left out."

The CNAs also had determined that work load depends on which wing you are working. As already mentioned, Pecan Grove Manor had a three-wing "T" shape. Each wing housed people with varied functional statuses. The logic of the wing designations would suggest that the "heavy care wing" would be the hardest work. It was on this wing that the most dependent, debilitated, demented patients lived. Yet, it was the "intermediate care wing" that was deemed the most difficult work setting.

Work on the intermediate care wing meant that the patients were physically dependent with regard to many things such as dressing and grooming, but also that they were able to make requests, state exactly how they wanted something done, and reason about their treatment. Those on the heavy care wing were passive recipients of care. Their communication limits were so great that CNAs could control virtually all of their circumstances.

Anyone who has a group of people making demands on him or her can find it tedious. CNAs working on the intermediate care wing certainly found the work the most demanding of all. However, in the context of an organizational culture, which places the greatest value on basic care, psychosocially linked factors are perceived as even more of an irritant. Consequently, CNAs described the nature of their jobs as "loving all these little old people," although emotive, psychosocial matters were actually left to little more than congenial behavior.

In summary, the "Cult of Time and Task" at Pecan Grove Manor placed a premium on physical tasks, such as bed and body care, at the expense of humanizing factors common to more time intensive, cognitive psychosocial care. Nursing home caregiving, as a ritual of fabricated life, masqueraded as a small but noble part of the biomedical health sciences. CNAs deliver caregiving tasks based on criteria ultimately derived from acute care hospital models, which are presumably indicative of quality care. The emphasis was on tangible, mechanically delivered tasks amenable to check-list review. The actual subtleties and skills related to providing psychosocial care were reduced to congenial behavior, with no formal evaluation. There was no perceived need to truly upgrade staff psychosocial care skills. There was no reward for it.

Meaningful versus Counterfeit Social Activities

Psychosocial care was expected to be delivered mainly as "activities." Activities at Pecan Grove Manor were frequent and of variable quality. The person hired as the activities coordinator would plan an activity, try to get patients to the chosen location, and conduct the activity.

For example, "band" activity consisted of the activities director gathering several patients in the ambulatory wing lobby to play various percussive instruments. She complained often that by the time she walked a few patients to the lobby and went down the corridors to get others and walk them back to the lobby, the early arrivals had become bored and wandered off to different parts of the building. Efforts to enlist the assistance of CNAs were futile, due to their insistence that they did not have time, or could not leave "the lights" (i.e., the patients' call lights) unattended.

In the "beauty shop," a room designed for hairdressing, licensed and volunteer beauticians served the patients. Sometimes hair dressing also became a spontaneous party, even attracting male patients and office workers to the door. One licensed nurse disliked the laughing and commotion in the beauty shop because it disrupted the sanctuary-like environment she considered proper. As she told me one day, she preferred to work on shifts in the evening and night hours because fewer families were present, most patients were asleep, and she could engage in "purdee quality nursing care." One of those involved in activities suggested that the CNAs disliked patients in the beauty shop in the afternoon hours because it prevented the CNAs from putting the patients to bed so they "wouldn't have anything to do."

Activities as therapy were suspect, too, because there were no assessments of patient improvements attributable to the activity program. Benefits to patients may have been slight, subtle, or nonexistent, but no one knew for certain. The visibility of physical care benefits overshadowed the relative invisibility of psychosocial improvement.

Activities in the religious and civil/religious categories were highly visible and received great attention from the administrative, nursing, and activities staffs. Most important were Christmas and Mother's Day. For example, the Mother's Day celebration became a community competitive potlatch in which conspicuous consumption brought status to the nursing home from the community. One Mother's Day celebration lasted about three hours. It cost Pecan Grove Manor $170 for radio spots, $200 for a band, $200 for flowers, $270 for costumes, and $130 for photographs, and more for miscellaneous items. Relatives of patients, employees, and townspeople totaled between 100 and 150 spectators. Patients, staff, and visitors all appeared to enjoy themselves. Yet, within a few weeks, reminiscing about the party had ceased.

One month before the Mother's Day event, a group of patients were involved in an activity that they still mentioned over one year later. Pecan Grove Manor was near a large lake with many recreational potentials. The activities director decided to arrange a fishing trip to a floating, enclosed fishing dock. The interior of the float was arranged so people could sit and fish in any type of weather. Complete services were available, ranging from a bait store and equipment rental, to a café.

Seven male patients were selected to go on this trip. Selection was based on level of functional ability, unlikelihood of inappropriate public behavior, and an expressed desire to go. Three men from the community were asked to help at the fishing site. They were expected to assist in baiting hooks, netting fish, and any other fishing-related tasks. They were invited to fish, too. The remainder of the party consisted of the activities director and myself.

Twelve people participated in the outing at a cost to the nursing home of $140. The five-hour event took place from 9 A.M. to 2 P.M. The activities director sent a small write-up to the local weekly newspaper, as is commonly done with patient birthdays. Other than this, the community-at-large was uninvolved and unaware of the fishing trip.

The effect of the trip on the patients and the activities director was quite noticeable. Patients were ready to go and positioned at the entrance doors 30 to 40 minutes in advance. Although everyone was ready for a rest at the end of the trip, the patients asked when they could go again. The activities director considered possible ways to continue such trips by buying some small Zebco rods and reels and some fishing tackle. A member of the administrative staff cautioned that the group of people wanting to go would increase in size. Overall, I had never seen these particular men so animated prior to the trip or known of a special activity that engendered such a sustained level of excitement and anticipation of another trip.

Mother's Day and the fishing trip were both entered on government forms as activities. Nonetheless, each event served different purposes that led to the retention or loss of the event. The Mother's Day events and other major productions were opportunities to symbolically communicate to the public Pecan Grove Manor's solid concern for the welfare of its patients. The more visible and lavish this public event was, the more status was given to the nursing home, and its reputation was sustained or improved. Conversely, the fishing trip was a low visibility, inexpensive event affecting seven patients. There was great opportunity for quality psychosocial improvement (judging by change in patients' affect) and maintenance but little chance for status accruement to the nursing home. Mother's Day will continue to be celebrated annually as part of the major public potlatches. Over a year later, the fishing trip had not been repeated, although the participants still reminisced about it.

CNAs Tend the Body, Housekeepers Tend the Mind

The work that I did as a CNA allowed for "off duty" time during which I could be at the nursing home to make other observations. Ten months into the fieldwork, I could lean against the handrail, think, and write notes. At this stage of the research, such open data collection was fully acceptable. Still, I was not visually blatant in my note writing. I avoided large notebooks and "in your face" note taking, preferring to use quiet moments to write phrases in pocket-sized notebooks for later elaboration in my refined notes.

It was during one of these quiet moments of note taking that I was literally leaning against a hand-rail along the corridor wall and overheard part of a conversation in a patient's room. The housekeeper's cleaning cart with mops, brooms, and buckets was next to the door. The housekeeper was in the room sweeping with a broom and responded to the patient, "That must have made you feel sad." After ten months of daily involvement in the conduct of long term care, I had "discovered" an unexpected source of caregiving.

The potential for housekeepers to engage in meaningful interaction with patients is naturally enhanced by their job performance demands (Henderson 1981). While the CNAs demonstrate to supervisors their diligence and hard work by quickly flitting from room to room, the housekeepers are in the opposite situation. Demonstration of job fulfillment for housekeepers involves a lengthy stay of about 20 minutes in patient rooms. This indirectly conveys a message of thoroughness of cleaning and provides a social field for engaging patient–housekeeper interactions. An 80-year-old male patient compared CNAs and housekeepers this way:

Well, all the CNAs don't have the time [to visit] 'cause [basic care] is more important. Now, Jane [housekeeper], she can come in here and clean that wash basin and talk all at the same time. And the CNA, if I am sick and they come in to give me some attention, why they got their mind on what they are doing . . . they don't know what time that intercom is going to say go to so-and-so room or a certain wing. Jane, she knows that she is going to clean this wing up before going over to that east wing.

A 77-year-old female patient had this to say about her encounters with the housekeeper:

Well, if I am crocheting, well, we will talk about that, or something that she has made. Usually, that's what we talk about—things that we are interested in. . . . I enjoy the fellowship with her. She is interesting to talk to. We [i.e., patient and roommate] stay in the room right smart and it is nice to have somebody to talk to.

When comparing the CNAs and housekeepers, she said, "She [i.e., housekeeper] just comes in and cleans up and . . . she's not in a big hurry. And we talk and visit some. . . . When they [CNAs] come in, well, whatever they come to do, why they will talk but they do just what they've got to do and then they just go on."

Another factor that promoted the psychosocial support role of the housekeeper is that she wears street clothes like patients instead of a white nursing uniform. Housekeepers were middle-aged and, in these particular cases, had previous experience as CNAs. Thus, while they had primary care experience, patient-caretaker distinctions diminished and were replaced by more ordinary social interactions.

I asked a housekeeper why patients talked with her so frequently. She said, "I think maybe it's because we're in the rooms longer, and we don't wear white, and they [the patients] seem closer to us. You know, we seem closer to 'em because they [the patients] will tell things that maybe they won't tell someone else. . . . Anita [i.e., the other housekeeper] will probably tell you the same thing. They [the patients] tell her things they don't tell the CNAs or even Miss Turner [the R.N.], you know."

Provisions of psychosocial support were invisible cargos. An instance of providing psychosocial support was not showy, did not involve mechanical instrumentation, but revolved about subtle personal demeanor and time to dispense this cathartic cargo. For example, one housekeeper said, "They [the patients] just feel closer to us because we are really in the wings longer and we have more time to talk to 'em . . . like little things I say, like . . . maybe they won't like a nurse and you don't run this nurse down, you know, you build her up and then maybe next time they'll just fall in love with this nurse. . . . But, it's just little things like that. But it don't really seem important—not even to the CNAs you know. But, to me and to them it is."

The lack of awareness of the psychotherapeutic benefit of housekeeper– patient interaction by the nursing staff was a common theme in conversations with housekeepers. One housekeeper quietly stated, "Sometimes, you know, now I know I never did feel like this, but some of the CNAs think the housekeepers are just the housekeepers, you know. But sometimes we understand the little people more than the CNAs do."

Because the other staff groups were unaware of the multidimensional role of the housekeepers, episodes of significant psychosocial support given to patients were not only unrecognized, such support was not promoted. Consider the following exchange in which a housekeeper conveyed the boundedness of her psychosocial function. The housekeeper said, "Like Miss Thompson, for instance, before she left [for irradiation of a cancer site], she was, you know, just very depressed, and I came in her room and just sat down on a stool and talked to her a little while and had her laughing before I went out." I asked, "You don't have to do it for your job?" She replied, "No, I don't . . . I just go ahead and talk to 'em if they're real lonesome. You know, a lot of them [patients] are really, really lonesome, and if you can just have a little time with 'em . . . they're just lonely little people and if you can say a word or two to make them happy or make 'em feel a little better—you have the time—I don't see anything wrong with it."

Other housekeeper–CNA distinctions operated to alter the patient perception of encounters with the staff. Being a patient meant the surrender of a large degree of personal autonomy. CNAs could enter patient rooms, inquire about bowel habits, sleep habits, mood, touch the nude body and genitals, all as a part of nursing care regimens. On the other hand, the presence of a housekeeper in the patient rooms carried no threat of bodily invasion or other nursing tasks that often resembled infant care. The subsequent reduction of role and status inequities enhanced the encounter in the direction of psychosocial independence and away from institutional dependence.

In summary, the patients perceived the housekeepers as expected daily visitors who could converse at length, carry information throughout the nursing home, and report on local community matters on a routine basis. Housekeepers, then, not only "kept house" but also acted as a patient resource and a consistent provider of psychosocial support, although outside the standard boundaries of therapeutic agents. Thus, while nurses tended to the body, housekeepers tended to the mind.

Food Procurement Strategies

Tours of the nursing home given to families of prospective patients were conducted by the head nurse. They showed the staff orientation to eating as a biologic phenomenon, uncomplicated by psychosocial factors (cf. Clark and Bowling 1990). All of the major points of interest in the nursing home were shown and discussed with the families. This included the dining room, which was described as "homey" and "complete with residential-style furniture."

The head nurse stated to the family members that nutritious meals were provided by the facility with expert help from a registered dietician. The implication was that all the patient had to do was eat. This view was very correct from the perspective of able-bodied staff members and families. However, this was very unrealistic from the perspective of patients, who had to learn to negotiate the physical environment in special ways to make proper use of the food service.

The food procurement strategy observed in use by patients involved a series of sequenced steps. First, as the clock approached 11:15 A.M., patients began to position themselves in their rooms so they could see obliquely down the corridor to the dining room area. Alternatively, they stood in the doorways of their rooms and looked toward the dining room area, watching for the dining room light to be turned on by one of the dietary staff. This was the first signal that serving preparation was underway.

Second, when the light was seen, the patients began to move down the corridor toward the lobby area, near the dining room. Mealtimes were the only times during the day when the lobby area was used by large numbers of patients. Otherwise, the empty furniture awaited use in straight line arrangement. At mealtime, however, the couches, chairs, and rocking chairs in the lobby were all filled by patients who used them as an intermediate staging zone prior to their final destination. Patients sat in the lobby area watching the dining room from within a few yards of the "residential style" tables.

Patients discovered it necessary to watch the dining room area to determine at which end of the dining room the serving would begin. For example, if serving began at the west end and you sat at the east end, there would be approximately 30 more minutes after the west end began serving before you received your tray of food. Therefore, it was necessary to again watch the activities of the staff in order to know when you should begin moving toward your table. As soon as the first tray was placed, those who sat in that vicinity of the dining room would immediately move to their dining room seats and await the arrival of their trays. As tray distribution progressed towards the opposite end of the dining room, people moved from the lobby to their dining room seats in order to best time their arrival in the dining room with the arrival of the food in an appropriately hot or cold condition.

Food procurement behavior can be observed in the following sample of time-tracked fieldnotes:

11:15	Six in lobby, plus two visitors (one was George), two in entrance. This A.M. at breakfast, Mrs. King tried to get the kitchen to move her to her room to eat because Nelson plays in her food. The kitchen couldn't understand her and moved her to another table. King became mad and now her son is asking for King to be served in her room.
11:25	Mr. Moran and Mr. McPherson leave their room to TV part of lobby; Mrs. Smith also. Mr. Keller is looking out of his room.
11:30	14 in lobby, plus one visitor; kitchen lights off, no trays there; south wing has trays in halls.
11:32	Four people on east wing look out doors toward dining room; now Mrs. Nichols, too; now Mrs. Lochmiller; now Louise. Mrs. Johnson had walked from the last room by all of the other doors—30 seconds duration. Mr. Jones 28 seconds from his room to TV area.
11:35	16 in lobby; others on east wing still looking out. Mrs. Beatty 1:16 seconds from her room to her table; sits at her table alone in dark dining room.
11:40	17 in lobby and entrance; one in dining room.
11:41	Lights on in back dining room, those assigned to back of dining room move immediately to it.
11:42	First tray served.
11:45	Nine in lobby and entrance; 10 sitting in front dining room in the dark.
11:46	Lights on in front dining room, Mr. McPherson goes; Mr. Keller said that the kitchen alternates starting points and occasionally starts in the middle. Mrs. Stanley 57 seconds from her room to her table.
11:52	First person finished (Louise, Mr. Roberts is pushing her in wheel chair back to her room).
11:55	Four in lobby and entrance; Mr. Moran pushes Mrs. Ault to TV area for her soap opera (Moran and Ault eat at same table). 52 seconds Mrs. Smith from first rocker to her table chair.
12:00	Five in lobby and entrance (four have not been served).
12:06	Last tray served. Mr. Keller related this story: Mr. Cairl told the "cooks" one day that they started serving at the wrong end and they told him that they'd serve at any place they wanted to. 12 in dining room left when last tray served.
	One minute 26 seconds Mrs. Beatty from her table to her room. 35 seconds Mrs. Stanley from TV to her room. Mrs. Johnson stopped to check bulletin board. The diet sheet was completed before 12 people had finished eating.
12:21	Last person finishes (Mr. Stepic). Mrs. Roberts still cleaning from back to front of dining room. All but three patients are finished eating.
12:40	Mr. Roberts finishes, lights off in dining room, he has coffee sitting alone at a dining room table.

In order for a nursing home patient to eat food that is in its proper condition, timing, the physical environment, and one's own infirmities have to be considered in a cluster. The steps to "food getting" were obviously of high importance to patients at breakfast, lunch, and dinner. These were the times of the day at which they were provided with nutritional food by the facility in a congregate setting. Other times, only snack foods or some small amount of food that happened to be in preparation from the kitchen were available.

The staff perspective of what it was like to "simply" eat at Pecan Grove Manor was very different from the experience of the patients. These food procurement behaviors took place daily at this facility and were generally out of awareness or considered unimportant by the staff. Nonetheless, the patients had discovered, without the assistance of the professional staff, a way of negotiating their physical environment consistent with their remaining capacities for the improvement of their routine experience of institutional life.

SUMMARY

It is clear that the patient career (cf. Roth 1963) is most directly influenced by that segment of the nursing staff known as the CNAs. The style of caregiving is one in which physical care is emphasized to the neglect of psychosocial care. Several reasons exist for this skewing. The nursing staff supervisors are trained in the traditional medical model as L.P.N.s or R.N.s. Their training emphasizes physical therapy with only a slight orientation toward psychosocial parameters. Federal and state inspection clearly promotes and rewards medical action. For example, Pecan Grove Manor prides itself on having patient charts up-to-date, meaning that all entries had been made on a daily basis, particularly daily remarks regarding each patient. "Charting" consumes the vast majority of the licensed nurses' time. This practice becomes so perfunctory, however, that patients who are away visiting or in the hospital have been unintentionally charted as not only present, but the recipient of "usual A.M. care" or "up and about, cheerful" (cf. Gubrium 1975).

The CNA/patient/long term care institutional environment operates collectively to produce a community of daily forced interaction. The longevity of patient/CNA interaction coupled with a mother–child interactional pattern leads to in-depth knowledge of patient behaviors. The CNAs, being minimally trained, make use of their own physical senses and beliefs about health and disease to make decisions regarding therapeutic actions.

Psychosocial care is de-emphasized due to the pressures of fulfilling physical care needs. Most important, however, is the relative invisibility of psychosocial care procedures and benefits. Additionally, benefits that accrue are likely to be relatively gradual in appearance. Lastly, there is no staff member who is trained to be perceptive of the psychosocial environment, while conversely there are plenty of staff members who have received formal education in business management and medical-model nursing. These factors are reflected in the topics for in-service training.

CNAs and patients alike have an enormously difficult task. The patient career consists of pretending to be socially functional while, by some appearances, being totally expendable. One is the victim of chronic disease and social circumstance. CNAs, dressed in white, pretend to be therapeutically functional while dispensing palliative care. Patients become the victims of therapeutic expectation but incurable disease. Thus, CNAs and patients engage in a variety of rituals to fabricate a facsimile of life. In this way, the stark reality of chronic disease and old age can be partly veiled.

4

Health Trajectories and Long Term Care Choices: What Stories Told by Informants Can Tell Us

Lisa Groger

This chapter is based on interviews with 20 African-American elders, who told how they had chosen either nursing home care or in-home services.[1] Their stories revealed that functional status alone did not explain why some informants found themselves in nursing homes and others managed on in-home services. Their stories also revealed that aspects of choice and autonomy were intertwined with elements of coercion—intended, perceived, or both—and that some residents would have found it hard to say who had made the decision about their nursing home placement. The findings indicate considerable intragroup differences in the decision-making process for an otherwise relatively homogeneous group of individuals.

YOU SAY "RESPONDENT," I SAY "INFORMANT"

In using the term "respondents" or "informants," researchers signal that they are from different disciplines. The difference in the names they use for their interlocutors also indicates different expectations. The respondent, defined as one who responds or makes a reply, is expected to settle for one of several predetermined choices. Information not covered by these choices remains untapped, no matter how relevant it may be. The data-gathering phase leaves little room for surprise. In contrast, the informant, defined as one who gives information, is not only allowed but expected to lead the discourse into unmapped territory and to help the investigator discover how to formulate meaningful questions. Groping and probing are essential elements of this method; surprises are hoped for, integrated into the ongoing inquiry, and used to shape subsequent questions.

Until recently, most mainstream gerontological research was conducted with respondents and quantitative methods, which imply a scientific rigor deemed by some observers to be lacking in qualitative studies. As a result, qualitative researchers who ventured into gerontology found themselves apologizing for their relatively small (sometimes very small) samples and for the nongeneralizability of their findings. There is a growing recognition, however, that one can learn a lot from a few people, and that discovering the significant questions, rather than generalizability, is the point of qualitative research. This recognition has coincided with the realization that the more sophisticated the quantitative methodologies, the more questions they raise and the more tenuous is their explanatory power (Golant 1992).

In our search for better explanations, we are once again letting people speak, as evidenced by the emergence of a literature on how to conduct qualitative gerontological research. Publications on methods in gerontology either ignored qualitative approaches altogether or included only token examples (see Lawton and Herzog 1989; Schaie, Campbell, Meredith, and Rawlings 1988) until whole volumes dedicated to the subject appeared (Gubrium and Sankar 1994; Morse 1992; Reinharz and Rowles 1988). These methodological explorations have been paralleled by ethnographies of life in nursing homes (Gubrium 1993; Savishinsky 1991; Shield 1988) and of the struggle of frail elders (Gubrium 1990; Rubinstein, Kilbride, and Nagy 1992). Goffman's (1961) classic work on processes and types of adjustment to total institutions can be seen as a precursor to nursing home ethnography. These richly detailed accounts from the insiders' points of view often complement findings from quantitative studies, and sometimes contradict or question them.

Functional status and decision making about long term care are two areas about which we have a considerable amount of information based on quantitative, large-scale studies. These studies have identified functional status as one of the predictors of institutionalization (see Hanley, Alecxih, Wiener, and Kennell 1990), and participation in the decision to institutionalize as one of the predictors of adjustment to, and satisfaction with, life in a nursing home (see Reinardy 1992). Whether these studies use few or many variables, they assume that everything else is equal. Everything else is never equal, however, and often the findings raise more questions than they answer. Even studies that deal with a relatively large number of variables usually cannot capture elements of context that may be crucially relevant to the subject of inquiry. Nor can they capture and interpret elements of ambiguity, ambivalence, contradictions, and feelings that are an integral part of experience. For example, an affirmative answer to the question "Can you prepare your meals?"—intended to measure functional ability—actually may reflect the level of effort individuals consider reasonable or desirable for accomplishing this task. The answer also may vary depending on respondents' perception of the meaning of "a meal," "preparing a meal," and even the word "can." A negative response from a male may indicate social norms rather than physical disabilities. Similarly, a closed-ended question such as "Did you or someone else decide that you should go to a nursing home?" may fail to elicit what happened because it reduces a complex process to a simple event.

To illustrate these points, I report the findings from a qualitative study that asked 20 African-American elders—10 nursing home residents and 10 home care clients—how they had chosen their long-term care setting.

DESCRIPTION OF METHODS

Using a semistructured, open-ended interview format, I explored the health histories of 20 African-American elders in a metropolitan area in Ohio. Because this phase of the research did not attempt to compare African-Americans with whites or other groups, its findings cannot be assumed to be specific to African-Americans. The nursing home residents (six females and four males) lived in three different facilities; the home care clients (nine females and one male) received services provided under a home care program in the metropolitan area. Ohio's PASSPORT program screens and assesses applicants for long term care and refers them either to a nursing home or to home care services.[2] Home care recipients were recruited through caseworkers at the Area Agency on Aging (AAA), which administers the PASSPORT program. The AAA also provided information on functional assessment, medical diagnoses, demographic characteristics, and informal support. Nursing home residents in the three opportunistically selected facilities were recruited by the administrators, who also provided data on the residents' health.[3]

All informants were cognitively competent and were able to give informed consent. I ascertained cognitive competence in conversation with the prospective participants before the actual interview. I rejected the use of a more formal measure because such measures might be culturally inappropriate for populations from which they were not derived originally. I considered informants competent if they could answer a series of questions about themselves and could sustain a conversation. Typically, I asked questions that were part of the interview: I asked about their health and about how they were feeling, and I let their responses shape my subsequent questions. My sample is highly biased in the sense that each of the three facilities that took part in the study had more cognitively impaired than cognitively competent African-American residents.

The major instrument used in this research was a one-time interview that allowed for open-endedness and contingencies while focusing at the same time on a set of central questions. Questions about informants' health histories were asked in a general and nondirective manner and were followed by prompts to explore all formal characteristics of the topic under question. I explored informants' histories of declining functional abilities with this opening question: "Tell me the story of what happened since you first became sick." I tape-recorded the interviews, which lasted from 45 minutes to two hours. This qualitative approach, which is exploratory and inductive, seeks to identify the informants' views and experiences; by doing so, it uncovers a reality and yields categories and concepts that the researcher could not have constructed a priori. In other words, this kind of open-ended but focused interview allows one to achieve the ethnographic objective of discovering what the meaningful questions are without having to engage in participant observation. This is clearly an advantage when the more time-consuming and sometimes inappropriate or impractical requirements of participant observation cannot be met. On the other hand, it limits one to working with cognitively competent informants, which is one of the limitations of this study [see Silverman and McAllister, this volume]. Another limitation is that the interview is the only major source of data. In an ideal, multiple-method approach, this kind of interview would be complemented by some participant observation.

Through close analysis of the verbatim transcriptions of the interviews, the researcher builds theories or models to explain the data. The aim is not to achieve representativeness but to capture as much variation as possible. The ultimate objective of the analysis is to discover categories, relationships, and informants' assumptions about the topic. First, each utterance is treated as an observation, without reference to its context, in a process of "open coding" (Strauss and Corbin 1990). Then each observation is elaborated in the context of the transcript and with reference to the literature on the topic. The next step requires the identification of the interconnection between observations or themes. Finally, themes are scrutinized for patterns, consistency, and contradictions (McCracken 1988). The procedure for analyzing narrative is basically the same as that used for analyzing field notes (Spradley 1980, Gubrium and Sankar 1994). The need to become intimately familiar and to stay in touch with large amounts of narrative, and the exploratory intent of the method, make a sample of 20 informants both small enough to be practical and large enough to supply sufficient information.

DIFFERENCES AMONG INFORMANTS

Text analysis of the verbatim transcriptions of the interviews in my study revealed three different health trajectory patterns. It also showed the extent to which the nursing home placement decision is a process rather than an event. Nursing home residents and PASSPORT clients seemed particularly well suited for exploring the pathways to different long term care arrangements because applicants must be in need of nursing home care to qualify for the PASSPORT program. Thus, in theory, PASSPORT clients and nursing home residents presumably were comparable in functional ability. As a group, however, the nursing home residents in my sample were five years older and more seriously impaired in their activities of daily living (ADLs). Five nursing home residents could not walk and needed assistance with dressing and/or eating; one was ambulatory but needed some help with dressing; four were completely ambulatory and needed no help with ADLs. Of the three home care clients who could not walk, two were considered temporarily nonambulatory because they were recovering from foot or leg injuries. Three home care clients were completely ambulatory; four had some problems with ambulation. In a comparison of the two groups by medical diagnosis—allegedly more accurate than ADLs for measuring African-Americans' health status (Gibson 1991)—PASSPORT clients were only slightly less afflicted. The two groups resembled each other in the incidence of diabetes, heart disease, and hypertension, but differed in the incidence of stroke, a potentially very disabling condition. Members of both groups were diagnosed with multiple chronic conditions; nursing home residents suffered on the average from 5.8 conditions (range 3–11), compared with home care clients' 5.4 conditions (range 4–8).

Nursing home residents differed from home care clients most notably in their health trajectory patterns or illness histories (Groger 1993). As a group, the nursing home residents also had thinner informal support, either because of childlessness or geographic distance from children and other kin, or because of tenuous social relationships. Differences in social support, however, did not explain why some of these elders were living in a nursing home while others, similarly impaired, managed on in-home services. One informant could remain at home only because her informal support supplemented the formal services she received. Others remained at home in spite of exploitation by potential informal helpers; yet others found themselves in a nursing home despite their good informal support. The combined concepts of health trajectory and coping history made more intelligible the informants' greatly variable perceptions of what constituted "adequate" informal support and illuminated the often startling discrepancy between their objectively measured health status and their subjective perception.

THE STUDY OF FUNCTIONAL STATUS

The ability to perform ADLs (activities of daily living, such as bathing and showering, dressing, eating, toileting, getting in and out of bed, walking, climbing stairs, and getting outside) and IADLs (instrumental activities of daily living, such as meal preparation, shopping, money management, using the phone, and doing housework) is a widely used indicator of functional status. Compelling arguments have been made in favor of uniform assessment instruments for measuring functional status (Kane and Geron 1991). Yet a uniform assessment instrument cannot be sensitive to the cultural, educational, linguistic, gender, and value differences it is bound to encounter, not only in representative national samples but also in regional and local samples. If measurement errors may result in inaccurate assessment of whites, the possibilities for error are multiplied when these instruments are used for minorities (Markides, Liang, and Jackson 1990). Differences in linguistic style, linguistic expression, behavioral style, and behavioral expression all may cause error when instruments derived from one group are applied to others (Jackson 1989). Considerable error may also arise from differences in respondents' interpretations of questions about their ability to perform ADL tasks (Wiener, Hanley, Clark, and Van Nostrand 1990).

Even when care has been taken to minimize these sources of error, ADL/IADL measures cannot capture such elusive but consequential qualities as "struggle for independence" and "refusal to define oneself as incompetent." Yet these were the characteristics of informants in my study who resisted nursing home placement against all odds and who lived with in-home services despite their severe functional limitations. Functional status as measured by ADL/IADL scales did not explain some informants' choice of a long term care setting. All informants needed some help with IADLs, the kinds of activities that PASSPORT choreworkers typically provide. Three of the home care clients were ADL independent, but so were four of the nursing home residents. The seven other home care clients, including two who supposedly were temporarily nonambulatory, had ambulation problems of varying degrees. Yet even the notion of being "permanently" versus "temporarily" nonambulatory begs the question of how that determination is made, and by whom. For example, an old person who is expected to be permanently nonambulatory after a leg amputation may walk again and manage on in-home services, while another who is expected to recover from a foot injury may become permanently nonambulatory and end up in a nursing home. I argue that different health trajectories, or histories of illness, had equipped informants in this study with different coping strategies that made them more or less vulnerable to institutionalization.

HEALTH TRAJECTORIES

Home care clients followed one of two trajectories; both of these were marked by the informants' struggle for independence and their refusal to define themselves as sick.

Home Care Clients: Long History of Illness

The first trajectory produced elders experienced in coping with illness as part of normal life. In spite of long-standing health problems, they defined themselves as competent. Their discourse also revealed a determined struggle for independence. They refused to assume the sick role even in a health crisis; this refusal made them more likely candidates for in-home services. A case example will illustrate these home care clients' determination to transcend their ailments.

Mrs. W, age 75, lives alone in a two-room apartment in a large, littered, desolate public housing complex. Her daughter died of a heart attack at age 40. Her own diagnosis includes epilepsy, a heart condition, poor vision, color blindness, a left-eye cataract, obesity, and diabetes. Her legs and feet are so swollen that she cannot wear shoes. Because she spends most of her time in a wheelchair, she has pressure sores.

Mrs. W greeted me with the statement that she was trying to reach Senator Metzenbaum's office and that she was a fighter. Her repertory of coping mechanisms consists of an array of culturally appropriate metaphors for assistance. She indicated that God and her mailman constitute her only informal support. God guided her finger to dial the PASSPORT phone number, and he makes miracles happen right there in her kitchen: the medicine she needs turns up, as does the nurse when she needs her. God has also helped her in defending herself against exploitative and predatory grandsons and great-grandsons. When asked how she felt on the day of the interview, she replied:

I feel wonderful. God let me live long enough to see this day. And I walk aroun' in here. And when I git tired I just sit down in this chair. . . . And the food. I enjoy my food. I praise the Lord when I'm eatin' 'cause it tastes good. Um-hm. I really enjoy my food better'n I used to. . . . My feet and legs are swelled. But they stay swelled so much, I guess I just don't pay it no 'tention. . . . And when my feet swell it leak a little bit. It's bound to leak like that when it swell.

Informants such as Mrs. W, who has a long history of illness, learned to deal with their long-standing ailments by considering them almost as normal. People around them were sick; they themselves had been sick so long that they had become used to it. This approach leads Mrs. S, another informant who has disabling asthma, to believe seriously that a sprained ankle is her only handicap. These women, having coped with illness for years while they went about the business of working, raising children, managing households, and scraping by on limited incomes, did not question their ability to continue to cope. By defining themselves as competent and by not allowing the environment to define them as incompetent, they refuse to enter the "vicious cycle of induced incompetence" (Kuypers and Bengtson 1984).

Home care clients' struggle for competence and autonomy and their determination to define themselves as competent are embodied by Mrs. B. Although virtually bedridden with crippling arthritis, she can say: "When I get to where I can't do for myself..." Other informants reflected the same feelings by stressing what they *could* do and what they insisted on doing, often with great effort and difficulty. (Attempts to defend oneself against abusive offspring are part of the struggle for independence of two home care clients.) The struggle for independence also manifests itself quite positively in attempts to manage liminality and to minimize disability. Mrs. S, who administers oxygen to herself for her asthma when she is "well," and who goes to the hospital for recurring crises, tells the story of her attempts to normalize her hospitalizations by making her hospital quarters as homelike as possible and by engaging in housekeeping activities "just like I do at home."

Home Care Clients: Crisis Strikes the Resilient

The pattern of resisting dependency was followed by two home care clients who had enjoyed relatively good health and who continued to define themselves as healthy even in a health crisis. They took crises in stride, were determined to recover, and returned to living alone at home, assisted by PASSPORT.

Mr. T, age 72, had a severe heart attack at the age of 64 and suffered "a light stroke" five years later, one year after his wife died. The stroke caused him to tumble down the stairs. When he talks about it, he minimizes both the injury from the fall ("I skinned my leg all up. I had a big sore on my leg, and that wasn't very much") and the stroke ("I just had a stroke... it wasn't that bad"). His narrative stresses his recovery: how he was never out of control; how his brother reassured him that he was "strong enough to overcome"; how he knew that he had strength; how he had bought a cane that he used until one day he forgot it in the grocery cart ("I walked away from that cane, and that was it"); and how his family encouraged him in his quest for competence and independence by not letting him go back to retrieve his cane.

Mrs. F expressed the same determination to overcome a potentially very disabling health crisis which culminated in a below-the-knee amputation when she was 80 years old:

Before I knew anything, I was diabetic. They done cut this leg off about four years ago. Oh, my goodness, that got to me. I stayed in the hospital so many days, and then I went home. I had my own home. I done pretty good, I got up and done my cooking. I didn't have too much trouble [walking]. I done pretty good to say I didn't have but a leg and a piece [prosthesis]. I had one leg and a piece, so I managed pretty well. I just kept getting better and better. I done what I wanted to do around the house. . . . My own doctor told me "You're in such good shape, you don't have to come back for three months." Well, I don't need no nursing care.

In both cases, the environment encouraged the informants in their efforts to define themselves as competent. Their ability either to cope with chronic illness or to overcome a health crisis distinguishes them from nursing home residents, whose reactions to a health crisis were quite different.

Nursing Home Residents: Crisis Strikes the Vulnerable

Eight nursing home residents who followed the pattern of accepting dependency were overwhelmed by their crises.[4] By definition, institutionalization is a last resort for people who are overwhelmed by the demands of independent living. Although this point is obvious, it is less clear what makes a health crisis more overwhelming for some elders than for others. In spite of individual differences in the specifics of their adjustment to crises, nursing home residents shared certain features that might explain their institutionalization. They were more likely to define themselves as incompetent after a health crisis and to accept other people's definition of them as incompetent. Home care clients' narrative indicated an active approach, as expressed by the preponderant use of the first person pronoun followed by active verbs: "I tried to," "I managed," "I learned," "I can." In contrast, the eight overwhelmed nursing home residents were the recipients of actions by others: "They decided I couldn't stay by myself," "They sent me here," "They thought it was best." When they used the first person pronoun, it was usually followed by what they couldn't do: "I'm a half person," "I was helpless," "I can't." Although all of the nursing home residents knew about in-home services, they considered institutionalization as their only option. Two examples illustrate how their accounts differ in tone and mood from those of the home care clients.

Mrs. K, a 79-year-old widow, is an ambulatory nursing home resident who suffered a heat stroke one Sunday morning in 1983. Her reaction to the event was incomprehension and helplessness. After two hospitalizations, each of which was followed first by a short stay with her brother and then by a return home, her physician and her brother decided that she should go to a nursing home.

I had this heat stroke. . . . I don't understand it. . . . I went home and I had been doing pretty good. Then I started feeling weak and sick, and didn't know what was wrong with me. . . . They decided I couldn't stay by myself.

Although Mrs. K was unhappy about the decision, she did not question or oppose it. She also accepted others' definition of her as incompetent: "My brother said I couldn't stay by myself. . . . The doctor told me that I couldn't come home and live by myself."

Mrs. N, 78, who had a stroke but is ambulatory, defined herself in a similar fashion as incapable. She speaks about others having declared her unable to live by herself. Mrs. N is still mystified by their description of her condition, but she accepts that evaluation and uses images of helplessness to describe herself:

I was having some kind of spells . . . and my doctor told me I couldn't stay at home. The people in the hospital said I had a stroke, but the way it made my legs turn under, buckle up, whatever you want to call it, like a little young baby that can't stand on their legs, well I don't know what it is, whatever it is, it's got the whole alphabet in it. . . . I couldn't be by myself.

These nursing home residents had accepted others' judgments concerning both their situations and their incompetence. Although they did not understand their diagnoses, they did not challenge them. In contrast to the home care clients discussed above, they felt acted upon by outside forces which they did not attempt to resist. These characteristics may well be the reason why most nursing home residents in this study participated only minimally in their placement decisions.

DECISIONS ABOUT LONG TERM CARE

The notion of patient autonomy is an important aspect of health care decisions (Coulton, Dunkle, Chow, Haug, and Vielhaber 1988; Coulton, Dunkle, Goode, and MacKintosh 1982; Dubler 1988; High 1988; Jameton 1988; Reinardy 1992; Smerglia, Deimling, and Barresi 1988). Yet this is only one of many dimensions of the complex decision process that leads to nursing home placement. From a strictly legal point of view, family members have no right to decide for a competent patient. In practice, however, family members play an important part in the decision in two ways: they can provide or withhold crucial informal support, and they can exercise their power of persuasion over the patient (Jecker 1990). Whereas the public part of the decision process involving patient, family, and professionals is amply documented in case studies (see Dill 1987a, 1987b), the private interaction between patient and family, by definition, is inaccessible to scrutiny.

The decision to institutionalize is all the more momentous because it is often irreversible, generates ambivalent and contradictory feelings, concerns many persons in addition to the patient, and raises legal, ethical, and philosophical questions about the very nature of autonomy, competence, individual best interest, and common good (Arras 1987; Collopy 1988; Dubler 1988; Hofland 1988; Jecker 1990; Kapp 1991; Moody 1987). It has been suggested that planning can enhance a person's autonomy and empowerment for dealing with health decisions in later life (Clark 1987), and that a relationship exists between well-being and participation in health care decisions (Harel and Noelker 1982; Kapp 1991; Reinardy 1992). According to this reasoning, a person who decided autonomously, or who participated in the decision to enter a nursing home, would be more likely to be satisfied with the outcome of this decision than someone who was institutionalized against her will, or who entered the nursing home reluctantly after having participated only minimally in the decision.

My findings suggest that participation in the decision about nursing home placement is not an all-or-nothing activity and that even seemingly minimal participation may give a feeling of empowerment to the person whose institutionalization is determined essentially by others. Protracted negotiation may make it difficult to say who actually made the decision. The placement decision for the nursing home residents in this study was shown to be a process, not an event. Informants' arrival in the nursing home represents only one point in a lengthy process involving multiple actors (self and others), multiple modes of interaction among the actors (independent decision, imposition, opposition, negotiation, agreement, delegation), distinct phases (assessing health status, examining preconceptions, evaluating options, seeking information, inspecting facilities, completing paperwork, disposing of the patient's belongings, and entering the nursing home), and outcomes that may change over time (dissatisfaction, satisfaction, and coping—that is, efforts to overcome dissatisfaction and to move toward satisfaction). When all of these factors are taken into consideration, the number of possible scenarios exceeds the number of participants in this study. Although the number of informants is too small to reveal definitive patterns of decision making, the study indicates considerable intragroup differences in the decision-making process.

The themes that emerged from the aggregate of nursing home cases point to a processual model of decision making involving three questions: *whether* to institutionalize, *where* to go, and *how* to dispose of the patient's belongings. One or more actors, including or excluding the person whose move is being considered (self), may participate to varying degrees in each one of these three discrete and necessary aspects of the decision. Although at some point these three aspects may be dealt with simultaneously, they are addressed in temporal order. This temporal or processual dimension is clearly discernible in the possible phases and the actual steps by which the decision proceeds; one does not deal concretely with the "how" unless one has decided on the "whether."

The question whether to institutionalize invariably requires a judgment about the patient's health status, other options, and available resources. For the informants in this study, the resources considered were informal support as possible alternatives to institutionalization, formal support such as PASSPORT, and Medicaid eligibility as a prerequisite for institutionalization. As the actors contemplated their own or someone else's institutionalization, they drew on their preconceptions about nursing homes in general and on their knowledge of, and familiarity with, particular nursing homes. Together these considerations influenced how they approached the task at hand.

Once the "whether" has been determined, concrete questions about the "where" are in order. During this phase, the same or different actors may gather information, inspect facilities, consult professionals, apply to facilities, and carry out any other necessary paperwork. When the activities of this phase are well under way or completed, the process culminates in disposing of the belongings of the person entering the facility. Although this process may rarely achieve the ideal orderliness, its elements (all of which emerged from the interviews) indicate the complexity and the processual nature of placement decisions.

The actors participating in the decision process can interact with each other in a number of ways that represent points on a continuum between total patient autonomy (self decides independently and informs others of decision) and apparent total relinquishing of autonomy (self delegates all aspects of the decision). Two informants were in the former extreme category; none belonged to the latter. The others fell somewhere between the two extremes: they had reached consensus via different modes of interaction, including conflict, or never had reached consensus at all. Table 4.1 summarizes the individual scenarios in terms of the actors involved, their mode of interaction, and the resulting adaptation by the resident. It shows a clear relationship between autonomy and satisfaction for only four residents. Two residents made their decision completely autonomously and are satisfied with it. Two others, on whom the decision was imposed, were opposed to it and remain dissatisfied with their situation. The other six cases illustrate the complex relationships among the component parts of the decision, in which different actors may participate to varying degrees. These six nursing home residents would have found it difficult to say whether they or others had made the decision, or who had had the "final say" (Smerglia et al. 1988). One could argue that they exercised their final say by ultimately accepting institutionalization as the outcome of a negotiated decision. One also could consider a deliberate delegation of the decision as a special kind of autonomous decision. Although none of the informants delegated all aspects of the decision process, such complete delegation is certainly conceivable.

Informants also differed in their ability to consider other options to institutionalization. Some of the perceived options—such as staying with one's children—may have been unrealistic; others may represent retrospective efforts to rationalize the outcome. Such retrospective rationalization can be viewed as one of the coping mechanisms that helped informants to progress from opposition or dissatisfaction to acceptance or satisfaction, as epitomized most often by the statement "I made myself satisfied." Three informants, who embarked on the decision-making process jointly with

Table 4.1
Individual Scenarios for Nursing Home Placements

Case	Decision	Actor(s)	Interaction	Adaptation	No. Months in NH
1 and 2	Whether Where How	Self	Autonomy	Satisfaction	25 and 216
3 and 4	Whether Where How	Others	Imposition Opposition	Dissatisfaction	76 and 24
5	Whether Where How	Others	Imposition Suggestion Acceptance	Coping	34
6	Whether Where How	Others	Imposition Opposition Resignation	Coping	19
7	Whether Where How	Others	Imposition Acceptance	Satisfaction	3
8	Whether Where How	Self and Others	Suggestion Opposition Negotiation	Satisfaction	29
9	Whether Where How	Others Self Others	Suggestion Acceptance	Satisfaction	15
10	Whether Where How	Self and Others Others and Self Others	Suggestion Negotiation Acceptance	Satisfaction Unhappiness	9

others in a "negotiated consent" (Moody 1988), finally reached satisfaction, or acceptance resembling satisfaction, but so did one of the three whose placement had been decided by others. The other two are coping in ways that indicate their desire to find satisfaction. Lack of autonomy in making all aspects of the decision did not automatically result in dissatisfaction. This point suggests that some elders indeed may be happy to be relieved of the sole burden of such an important decision (Kapp 1991).

In spite of the informants' relatively long nursing home residence (see Table 4.1), their reaction to the placement decision should be viewed not as an outcome but as an adaptation which changed between the time of placement and the time of the interview, and which may still be changing. In writing about 502 newly admitted residents, Reinardy (1992:102) states that perceived control may be an accurate predictor for the period following the baseline but "becomes questionable . . . as a retrospective measure for what has come before. It may be biased, for example, by the informants' initial experience of the nursing home" (p. 102). One also could argue that the previous events color the initial experience of the nursing home. For example, dissatisfaction with the disposal of one's belongings may result in post-admission adjustment problems that are unrelated to the post-admission experience, as was the case with one informant in this study (Groger 1994). The drama and the process begin before and continue after institutionalization, and assimilating this experience is part of the process. Coping strategies such as retroactive rationalization may enable residents to achieve some kind of satisfaction with their situation.

The considerable differences in the scenarios reflect the complexity of the decision process. How easily this process unfolds depends, among other things, on the actors' prior experience with nursing homes. Positive experience with nursing homes helps them to overcome some of the most negative stereotypes, and thus can ease the process considerably. One's own caregiving experience may result in higher expectations that one's children will make similar sacrifices, or it may have the opposite effect. Finally, a person's life experience and personality will affect the decision process. In some cases, after a life of poverty, a person may even experience institutionalization as a release from the struggle for daily necessities.

DISCUSSION

The stories told by informants give us glimpses of a complex reality that might not have been captured by the standard closed-ended instruments used to measure functional status and participation in health care decisions. Open-ended questions are generally more appropriate and useful for research on subjects about which little is known, particularly with minorities (see Jackson 1989). The usefulness of these qualitatively derived concepts should be explored on a larger sample and cross-culturally. Could the notion of health trajectories that are embedded in my informants' narratives be confirmed with a larger sample of African-Americans? To what extent and in what form would they also emerge from interviews with members of other groups? Similarly, one might use the decision model as a map for exploring patterns of variation and regularities within any group and for examining differences between groups. One also might use it for exploring decision processes that do not result in institutionalization. What combination of perceived options, perceived and actual resources, and assertiveness of the various actors results in one outcome or another?

The discourse of participants in this exploratory study revealed differences in coping behaviors between nursing home residents and home care clients. Home care clients demonstrated a fierce determination to remain "independent" in spite of chronic and disabling ailments. In contrast, nursing home residents were helpless in the face of a health crisis and were more likely to define themselves as incompetent. Until and unless we can be sure that such a negative self-evaluation is the result rather than the cause of institutionalization, intake assessment should be sensitive to such salient personality traits. The findings from this study suggest that informants' past history of dealing with illness may indicate how they will react to a health crisis in the future; this point should be taken into consideration in evaluating their risk for institutionalization.

5

Ethnography and the Nursing Home Ombudsman

Lynn D. Mason

INTRODUCTION

Staff and volunteers in the national Long Term Care Ombudsman Program promote, monitor, and mediate resident rights issues in nursing homes and board and care facilities. The view presented in this chapter is that ombudsmen activities are inherently ethnographic and can be strengthened by consciously using the insights and methods of "folk description." Qualitative research is an essential aspect of rights violation documentation, complaint resolution, and quality of life monitoring. In turn, qualitative nursing home research can benefit from the unique vantage point of the ombudsman-advocate. This perspective comes from three years as a volunteer ombudsman in two Denver nursing homes and from earlier training and teaching in cultural anthropology.[1]

The Long Term Care Ombudsman Program was initiated in the early 1970s in response to growing public awareness of nursing home abuses (cf. Sarton's *As We Are Now*, 1973) and the need for stronger consumer protection activities to supplement government regulation. The reform movement was sparked by the scathing reports of Mendelson (1974), Butler (1975), Moss and Halamandaris (1977), Vladeck (1980), and other vocal critics, nurtured by the grass roots investigative advocacy of the National Coalition of Nursing Home Reform (1985), and brought to maturity in the Institute of Medicine's report, *Improving the Quality of Care in Nursing Homes* (1986). These efforts aggressively promoted higher care standards and affirmed that residents' views and expressions of self-determination really matter.

The Ombudsman Program (OP) is authorized in the Older Americans Act and administered by the Administration on Aging primarily through state and local area agencies on aging. Each state's mandated ombudsman is expected to (1) investigate complaints made by or on behalf of nursing home residents; (2) monitor the development of federal, state, and local laws and regulations related to long term care; (3) provide information to families, agencies, policy-makers, and other interested parties; and (4) coordinate training for staff and volunteers in each area agency. By 1988 the OP supported over 1,200 paid staff and 9,000 volunteers, who in turn processed 130,000 complaints annually (Fraser 1993).

The OP was upgraded significantly, along with resident rights, in the 1987 Omnibus Budget Reconciliation Act (OBRA). For the first time in the history of nursing home regulation, "quality of (resident) life" became an inspection survey issue, and "quality of care" was linked to specific planning and outcome measures. Promoting resident rights became a requirement for nursing home Medicare/Medicaid participation, and direct access by ombudsmen to residents and their records (with their consent) and state surveys also was mandated.

OMBUDSMEN RECRUITING AND TRAINING

Nursing home ombudsmen are ostensibly impartial and accessible to residents, families, staff, and administrators alike—in the spirit of the 18th-century Swedish political ombudsmen, after which the OP is modeled. In most encounters, however, they will be found advocating most strongly for residents and their well being. Local ombudsman programs typically seek staff and volunteers motivated to serve institutionalized elderly in several roles, including advocate, educator, investigator, observer, conflict mediator, and friendly visitor.

Personal qualities considered essential in the successful volunteer ombudsman include an ability to recognize and work sympathetically through the physical and mental problems and limitations of one's clients, a tolerance for ambiguity and resentment, and respect for cultural, ethnic, and personality differences among residents, staff, and others (Colorado Ombudsman Program 1989:5). Strong kneecaps for kneeling on hard hallway floors to talk with wheelchair-bound residents are also helpful.

Volunteer and staff training is guided by a curriculum produced by the National Association of State Units on Aging (NASUA) and modified by many states to suit local needs. Colorado, for instance, requires 20 hours of volunteer training prior to placement and at least eight hours every year of "continuing education" in the form of seminars, training workshops, lectures, and volunteer support activities.

Trainees are exposed to materials on such topics as the long term care system, life and work in nursing homes, biopsychosocial aspects of aging, medical vocabulary, empowerment strategies, and conflict resolution. Topics featuring some ethnographic slant related to investigative research include: verbal and nonverbal communication; active listening; sensitivity to diverse values and impaired mental and physical states; interviewing techniques; using the five senses to detect abuse, substandard care, and other problems; documenting complaints and analyzing evidence; and reviewing records (NASUA 1992; Colorado Ombudsman Program 1989).

The Colorado training manual briefly discusses interviewing skills in terms of setting, timing, goals, establishing rapport, maintaining objectivity, using open-ended and closed-ended questions, and explaining to residents and staff how information will be used. Note taking tips are offered, although ways of organizing and coding field notes are not suggested. The training materials discuss how people use personal and social space but do not mention ethnic variability or cite Edward Hall's original research (1966) in proxemics, the study of cultural differences in interpersonal spacing. The sensory world of the aged is explored cursorily using several sensory limiting and deprivation exercises (e.g., reading small print with Vaseline-smeared eyeglasses and wearing gloves to open small tamper-proof medicine bottles). Participant observation is not named as such but is implied in the statement that "many complaints can only be understood and verified by sharing in the experience of the complainant." Trainees also are encouraged to participate with residents in organized activities, such as meals, resident council meetings, and social events (Colorado Ombudsman Program 1989: 59).

NURSING HOMES AS GRASS HUTS: ETHNOGRAPHIC POSSIBILITIES AND APPLICATIONS

Following their formal introduction to key staff and several residents at assigned nursing homes, ombudsmen begin self-paced visiting and documentation of concerns and complaints. The ethnographic parallels and openings quickly become apparent. Like the ethnographer, the ombudsman seeks to reveal and document the "inside situation." As Jennie Keith points out, until recently "the activities and attitudes of old people among themselves were as unknown as any unexplored tribal village. The qualitative aspects of older people's lives in any setting are still exotic data" (1986: 8).

Culture shock is common to both ethnographer and ombudsman. Those entering nursing homes for the first time experience varying levels of discomfort, disbelief, and bewilderment before settling into personalized investigative routines. Their first impressions might be similar to those of Sallie Tisdale, who described her nursing home work setting as "a place of misfits . . . (with) a language of its own, customs of its own . . . (and) slightly out of plane, not quite polite, designed for people who have no other place to go, no other place to be, who don't mingle with the rest of us" (1987:xiii).

The ombudsman's ongoing tasks include explaining one's presence and purpose to wary staff and curious or confused residents. Part of the inevitable discomfort arises from the realization that so many individuals appear to be suffering and that the ombudsman can play only a minuscule part in documenting and alleviating that suffering. As Joel Savishinsky discovered while conducting his nursing home volunteer pet therapy research, the "emotional costs of doing research (are) paid in the coin of discomfort, disillusionment, and uncertainty. From the very start there was the question of whether people could really be happy living in such places" (1991:19). The ombudsman's activity is intrusive, and doubts about when to intrude and whether intruding and intervening really will make a difference may nibble at one's confidence. How does one begin conversations with those who are strapped in wheelchairs in the hallway dozing or gazing into space and seemingly oblivious to everyone and everything around them? What are the appropriate openings? What do you do when they rave or stare at you and say nothing?

Like the ethnographer, the ombudsman tries to make sense of a "separate" community in which social organization, behavior, values, and meaning constitute what needs to be documented and interpreted. The key questions for both are: "What is going on here?" "How do I know it?" and "How do I validate it?" Both recognize the importance and humanity of understanding their subjects by observing and interacting with them in their own territory and inviting them to "speak their minds." Both attempt to control personal bias and ethnocentrism and are sensitized to the ethical considerations surrounding investigator–informant relations. And both organize their tasks around research problem definition and design, data collection and analysis, and reporting.

RESEARCH PROBLEM AND DESIGN

Residents generally become quite receptive to the ombudsman's advocacy and research efforts—especially when the latter are explained in relation to improving their care. The central research issues for the ombudsman are quality of life and care in general and resident rights in particular: how they are defined, perceived, expressed, encouraged, and violated or ignored.

Resident rights currently are defined broadly to include civil, legal, and personal conduct that fosters autonomy and well-being. They encompass dignity and respect; access to information (including medical records);

self-determination in choice and participation; privacy and confidentiality; socialization and activities; visitors and communications; finances and property; grievance procedures; freedom from abuse and restraints; and due process in admissions, transfer, relocation, and discharge. Within these general categories are over 30 explicit rights that residents are supposed to be informed about upon admission and which are required to be posted for their viewing (Table 5.1).

The official version of resident rights—defined primarily by policy-makers with some input from advocates, caregivers, and articulate residents—is a normative template imposed by the regulatory system on staff and residents. Against this ethical model of how residents should be treated and allowed to act, the insiders' views and actions can be compared. (Cf. Pelto 1970:84 for his discussion of the application of "embedded emicism" in fieldwork settings where it is important to gather information as much as possible from "the actors' point of view.")

The regulatory emphasis on resident rights parallels the contemporary focus in biomedical ethics on the patient bill of rights, in particular the promotion of patient autonomy and informed consent. Self-determination is widely rationalized and expressed as a core American value and, not surprisingly, it has become a predominant factor in health care decision-making protocols. Its advancement has succeeded most often in acute care settings. In nursing homes and other chronic care arenas in which frailty, physical disabilities, and mental deficits fill the work day, autonomy (viewed in terms of effective deliberation and voluntary, intentional action) is conspicuous by its restraint and constraint. In fact, as Rosalie Kane points out (1990:5), "infringements of personal autonomy are so commonplace and efforts to protect agreed-upon areas of autonomy so unsuccessful that many observers have come to accept rather severe limits in personal autonomy as the 'way things are.' "

Trained and encouraged to challenge the "way things are" in nursing homes, the ombudsman looks for and documents autonomy denied, curtailed, or successfully expressed. A dozen reasons why residents don't routinely insist on and exercise their rights have been suggested by the National Citizens' Coalition for Nursing Home Reform (NCCNHR 1985: II, 17–18) and summarized in the training curriculum (NASUA 1992: 94–96). Reasons listed include the following: (1) residents are intimidated by the idea of appearing in any way to criticize the nursing home; (2) most residents do not know that they have specified rights and what those rights are; (3) residents have few relationships within which to practice interactive or assertiveness skills; (4) residents who are aware of their rights still must choose their battles and contend with daily violations of their individuality and dignity to avoid retaliation or worse consequences; (5) since violations are a routine part of daily care, they are perceived as normal or inevitable; and (6) many residents experience tensions between their desire

Table 5.1
Nursing Home Resident Rights

All residents (or their proxies, when appropriate) have a right to:

- Freedom of choice in selecting a health care facility.
- Adequate and appropriate health care.
- Knowledge of available choices.
- Independent personal decisions.
- Encouragement and assistance from the staff in exercising these rights.
- Vote (inside and outside the facility).
- Participate in activities inside and outside the facility.
- Present grievances on behalf of him/herself or others without fear of reprisal.
- Participate in the resident council.
- Be informed (address and telephone number) about the nursing home ombudsman.
- Manage his or her own financial affairs.
- A quarterly accounting of any financial transactions made in his or her behalf.
- Be fully informed, in writing at admission and during stay, of services available and related charges.
- Be adequately informed of his/her medical condition and proposed treatment.
- Participate in the planning of all medical treatment.
- Refuse medication and treatment . . . and to know the consequences of such actions.
- Participate in discharge planning.
- Review and obtain copies of medical records.
- Have access to a translator (if non-English speaking) to facilitate communication.
- Communication assistance when sensory impaired.
- To have private and unrestricted communications with any person of his/her choice.
- Privacy for telephone calls.
- Receive mail unopened.
- Private consensual sexual activity.
- Be free from mental and physical abuse.
- Be free from physical and chemical restraints.
- Copies of the facility's rules and regulations, including an explanation of his/her rights and responsibility to obey all reasonable rules and regulations.

- See facility policies and the state survey reports.
- Be transferred or discharged only for medical reasons or his/her welfare, or that of other residents, or for nonpayment and to be given reasonable advance notice of any transfer or discharge.
- Privacy in treatment and in caring for personal needs.
- Confidentiality in the treatment of personal and medical records.
- Security in storing and using personal possessions.
- Be treated courteously, fairly, and with the fullest measure of dignity and respect.

Adopted from Omnibus Budget Reconciliation Act of 1987.

for independence and their need for assistance. One or more of these observations could inform the ethnographic research frame for the ombudsman's activity.

Authentic autonomy, however, cannot be understood or promoted in a cultural vacuum separate from "community." It must, in a very practical way, be "negotiated" in socio-historical context rather than assumed or forced (Collopy, Boyle, and Jennings 1991:7–9; Moody 1992: 158–183). An important component of the quality of life/resident rights issue is how frailty and physical and mental illnesses compromise the residents' ability to comprehend and exercise their rights. Ombudsman training and continuing education provide fairly detailed information about the biological aspects of diseases and their effects on resident cognition, mobility, and behavior. Little time and text, however, are devoted to what might be called the "meaning" dimensions of resident health status. Here the distinction made by Arthur Kleinman (1980:71–80) and other medical anthropologists between "disease" as a biomedical construct and "illness" as a patient-centered, experiential construct could help in probing more deeply into how individual residents bring their histories, values, families, and health problems to bear on their present circumstances. As Kleinman has shown, chronic illnesses are culturally patterned and explicable through an intensive, systematic, and imaginative empathy with those who tell their stories (1988:23). The mini-ethnographic method he proposes for health practitioners is equally useful to ombudsmen, whose purpose is enriched by placing themselves, however briefly, in the lived experience of a resident's illness and suffering (1988:230– 232).

The ombudsman's activity is very favorable for collecting retrospective and contemporaneous life histories (Frank and Vanderburgh 1986: 187–188). By documenting not only disease behaviors but also residents' narratives, feelings, and perceptions about their illnesses, the ombudsman can be a better judge of true violations of autonomy as well as individually tailored strategies for promoting self-determination. At the same time, the ombudsman can contribute to a larger purpose that connects those researchers, advocates, and health care providers who care for those who suffer. This engagement has been most eloquently described by Sue Estroff in her summary of her research with the mentally ill:

I was there to witness, experience, understand, and communicate the suffering and despair . . . of others who are different from us. We anthropologists are here to view with clarity and humanity those amongst us, or any other human group, who lead lives of dire circumstances, who have little and who need much, who are differently able and whose place in human societies is often meager and painful. Hauerwas (1979:230) has said in reference to medicine what also holds for anthropologists, "It is the burden of those who care for (or learn about) the suffering . . . to teach the suffering that they are not thereby excluded from the human community. In this sense (anthropology's) primary moral role is to bind the suffering and the non-suffering into the same community." (1984: 368)

Ombudsmen preparing for their "fieldwork" can glean many ideas and hypotheses from reading the work of other nursing home researchers, several of whom have combined ethnography with other roles, e.g., nurse (Powers 1988b; Tisdale 1987), nursing assistant (Henderson 1981; Vesperi 1987; Diamond 1986), social worker (Schmidt 1990), pet therapy volunteer (Savishinsky 1991), gerontology consultant (Gubrium 1975), and resident (Laird 1979). (See also Watson and Maxwell 1977; Kayser-Jones 1981; O'Brien 1989; Shield 1988, 1990.) Their work illuminates the intricate institutional and interpersonal contexts in which resident rights and other quality of life components are both fostered and discouraged.

In these unintentional communities, appearances are often deceptive and life is full of subtleties. Many residents "curl in" socially but are "busy" even when "just sitting" (Diamond 1986:1289–1291; Gubrium 1975:159). Status and dignity are subject to negotiation (Schmidt 1990), and infantilization is often the reward for dependency and lack of bargaining resources (Kayser- Jones 1981:111–120). Home is where the heart may be, but the rest of one's self is given over to batching, medical management, and other indignities of the "total institution" (Foldes 1990: 27–28; Goffman 1961:1–124). Days and nights are ruled by routine, restriction, and regulation. The ubiquitous preoccupation with eating and excretion (Laird 1979) is punctuated by celebrations of small accomplishments (Gubrium 1975:ii). "Boredom perches on the bedclothes . . . and incessant cries for help are the work songs of the field" (Tisdale 1987:18, 82). In these "brave new worlds" (Savishinsky 1991:18), countless acts of kindness mingle with innumerable "little murders" of the spirit and personhood.

Consciously or not, ombudsmen engage in research design to the extent that they are involved in "combining the essential elements of investigation into an effective problem-solving sequence" (Pelto 1970:331). Ombudsmen quickly learn that without a formalized procedure for gathering and analyzing their data, complaint investigations will bog down and essential data will go unrecognized and unrecorded.

Of several available guides to ethnographic participant observation and ethnographic interviewing, Spradley's step-by-step approach is perhaps the most accessible to prospective researchers (1979; 1980). Along the spectrum of participation (from none to complete), the ombudsman's work calls for "moderate" participation to "maintain a balance between being an insider and an outsider" (1980:60).

Spradley's descriptive question matrix (1980:82–83) offers a helpful way to plan and organize observations and interview questions aimed at discovering patterns related to space, objects, acts, activity, events, time, actors, goals, and feelings. The filled cells in Table 5.2 exemplify the kinds of information that ombudsmen collect: where possessions are kept, areas of personal space, how "feeders" are fed, how residents are notified of activities, when and where resident councils are held, how negative feelings about residents are expressed.

Spradley's discussion of "overcoming years of selective inattention" in order to develop "explicit awareness" of background details speaks directly to what the ombudsman must attend to (1980:55–56). Details are often critical clues, as Savishinsky learned from one of his informants: "The little things got to residents, Louise felt, because these were all they had left: the tone of a greeting, the type of bread, the place for the call bell. What seemed picky was really powerless people trying to practice the art of assertion" (1991:159).

DATA COLLECTION AND ANALYSIS

Participant Observation

The ombudsman's action plan is very well suited to participant observation, the fundamental strategy of the ethnographic enterprise. Participant observation offers a way to get at "grass hut" data in a way that observation or interviewing alone cannot. The benefits of participant observation include lessened reactivity to one's presence over time and, as a consequence, increased validity in one's data, enhanced intuitive understanding of what is going on, and increased sensibility in the questions one learns to ask in the working language of the setting (Bernard 1988:150–51). As Werner and Schoepfle aptly put it, systematic swings between observation, participation in selected activities, and interviewing help the investigator "home in" on the heat of target concerns (1987:78).

Table 5.2

Ombudsman-Researcher: Descriptive Question Martrix

	Space	Object	Act	Activity	Event	Time	Actor	Goal	Feeling
Space		1		2					3
Object			4				5		
Act			6	7		8			
Activity				9					10
Event					11		12		
Time	13								
Actor									14
Goal			15	16					
Feeling		17							18

1. Where are residents' possessions kept? How safe are they from theft?
2. In what environment are resident councils conducted?
3. What feelings and perceptions do residents have about their favorite "spots"?
4. How and under what circumstances are restraints administered?
5. Do residents have unrestricted access to mail and phones?
6. What happens when care or therapy are resisted or refused?
7. How are residents encouraged to make choices among available activities?
8. How does the time of day affect resident behaviors?
9. What kinds of activities are offered to residents?
10. How do specific activities contribute to residents' sense of well-being?
11. Are holidays and special events sensitive to cultural and religious diversity?
12. Are residents encouraged to participate in their care planning conferences?
13. When and where can residents find privacy?
14. How do staff exhibit negative feelings about "problem" residents?
15. Are rehabilitation goals resident-specific, appropriate, and practical?
16. What are the explicit and implicit goals of medication regimens?
17. What feelings and attitudes do residents have about their food?
18. How is dignity conveyed by staff and expressed by residents?

Participant observation also helps the ombudsman-advocate to establish rapport—a prerequisite for expecting evaluative information from angry or frightened, vulnerable residents. Mary Gwynne Schmidt notes that "the interviewer [of the old old] can give his prospective respondents an opportunity to look him over by functioning first as a participant observer" (1975:545). I found that while most able residents initially were quite willing to talk about themselves and their present situations in general (including allusions to "things not being right or good"), many initially were reluctant (or simply refused) to share specific concerns or complaints. And for good reason: they doubted I could be trusted to treat their concerns anonymously or diplomatically to any satisfactory end. By participating in activities as well as regularly appearing for visiting rounds, I showed sufficient interest in their lives for many to speak more candidly. Still others hinted or said they could tell me an "earful about what goes on around here" but preferred to wait for the right time—that is, I suspect, after they had had several more opportunities to "look me over."

The number and variety of organized nursing home activities are critical in the notion of quality of life, and ombudsmen can get a fuller sense of resident life by participating in those events. Different activities yield different kinds of useful details. Resident council meetings, for example, provide excellent opportunities to observe how likes and dislikes, praise and grievances, choices and refusals, and interest and indifference related to their care and social interactions are expressed verbally and nonverbally by those who choose to attend. Some residents prefer to give their opinions to the ombudsman in private and with the understanding that their concerns will be reported anonymously; others like an open forum where their views can be discussed and confirmed or supported by others.

During exercise classes one sees residents in motion and their physical responses to instructions and games. These observations then can be compared to charted physical assessments and care plans and the residents' own statements about their condition and "body image." A common source of tension between some staff and residents involves resident expectations of physical assistance. What are the rights (and obligations) of residents who ask for assistance in bathing, dressing, eating, and transferring? When and to what extent should staff provide assistance? When residents complain of receiving little or no care and assistance, how does one determine if they are being appropriately encouraged by staff to attain the highest practical level of rehabilitation or are simply being neglected?

Bingo games, ice cream socials, and other recreational activities are good settings to gain a wider perspective on residents' social interactions with other residents and staff and to informally assess their mental status. Many residents complain that there is "not enough to do" or that scheduled activities are repeatedly canceled. Others refuse or are unable to participate in any organized activity, including group eating. Television and smoking lounges are useful places, not only for observing and engaging in social interaction but also for taking a break to sit down and write notes and plan where next to go and whom to see.

Interviewing

Interviewing residents (and staff) is perhaps the most challenging aspect of the ombudsman's routine—not because ombudsmen are reluctant to talk and ask questions or unskilled at doing so, but primarily because time constraints imposed by their work schedules limit the choices among interviewing styles. Salaried ombudsmen in most regional agencies are responsible for monitoring numerous facilities and usually must focus their attention on specific complaints and resulting interaction with regulatory officials. Volunteers generally cannot devote more than a few hours (often less) to a given facility each week. As a result, they do not have the full-time field researcher's advantage of larger blocks of time to conduct extensive interviews.

Informal, unstructured, and semi-structured interview formats are appropriate for the ombudsman's work (cf. Werner and Schoepfle 1987; Bernard 1988; Spradley 1979). The most useful format depends primarily on the circumstances; that is, whether one is responding to a specific complaint, walking the floors to "see how things are going," sitting down with a resident who wants company, or all of the above in the same visit. As with effective participant observation, asking the right questions and getting useful answers involve negotiation, time, and trust. One seldom can predict what will happen after entering a facility, so it helps to have a flexible protocol.

Many of the most vulnerable residents cannot communicate clearly, and some not at all. Dementia, depression, confusion, dysphasia, deafness, and other conditions often intrude. Memory deficits, such as telescoping, are common. Two cardinal rules ombudsmen need to keep in mind are: go slow and keep trying. Schmidt reminds us that "even chronic confusion is not necessarily a bar: the trick is to not accept the local assessment. . . . Often persons who do not know where they are are perfectly clear about how they feel" (1975:546). [See also Silverman and McAllister, this volume.]

Disregarding or discounting a resident's feelings in the absence of full decisional capacity often lies at the heart of what Kane and Caplan refer to as "everyday ethics" in nursing homes (1990). One of my cases involved an unmarried man and woman who became enamored and asked for a privacy room. The nursing staff resisted because it seemed that Henry was doing all the talking and appeared to be "domineering" and "overly aggressive" in his courting of Julie. He was Anglo, she was Asian-American. His health problems were primarily physical; he had an indwelling catheter that prevented intercourse. She had been admitted with a stroke and periodically had to be tube fed due to failure to thrive. She had never been married and, according to her sister, was very religious. They met in the television lounge and became inseparable. After Henry was discovered embracing and fondling Julie in her room, the nursing staff refused to allow him to visit her. He complained that he wasn't doing anything wrong and that he and Julie should be allowed privacy.

After talking several different times with Julie in different settings, it was apparent to me that, while her orientation to time and place was inconsistent, her affection for Henry was persistent and genuine. She talked about being "in love" with him, and she expressed concern when he was sick and unable to visit her. She also asked for a privacy room. Her sister concurred with the social worker, assistant administrator, ombudsman, and director of nursing that Julie was capable of deciding for herself if her relationship with Henry was to involve physical intimacy. While staff remained concerned about Julie's safety and divided over her capacity to make such a decision, a private room was made available.

Behavioral Observations

In part because of communication barriers, much of the ombudsman's time is devoted to direct, reactive observation of staff and residents. Several techniques can be used to gather useful information. Interactive behavior can be recorded for specified periods of time from various vantage points, e.g., the television lounges, which in the two facilities I visited also include clear views of the nurses' stations. Different ways of coding continuously monitored behavior have been devised (Bernard 1988:272–278). One option is a Bales-type scale modified to measure the incidence of 13 universal types of interaction (from positive to negative) among four directional dyadic relationships: staff to resident, staff to other staff, resident to staff, and resident to other resident (Table 5.3). This kind of measurement is useful for highlighting particular settings or scheduled events within the nursing home where problems occur with greater frequency and which warrant closer scrutiny.

Because the ombudsman's presence is reactive—ombudsmen always wear name tags and many staff perceive that they are "looking for problems"—another potentially useful technique is time allocation spot sampling, in which the researcher simply appears at randomly selected times and places and "records what people are doing when they are first encountered" (Bernard 1988:280–281). That approach worked best for me at the facility with a front and back entrance and two stairways to each of four floors. I could initiate observing and visiting on any floor without first being sighted or announced by the front desk staff. The only way into the second facility, however, is through the front entrance and past the receptionist and director's office. When I first started visiting there, I was often shadowed

Table 5.3
Bales Scale for Observing Interaction

FACILITY: DATE: LOCATION/EVENT:

Action/Reaction	S→R	S→S	R→S	R→R
1. Shows solidarity, raises other's status, gives help, reward				
2. Shows tension release, jokes, laughs, shows satisfaction				
3. Agrees, shows passive acceptance, concurs, understands, complies				
4. Gives suggestions, direction, implying autonomy for other				
5. Gives opinion, evaluation, analysis, expresses feeling				
6. Gives orientation, information, repeats, clarifies, confirms				
7. Asks for orientation, information, confirmation, repetition				
8. Asks for opinion, evaluation, analysis, expression of feeling				
9. Asks for suggestion, direction, possible ways of action				
10. Disagrees, passive rejection, formality, withholds help				
11. Shows tension, asks for help, withdraws out of field				
12. Shows antagonism, deflates other's status, asserts self				
13. No reaction				
R = Resident S = Staff				

by a designated staff member between two wings and four floors. Random appearances under those circumstances obviously could not yield very reliable information.

The relevance of map-making and documenting proxemic relationships cannot be overemphasized. Space (and the lack of it) dramatically affects resident mobility, privacy, social interaction, and overall well-being. The architecture of most nursing homes favors "nursing" over "home" and ensures that one's personal space is continually breached throughout the day and night.

Aside from the "bed and body work" that incessantly attends rehabilitation and maintenance (Gubrium 1975), residents find their control of space and mobility constrained in many other ways that could, with some attention to creative reconfiguration, be alleviated. Few residents outside of private-pay facilities are given private rooms. Most multiple-resident rooms do not exceed the minimum requirement of 80 square feet per occupant. Privacy curtains seldom enclose more area than one's bed. Room doors cannot be locked, and staff frequently enter without pause and little more than a quick knock. Mealtimes are the occasion for long wheelchair lineups in the hallways and long waits for the elevator. Activity rooms and lounges are not spacious enough to accommodate all possible comers, and residents in wheelchairs often jostle for space and maneuver like drivers in a slow motion bumper car ride.

In sum, proximity conspires against privacy. There are few places where residents can find solitude if they wish it. As Savishinsky noted in his research, "Patients had difficulty controlling their doors, drawers, clothing, belongings, and surface of their bodies—all of which were exposed. . . . " Residents often resort to "hiding in public," and for some who cannot find sanctuary in "disputed territory, . . . not to be left alone is the final indignity" (1991:117–118).

Of several possible unobtrusive methods (cf. Webb et al. 1966), reviewing resident charts is one of the most useful for obtaining informative data related to resident health status and behavior, medications, and staff perceptions of resident progress, compliance, and so on. However, the consequences of requesting access to and then making notes on resident records can be disruptive and unsettling to staff, since the ombudsman must obtain the resident's or guardian's permission to view records and usually does so only when investigating specific complaints or suspicions of poor care or abuse. This method of collecting data is, therefore, intermittent and not an option for surveys, sampling, or casual browsing.

Participation in resident care conferences is another—and usually less confrontational—way to obtain the same kind of information. Conferences typically are held quarterly, or more often if the resident's health status changes substantially. They are attended by representatives from the several departments (nursing, social work, activities, dietary, administration,

physical therapy) and interested family members. Once again, the ombudsman can attend only with the resident's permission, but residents and even
staff often welcome the ombudsman's presence. Such conferences are opportunities for two or more parties to share their thoughts, opinions, and
concerns about the individualized institutional care being planned and
received.

Field Notes and Reports

Volunteer ombudsmen in most states are asked to file monthly reports
on contacts made and complaints investigated. A minimal system is thus
needed for recording, coding, and managing data. Activity logs and diaries
are also useful. It is as important for the ombudsman as the ethnographer
to distinguish carefully between (1) the thoughts, observations, and statements of the investigator and those of informants and (2) information that
is given privately to the researcher and information volunteered in the
presence of others. No less important to the ombudsman than to the
professional researcher are data reliability and validity. The ombudsman's
documentation and personal testimony not only influence nursing home
life, they can be admitted into review board hearings and legal proceedings
involving abuse, neglect, and other serious infractions of rights and care
standards. Careful and thorough data gathering can make a critical difference between verifying a reported event or episode as fact and documenting mere hearsay.

The ombudsman's fieldnotes and interviews can be easily coded, which
facilitates analysis and report writing. Table 5.4 shows a four-letter coding
scheme for relevant variables. A "C/" turns them into complaint-specific
codes. As coded variables appear in the numbered pages of the field notes,
they can be keyed into a simple computerized indexing program. The
cumulative index then can be scanned to determine patterns in the chronol-
ogy and frequency of documented issues, events, complaints, and associated factors.

In Colorado the only written documentation required from volunteer
ombudsmen by their sponsoring agencies are contact and complaint reports. These are submitted on standardized forms and then compiled by
staff for submission in abstracted form to the state ombudsman. States in
turn submit their statistical summaries to the Administration on Aging
(AoA) office in Washington. While this complaint data base is potentially
very valuable to care providers, researchers, and policy-makers, it is weak-
ened by nonuniformity in the collection and analysis of complaint data
among state reporting systems. The AoA format covers 136 complaint types
in 9 categories. However, it is not mandatory, only suggested. As a result,
some states use it unaltered, some have elaborated on it by reporting more

Table 5.4
Topical Codes

Subject Codes

ABUS	Abuse/Neglect/Exploitation
ABUS/F	Financial
ABUS/M	Mental
ABUS/N	Neglect
ABUS/P	Physical
ABUS/V	Verbal
ACTS	Activities and Social Services
ADIR	Advance Directives
ADLS	Functional Status
ADMI	Administration
ATED	Admission/Transfer/Eviction/Discharge
AUTO	Autonomy/Choice/Exercise of Rights
AUTO/C	Right to Complain/No Reprisal
AUTO/D	Dignity
AUTO/P	Privacy
AUTO/R	Refusal of Treatment
CARE	Care/Rehabilitation
CARE/A	Assistance/ADLs
CARE/D	Dental Services
CARE/N	Nursing/Hygiene
CARE/O	Other/Auxiliary
CARE/P	Physician Services
CDOH	Co. Dept. of Health
CERT	Certifying/Licensing Agency
DIET	Dietary
DRES	Clothing/Appearance
ECON	Economic/Exchange
EMED	Ethnomedicine
ENVI	Environment
ETHI	Ethical Issue
ETHN	Ethnic Factors
FALL	Falls/Falling
FAMY	Family/Kin
HIST	Personal History
INFO	Access to Information

LANG	Language/Communication
MCMD	Medicare/Medicaid Process
MEDS	Medications
MIND	Mental Status
MORB	Pathology/Health Status
MORT	Mortality/Death
PBEH	Problem Behavior
PERS	Personality
PROP	Financial/Property
PROX	Use of space
REAC	Reactivity
RECO	Records/Charts
RELI	Religious Factors
REST/P	Physical Restraint
REST/C	Chemical Restraint
REST	Restraints
RC	Resident Council
ROOM	Roommate
RR	Resident Rights and Care
SOC+	Positive Social Interaction
SOC-	Negative Social Interaction
SOCI	Social Interaction
STAF	Staffing
SYST	System/Family/Other

Complaint Codes

C/ABUS/F	Financial
C/ABUS/M	Mental
C/ABUS/N	Neglect
C/ABUS/P	Physical
C/ABUS/V	Verbal
C/ACTS	Activities and Social Services
C/ADMI	Administration
C/ATED	Admission/Transfer/Eviction/Discharge
C/AUTO	Autonomy/Choice/Exercise of Rights
C/AUTO/C	Right to Complain/No Reprisal
C/AUTO/D	Dignity

(continued)

C/AUTO/P	Privacy
C/AUTO/R	Refusal of Treatment
C/CARE	Care/Rehabilitation
C/CARE/A	Assistance/ADLs
C/CARE/D	Dental Services
C/CARE/N	Nursing/Hygiene
C/CARE/O	Other Auxiliary
C/CARE/P	Physician Services
C/CDOH	Co. Dept. of Health
C/CERT	Certifying/Licensing Agency
C/DIET	Dietary
C/DRES	Clothing/Appearance
C/ENVI	Environment
C/ETHI	Ethical Issue
C/ETHN	Ethnic Factors
C/FAMY	Family/Kin
C/INFO	Access to Information
C/MCMD	Medicare/Medicaid Process
C/MEDS	Medications
C/PROP	Financial/Property
C/RECO	Records/Charts
C/RESI	Another Resident
C/REST/CP	Chemical Restraint
C/REST/P	Physical Restraint
C/ROOM	Roommate
C/STAF	Staffing
C/SYST	System/Family/Other

information than asked for, and others have modified the complaint categories (Netting, Paton, and Huber 1992:843–844).

Potential Analytic Contributions

Beyond descriptive narratives and detailed case studies, the contributions that ombudsmen-researchers could make to nursing home reform, elder empowerment, and qualitative research would derive from more focused research designs and analyses related to "grounded theory" discovery (Glaser and Strauss 1967) and other social science paradigms. Key

concepts and postulates in symbolic interactionism and cognitive anthropology, for example, underlie the Ombudsman Program's implicit interest
in how nursing home realities are socially and mentally constructed and
how individuals attempt and can be helped to maintain control over their
identities and situations.

The ombudsman's data could be presented in a variety of analytic
formats, including observational matrices, activity flow charts, social network maps, and taxonomic diagrams. Decision models, which are designed
to predict choices people will make under specified circumstances, are a
potentially valuable outcome of the investigator's information on the circumstances and conditions under which complaints are made. Such models
would help volunteers to focus attention quickly on those who do not or
cannot express dissatisfaction but who may be at risk for poor care or
abusive treatment. From a cognitive view, resident rights constitute an
interesting "domain" of cultural meaning, appropriate for taxonomic and
componential analyses. The variations and discrepancies mentioned earlier
between the "official" and "insider" views of resident rights could be
illuminated using more structured interview protocols, such as free listing,
frame elicitation, triad tests, and pile sorts (cf. Bernard 1988:319–345).

CONCLUSION

The Ombudsman Program itself would make an interesting ethnographic study. Its impact varies with local leadership, creative use of limited
funding, community commitment, and volunteer access to facilities. State
and substate programs vary by structure, approach, staffing, and volunteer
coordination (Berry 1990; Monk, Kaye, and Litwin 1984; NASUA 1988;
Schiman and Lordeman 1989). Despite insufficient federal funding, the OP
works—due to staff and volunteer dedication and to what might be called
the "witness principle," suggested by the movie *Witness*. (The film depicts
life in a Pennsylvania Amish community whose members protect neighborhood families from threats of violence by quickly congregating when a
house bell is rung.) Bad behavior tends to decrease when alerted bystanders
are looking on.

Any investigative research undertaken by ombudsmen is tempered by
the call to effective advocacy. Because ombudsmen seek ways to support
quality of life changes (institutional as well as individual), their findings
are intended to influence policy development as well as community (i.e.,
resident and family) empowerment. In this respect they share similar
objectives (including ethnographic methods) with social scientists oriented
to applied, action, and advocacy research.

In Colorado, and presumably elsewhere, the affinity and collaboration
of ombudsmen with empowerment-oriented social workers are particularly close. Both groups are committed to a goal of developing "a partner-

ship with elderly residents which will encourage their fullest possible participation in problem- solving activity. . . . [While] the culture of nursing homes is, for the most part, antithetical to empowerment goals . . . commitment to resident rights in daily living in nursing homes and the struggle for organizational and societal change that will make this possible, is the essence of empowerment-oriented practice with nursing home residents and their families" (Cox and Parsons 1994:214).

A prerequisite for positive change is good information. Rosalie Kane and her colleagues have suggested that:

The first step toward any social change is paying attention. . . . At a time when many excellent scholars are preoccupying themselves with studying the functional limitations and acuity levels of nursing home residents, mapping the amount of time needed to care for residents, . . . and refining "case-mix adjusted" payment systems, . . . we would hope to see more explorations of the preferences and wishes of nursing home residents, weighed against their perceptions of their actual experience. We view this as a form of paying attention. (1990:307–308)

Paying attention is the ethnographic way. By consciously adopting it, ombudsmen can enlarge and systematize their engagement with the suffering, protest, and fragile identities that permeate the culture and lived experience of institutionalized residents. Here, indeed, is the promise of ethnography "in the service of mankind" (Spradley 1980:16).

6

In and Out of Bounds: The Ethics of Respect in Studying Nursing Homes

Joel Savishinsky

INTRODUCTION

It has been traditional for anthropologists to work in small-scale societies in order to be able to convey their reality to the larger world. Nowadays, however, researchers are just as likely to be studying medical culture within complex societies so as to understand how the reality of that larger world impacts on life inside the smaller setting of nursing homes and hospitals. Ethnographers were among the first to show how cultural systems of meaning and power affect the workings of geriatric facilities. Jules Henry's early study (1963) of three American nursing homes demonstrated how differences in organizational culture shaped the quality of life that frail older people experienced. Gubrium's pioneering monograph *Living and Dying at Murray Manor* (1975) revealed how one institution in the Midwest could be perceived in very distinct ways by the clientele and staff who occupy different positions in its system of care.

Subsequent ethnographies have employed a number of different methods and viewpoints. Using network analysis in a New York state facility, Powers (1988), a nurse and anthropologist, documented the distinctive styles and strategies that elderly residents used to construct their social support systems. Anthropologist Carobeth Laird entered Golden Mesa, an Arizona institution, at the age of 79; in *Limbo* (1979) she recorded her increasingly tenuous grip on identity and sanity as the facility's regime depersonalized and demeaned her. Vesperi (1987) worked as a nurse's aide and focused on the expectations that her peers and the nursing home residents brought to their relationship. She showed how the outcomes of institutional treatment in the Massachusetts home where she was employed commonly failed to fulfill the desires of both these groups. Diamond (1986, 1992) also worked as a nurse's aide, examining three different institutions in the Chicago area. He drew on ethnographic methods to describe the "invisibility of caring work" done by aides and "the commodification" of the care they delivered (1986:1291–1292).

In a comparison of two American institutions, one with a predominantly black clientele and the other primarily Jewish, Watson and Maxwell (1977) were able to quantify the much closer relations that minority staff had with residents in the former home. Their work raised important questions about the way race, class, and ethnicity affect the manner in which nursing personnel meet their responsibilities. O'Brien (1989), studying a church-run facility in the eastern United States, emphasized the supportive and cohesive role of religion in many residents' lives. She noted how it supported a congruence in the moral outlook of older people and their caregivers. Drawing on exchange theory to study national differences in long term care, Kayser-Jones (1981) contrasted a proprietary facility in California with Scottsdale, a National Health Service institution in Scotland. She documented how the effective organization, stability in staff, greater resources, and stronger community ties of the Scottish home enhanced the quality of older people's lives and contributed to a more conscientious regard for their privacy and personal rights. Lastly, Shield's recent study of Franklin (1988, 1993), a Jewish facility in the Northeast, explored how the lack of meaningful rituals and transitions in American culture can render late life—and nursing home life—into an unfulfilling experience for the elderly. It was an instance of what Turnbull (1983:96) has called transition without transformation.

These and other ethnographic studies (e.g., Henderson 1981, Johnson 1987) reveal the many ways in which models of the life cycle, work, and medical care contribute to the reality of nursing homes. They document the impact of the outside on the inside. Another very important, though elusive, dimension of this relationship turns on the way cultural values affect the behavior of institutional staff, patients, families, and community volunteers. The realm of moral ideas has a special salience for how these groups interact within these medical contexts. Two areas that are particularly compelling in this regard are cultural concepts of ethical conduct and personal privacy. Codes of ethics become critical where caregivers, relatives, and other visitors have special responsibilities and more power than the people they are serving. Privacy becomes a problematic matter in settings where older individuals have diminished control over their surroundings and where others have access to their bodies.

This chapter examines the interplay between people's behavior and these moral notions at a small, nonprofit geriatric institution in a rural area of upstate New York, and it concludes by contrasting the situation found there with what ethnographers have described in other institutional settings. Elmwood Grove Nursing Home is an 84-bed, skilled nursing facility, staffed by about 120 employees and visited by dozens of relatives and community volunteers.[1] Located in the downtown area of a small community, the facility has a long history going back to its origins as a tuberculosis sanatorium for young children in the 1920s. Subsequent decades saw its evolution into a chronic care geriatric facility as the region's medical needs changed. In both its original and its contemporary form, Elmwood Grove has been firmly embedded in the surrounding village and nearby communities. Most of its residents and staff come from the immediate area. It has been governed since its early days by a Board of Directors drawn from local families and civic leaders.

Research began when a local voluntary organization asked me and my students to evaluate a pet therapy program that its members conducted at Elmwood Grove. Using cats, dogs, and other pet animals, this organization's volunteers were making weekly visits to Elmwood and other institutions in order to give them a more "home-like" feel. The pet program's approach and purpose drew on the animal-assisted therapeutic models developed by Levinson (1972), Corson (1980), Bustad (1980), and others, and on the kinds of clinical applications that have been surveyed and analyzed by Wilson and Netting (1983), Cusack and Smith (1984), and Beck and Katcher (1984). Given the public's generally critical attitude toward recreational activities found in nursing homes (Curtin 1972), a perception illustrated by the fact that programs are usually reduced to the "BBCs" of bingo, birthdays, and crafts (Johnson and Grant 1985:135), we felt there was special merit in examining the meaning of this therapeutic innovation from an ethnographic perspective.

In addition to assessing the local pet program's impact, we were asked to make recommendations to enhance its effectiveness. By the time our 18-month evaluation was completed, however, we had not only documented and contributed something to the pet program's role within Elmwood Grove, we had also become intrigued with the very nature of life and work within the institution. The initial project led to a more comprehensive and continuing study of the nursing home as a whole. Over the next five and a half years, the research expanded to include an examination of the adaptations of residents, the experiences and viewpoints of personnel, and the role and impact of family visitors and community volunteers. Methods that were employed in this evolving study have included participant observation, interviewing, mapping, life-history analysis, still photography, and video.

In doing the research we were also confronted with a series of ethical issues in our role as ethnographers. As our relations with residents, caregivers, and visitors deepened, we found ourselves negotiating a series of ambiguous behaviors and boundaries. In the years since this study began, some of the most perplexing moral dilemmas have centered on the balance between publicity and privacy, the use of informed consent documents, the tension between candor and confidentiality, the uncertain balance between reciprocity and advocacy, and the difficulty of drawing boundaries around the research itself. I will examine each of these issues in turn.

The Projection of Privacy

One of the hardest borders to determine was that between public and private. Volunteers, including those in the pet program, sometimes engaged in a kind of "moral anticipation" when it came to the issue of residents' privacy. Assuming that the elderly did not want to be disturbed, visitors were often reluctant to approach people they did not know, explaining this to themselves as a respect for an individual's personal space. This extended not only to such "private" places as people's rooms, but to such open and accessible areas as corridors, the entryway, and TV rooms. Pet volunteers, for example, were anxious about starting conversations with residents sitting in hallways and lounges, feeling that such initiatives were intrusive to people forced to live their lives in such a public setting. Community visitors preferred to be first introduced to residents by staff, but while the home's personnel tried to accommodate this desire, their busy schedules often precluded such introductions. On many occasions, visitors were compelled to take the risk of violating their own assumptions about privacy and its purported ethical basis. They found that residents were delighted to have others speak to and spend time with them, even people who were strangers. It was the volunteers' own reticence, rather than residents' personal space, that was at issue. The visitors' ethical rationale really involved what could be called the "projection of privacy."

There were two features of meaning that volunteers had trouble recognizing in the early stages of their involvement. One was that their notions of public and private space were not congruent with those of residents and two, the elderly were often desperate to be seen, heard, and acknowledged. As institutionalized people, older women and men were often more concerned with getting personal attention than with preserving privacy. Though residents were trying, as Dianne Willcocks and her colleagues (1987) once put it, to lead "private lives in public places," they also wanted people to engage with them so that they could stand witness to their lives. The relationships with volunteers that formed and deepened over time provided a context within which elderly individuals, stimulated by the presence of sympathetic visitors and domestic animals, were able to reminisce in a way that approximated the "life review process" described by Butler (1968). The willingness of many residents to be approached, and their desire that volunteers keep returning to see them each week, reflected the fact that they also found more meaning in these human contacts than outsiders had dared to imagine. Elders were sometimes anxious, not about protecting private space but about finding an appropriate chance to share private possessions: love poems from a deceased spouse, letters from a grandchild, the old lesson plans kept in the drawer of a retired teacher. Many volunteers were surprised at the intensity of the relationships they developed with residents, leading one long-term visitor to speak of these bonds as a kind of "unexpected intimacy" (Savishinsky 1991).

While a moral risk had turned into a moral reward for volunteers such as these, there were also other kinds of encounters and outcomes where privacy and power issues remained problematic. Every visitor met some residents who rebuffed overtures, saying that they did not want to talk, or did not like cats, or that the dog being offered was too painful a reminder of a deceased pet from their past. Such rejections elicited two kinds of response from volunteers. The "projectors" of privacy took the rebuffs as a confirmation of their initial reluctance to impose on elderly people's space. Other visitors saw in these encounters an affirmation of the autonomy and power of residents: if the elderly could reject requests, then they had more control over their lives than volunteers had at first assumed. For visitors who viewed such events in this light, the moral of the tale was the reassurance that they did not have a monopoly on power, and that the locus of control sometimes resided with the very people who appeared to be powerless.

The Seamlessness of Ethnography

If the fear of invading people's privacy took some surprising moral turns, so did the process of getting people's permission to include them in our study. The use of an informed consent document for formal interviews was dictated by Elmwood Grove's policy governing patient rights, as well as the Human Subjects Research Committee at Ithaca College, where I teach. Consent forms were utilized not just with residents, however, but also with staff, volunteers, and family visitors whenever structured interviews were conducted. Almost no one who was asked for an interview refused. Nor, when the use of a tape recorder was suggested, did anyone object to having our dialogues preserved by this means.

Nevertheless, the utilization of formal consent documents left a number of ethical and practical considerations unaddressed. First, work with confused or demented residents presented a special problem. Could researchers freely interact with such people? Could these residents give consent that was truly informed? At Elmwood Grove, the answer to the first question was an unrestricted yes; the response to the second was more individualized and qualified, and rested, ultimately, with institutional policy [see also Shield; Silverman and McAllister, this volume].

Elmwood was a small and relatively unbureaucratic facility where most administrators, floor staff, residents, and visitors were on a first-name basis. Once we were able to establish a presence for ourselves as researchers and volunteers, my students and I were able to avail ourselves of the same informal pattern of etiquette. This enabled us to move throughout the home with relative ease and freedom. Though we never tried to deny or hide our role as anthropologists, that part of our identity receded for many people at Elmwood, most of whom came to look upon us primarily as volunteers and visitors. Walking around with our pets as companions and props, rather than with notebooks and clipboards, helped reinforce that image. One result was that we could interact as freely with the disoriented and forgetful as we could with other residents. A good deal of what we learned about the daily lives, thoughts, and feelings of such confused individuals came from this kind of informal participant observation.

When it came to the question of more formal interviews, such as structured interviews, the tape recording of conversations, and photographing or videotaping people, the home's rules about informed consent came into play. Elmwood's basic stricture was that residents who were regarded by the institution and the family as not being competent could not be directly approached for such formal and structured activities. Instead, we were asked to go through an administrator, usually the social worker or director of activities, to obtain permission. Officially, this process involved the appropriate staff person getting the family's verbal approval and, through conversation with the resident concerned, ensuring that this person was comfortable with and aware of what was going to happen. The social worker or activities director would then sign the consent form on behalf of the resident.

Adherence to the formal nature of this process was difficult for us to verify as researchers since the conversations it rested upon did not take place in our presence. Only a few requests for interviews were ever denied, and in each case it was because family members felt that their relative might be upset by the experience. These were residents, however, with whom we regularly met in much more informal ways. So, where we did not try to convince the families to change their minds, the view that we and staff had of these people's capacity to participate clearly differed from that of their relatives.

Observing these ethical guidelines about formal consent did not significantly compromise the conduct of the research. Anthropological methods, and institutional policy and culture, gave us access to these same residents under other circumstances, which were the very same circumstances under which we normally approached everyone else at Elmwood. The very nature of participant observation gave us access to a range of verbal, visual, and behavioral information, the gathering of which rarely involved formal consent from the people being studied. There were, of course, institutional rules and patterns of cultural etiquette that limited such access. For example, the use of toilets and bathrooms carried at least a minimum degree of privacy. People engaged in emotionally intense conversation assumed that others would respect their space. Elmwood's competent residents knew that their rooms were not be entered without a knock on the door and verbal permission from the inhabitant. At the same time, interactions in public places, such as sitting down next to someone in a lounge or dining room or stopping to chat with someone in a hallway or nurses' station, were less restricted. They carried no expectation of formal approval. It is interesting to note that we also conducted formal interviews in the very same locations, sometimes with the very same people, and on those occasions we felt called on to use an informed consent form. Public places such as these could sometimes offer, ironically, more privacy than residents' rooms. The relative quiet of a "semi-private" room enabled a roommate or her visitors to hear conversation, whereas the noise and bustle of a lounge or nurses' station could protect the intimacy of talk.

Technically, getting consent from people to speak with them at length in either the public or private places fit the institution's rules, but interpersonally it did not make a great deal of sense. This dilemma and this discomfort arose because policy and rule-makers, in both academic and institutional settings, do not know or understand much about ethnographic research. Its particulars involve sharing the day-to-day flow of people's experiences rather than using tests, questionnaires, biomedical monitoring devices, and other such instruments, all of which extract people from their family lives and package artificial encounters with them inside a wrapping of frozen time. Getting permission to pull people out of their lives may make a kind of formal ethical sense, but getting permission to let you share and be part of what normally goes on does not. This is especially true when the very act of securing consent turns a natural kind of being together into something artificial, concocted, and self-conscious. It undoes the very virtue, rhyme, and reason of anthropological method itself by hemming borders and stitching boundaries around what is ideally the seamlessness of ethnography.

Thick Quotations and Thin-Skinned Administrators

A third dilemma revolved around the conflict between what could be called "thick quotations"[2] and "thin-skinned administrators." In studying the way nursing home residents adapted to an interpreted institutional life, my students and I found considerable variation in the degree of acceptance, gratitude, and criticism towards Elmwood expressed by those who lived there. A common source of complaint among many individuals, including those basically content with the quality of their care, centered on the nature of institutional food. In an attempt to honor an ethical commitment to report people's feelings accurately, we once quoted at length an anonymous resident's pointed, negative, and graphic remarks about meals. His words, focusing on the quality and appearance of the food, appeared in one section of a technical report that we presented after the second year of our project. The document as a whole covered a broad array of topics, but focused on people's reactions to the pet program and their general process of adjustment to institutional life. It included descriptions of how residents spent a "typical" day at the facility and what their relations with staff, roommates, volunteers, and their families were like.

As we had promised in the research agreement signed with the nursing home at the start of our study, copies of this report went to Elmwood's administrators. While we naively thought that there was nothing controversial in this document, we turned out to be very mistaken. A top official at the institution was outraged at our decision to include the passage on food in the report, feeling that we had compromised the reputation of this facility and its dietary staff. He felt that nursing homes in general had enough of an image problem without the extra burden of bitter, unsubstantiated, and injudicious remarks from a "well-known malcontent."

Frank Healey, the resident whom we had quoted, was indeed a very critical individual who was upset not only with the meals but with the increasing number of demented individuals who were coming to live at Elmwood. He compared some menu items to dog food, and bemoaned the lack of people with whom he could have an intelligent conversation. Though he was especially sharp-tongued and prone to melodrama, Frank was not alone in voicing complaints about meals or the home's mix of residents. It was his choice of words rather than issues that was so provocative.

While the quote from Frank on meals was not factually in error, the reaction it brought forth made us realize that we had underestimated the sensitivity of some personnel to criticism, and had failed to consider this man's remarks from the perspective of what they would mean, and how they would feel, to others. Dietary staff were offended, and cited a number of positive opinions about food that were not represented in the residents' comments contained in the report. The central issue, then, was not one of accuracy, but of balance. We had failed to put Frank's comments in context, to provide a more diverse set of appraisals of the quality of meals, and to note, as we were only just beginning to realize, how often patients displaced their other discontents with life onto the quality of the food they were being served. What had struck us as a common, everyday, and minor complaint was thus a matter of some concern and substance to other people, and it would have been far better, and far more responsible of us, to contextualize and compare his remarks instead of leaving them to stand on their own.

The issue of balancing candor and confidentiality takes many forms in a nursing home, and the example of the food quote is, of course, only one case in point. Relations between residents and staff can raise far deeper moral questions, and researchers may get enmeshed in these as well. A critical and recurring situation, for example, revolves around how much residents should be told about their medical conditions. At Elmwood Grove, some patients let it be known that they wanted to be told everything. Other people and their families were far less explicit. This left staff and ethnographer in the position of having to guess, or read nonverbal cues, in order to determine how much they could or should say to these women and men. There were numerous instances where personnel shared their knowledge and their dilemmas with us. As one charge nurse expressed this quandary, it was not the commonly heard problem of the patient's "right to know"; the issue, rather, was "the patient's right *not* to know." A colleague of hers added that this dilemma had its reciprocal for the staff in the question of whether or not personnel had the right *not* to tell people distressing news. Both staff and ethnographers confessed to one another that they sometimes ignored, denied, or camouflaged some of their disturbing knowledge when speaking to residents and relatives. The motives combined protection with self-protection. As one aide put it, "We sometimes lie, or omit things, not just to make it easier on them, but to make it easier on ourselves." Her supervisor expressed it as the wish "not to always be the bearers of bad tidings."

Advocacy versus Reciprocity

A fourth issue grew out of some very ambiguous situations created by the residents whom we got to know over time. These people provoked uncertainty by asking us for help or favors we were not sure we could or should provide. Requests ran the gamut from the mundane and physical to the social and moral. For example: "Could you please wheel me to the elevator and take me down to the first floor?" Or: "I would like it if you would loosen the belt and these straps around my chest." But then there was: "Please, here's the number, please call my lawyer and tell him I've changed my mind about the house. I can never get through to him on the phone here." Or: "Did you see my daughter when she was here today? I wish someone would talk to her about her son. He's making such a mess of his life. You've met her. You know her. Would you please ask her or say something to her?!"

In the normal course of events outside the home, questions such as these from friends, relatives, or acquaintances are, if not all that common, at least not all that troubling. One can judge their appropriateness, measure the degree of intimacy, and weigh the feasibility and probable outcomes of getting involved. However, inside the nursing home, the issues of propriety, proximity, and practicality were often about as clear as institutional coffee. It was not evident what was authorized or expected or implied in our relationships. People who were giving us so much of their time and history and friendship certainly deserved and expected something in return. But what . . . and how much? Ethnographers generally agree that the very nature of anthropological fieldwork calls for some kind of mutuality. In traditional field settings, for example, researchers usually do not hesitate to help people farm their fields or catch fish, care for children or dress wounds, provide transportation or contribute to feasts. The ethical dilemma in the nursing home, however, was figuring out where reciprocity ended and became instead, advocacy.

This issue arose not just with the elderly patients but with staff and volunteers as well. Community visitors felt that their contribution to the nursing home was substantial but unheralded. Was it the responsibility of the ethnographer to redress this oversight? Staff were sensitive to a different problem of perception, namely, that they have commonly been seen as the "bad" people in the institutional world, whereas they perceive themselves as the overworked, underpaid, and periodically abused "good guys"—conversationally putting aside the fact that 90 percent of them were women. Did our role as researchers include publicizing their views?

This problem of advocacy, while troubling in our relations with volunteers and personnel, was further magnified in the case of residents because of two additional factors. One factor was the dependency of the very people we were befriending, and the second was Elmwood's emphasis on promoting such self-sufficiency as residents could achieve. Elderly people's reliance on others, which was the very situation which had prompted and now defined their institutionalization, made it hard to refuse their requests, just as a respect for the home's goal of autonomy was a caution against doing too much for them. The dilemma was very strong when dealing with individuals who were especially frail or isolated. In the case of people who had few if any visitors, taking on the role of advocate was a constant temptation. There were times, to be candid, when we dealt with this attraction by following the advice of that great Victorian anthropologist, Oscar Wilde, who once said that the best way to deal with temptation was to give in to it.

Inside and Outside

There was a dilemma derived from a rather different temptation, which was the desire to draw strict boundaries around the research itself. In the past, when anthropologists worked in isolated communities bereft of lawyers, telephones, and fax machines, it was relatively easy for an ethnographer to define his place of research and then leave the field to retreat to his own society and his study. Today, however, in an age of instant communication, distance and detachment are much harder to achieve.

Such difficulties are greatly compounded when the anthropologist's host community also happens to be his own hometown.

For my students and myself, the sequestered nature of institutional life sometimes blinded us to how open-ended and unbounded our project was. We could leave the nursing home at the end of the day, but could not always leave it behind us or take our personae and sense of presence with us. This was brought out in a simple, direct, and unexpected way during a confrontation in which my student, Lisa, was involved. Having become a regular at Elmwood Grove over the course of one fall semester, she began her second term there with a cadre of friends and "regulars" at the facility. In the midst of the spring semester, however, Lisa was unable to go to the home for three consecutive weeks because of an unplanned sequence of exams, personal illness, and vacation. On Lisa's first visit back at Elmwood in late March, she walked into the room of resident Bonnie Dumond's room and was taken to task in a half-joking but ardent way for her prolonged absence. Bonnie showed her the lunch tray cookies she had been saving up since February for Lisa's unrealized visits—cookies that were now stale but still fresh with accusation. When Lisa came by my office for supervision late that day, she collapsed heavily in a chair and began to unburden herself by saying: "They make me feel as guilty as my parents."

Bonnie's words and sentiments and snacks did not amount to an accusation of unethical behavior, but they clearly made explicit the implicit moral quality of the relationships that volunteers and researchers formed in the course of their work. If it was hard to keep our personal lives separate from and outside the facility, it was also difficult to contain the study's engagements within Elmwood's walls. We found that even research inside the circumscribed world of the nursing home inevitably drew us out and into relations with people from the surrounding town. Most residents had families, whose members we first met inside the facility, but whose friendship we also cultivated in coffee shops and living rooms as we tried to learn more about how institutionalizing an aging relative had affected their lives. Some of the ties and expectations we developed in this way were as strong and as long-lasting as those formed with residents themselves. These "outside" relationships became ethically problematic for us under two sets of circumstances which arose as our study progressed: one situation was occasioned by the deaths of residents and the other was posed by the end of the research itself.

Death concluded some relationships, but simply put others in a different framework. Though people died, we realized we were still connected to their sons and daughters and spouses and siblings, and that we shared with them the status of survivors. The "social contract" between us was not spelled out in research agreements or consent forms, and was certainly not part of our consciousness in the early part of the study. It was an ethical outgrowth of the project's human dimension. Despite our desire to keep the scope of the research and the number of subjects within reasonable bounds, we ended up paying condolence calls, we stayed in touch by telephone and letter, and we ran into recently bereaved people and spent time conversing, consoling, and reminiscing with them.

When the formal part of the project ended after seven years, its termination was no easier to define than the relationships that outlived residents. People who still lived in the nursing home knew that we were nearby, as did their families. None of them saw the finish of the study as moral license for us to withdraw, and they communicated that by treating us in the same way they always had, and by expecting us to reciprocate. There was no reason for visits to stop or friendships to terminate. It became clear that our status as anthropologists was only one part of our identity for them, and not always the most salient one. We were also members of the same community, as capable as ever of relating to them in the usual way. Academic calendars and research schedules were not compelling reasons for us to abdicate that role.

In essence, the boundaries we defined for the purposes of the research were not congruent with the networks of ties within which people lived. While we could put this aside in theory, to ignore it in practice would have violated some of our culture's foremost rules of intimacy as regards reciprocity, mutual support, and open-endedness. Formal vows apart, friendships were no more dissolved by death or distance than are marriages. The ties that bound us gave a new, if somewhat benign, twist to Rousseau's assertion in 1762 that "People are everywhere born free, but everywhere they find themselves in chains." From an ethical viewpoint, the perception of the social contract held by elderly residents and their relatives had turned the boundaries of the study inside out.

DISCUSSION

In the decades since mid-century, changes in demographics and health care policy in the Unites States have led to a substantial increase in the number and use of nursing homes. Not only has the size of the resident population grown, but so have the levels of their frailty and the prevalence of chronic as contrasted with acute conditions. Periodic scandals and exposés concerning the abuse and neglect of nursing home patients since the 1960s have also prompted new regulations for institutional care at both the federal and state levels [see Mason, this volume]. Furthermore, the enhanced scrutiny of long term care facilities, the increased role of public funding sources for their patients, and the changing health status of residents have likewise contributed to new levels of attention to ethical problems within the nursing home field. Among the issues that have been widely considered are elder abuse and neglect; quality of life and quality of care standards; the implementation of "right to die," Do Not Resuscitate (DNR) orders; and other end-stage directives. Also considered are the financial roles of families, communities, and governments in paying for long term care. Furthermore, the professional responsibilities and reward systems of administrators, clinicians, other caregivers, and conflicts of interest among proprietors, doctors, and other providers have demanded attention (Kane and Caplan, 1989).

While the growth in long term care has also led to an increase in practical, policy-oriented, and theoretical research on institutions, there has not been a lot of attention given to the ethical issues that researchers themselves face in the conduct of their studies. The preceding sections have identified five areas where moral dilemmas arose in one research project, and they invite at least brief comparison with the experiences of other ethnographers.

Privacy

Virtually every descriptive nursing home study has commented on the scarcity of privacy for residents (Laird 1979:70; Kayser-Jones 1981:46–48; Wilcocks et al. 1987:passim; O'Brien 1989:172–174; Savishinsky 1991:117–119). Gubrium observed that particular places at Murray Manor were variously public or private at different times (1975:9, 18, 31), and he and Shield noted specific areas of contention, such as Murray Manor's bathrooms (Gubrium 1975:13, 27), and the locking or unlocking of doors at Franklin (Shield 1988:71–72). Ethnographers rarely comment, however, on how they themselves negotiated these issues as an ethical dimension of their work. Diamond (1992), in his dual role as nurse's aide and researcher, does note that he was able to overcome his qualms about bathing elderly women only when he realized that the embarrassment at such times lay with him and not his female patients. As one of these women expressed it to him, "Don't worry, you'll get used to it" (1992:86). Such instances of the ethnographer "projecting" privacy onto situations are probably far more common than published accounts reveal.

Consent

Ethnographers have commonly noted a willingness on the part of residents and staff to discuss their experiences (e.g., Shield 1988:19), though rarely do researchers indicate whether or not, or under what circumstances, informed consent documents were used. Gubrium makes an important observation about the covert way administrators themselves obtained documentation about residents at Murray Manor. He notes that "serious interviews [of residents by top staff] are publicly performed as visits . . . [and so] much of what transpires in them are social pleasantries" (1975:64).

Top staff here clearly blurred the boundaries between formal and informal interaction in a way that ethnographers frequently do.

In most of the ethnographic studies that have been done on nursing homes, the institutions have clearly agreed to allow the research to be conducted (e.g., Gubrium 1975; Watson and Maxwell 1977; Kayser-Jones 1981; Powers 1988; Shield 1988; O'Brien 1989; Savishinsky 1991). However, the acquisition of such formal institutional consent is less clear in other studies. In at lease one case (Diamond 1986; 1992), the ethnographer's purpose was manifestly not revealed to administrators because, Diamond decided, this would have made it impossible to proceed with the project. Diamond has written that no one hired him when he said he wanted to do research, and so the study "was forced increasingly to become a piece of undercover research" (1992:8). While Diamond, as a sociologist, supports his decision by citing other sociological writings on disclosure (1992:247), his approach could be seen as conflicting with the American Anthropological Association's ethical stance (1990): "The aims of all their professional activities should be clearly communicated by anthropologists to those among whom they work." Recent concerns with informed consent and individual rights suggest that ethnographic studies need to strive for greater methodological and ethical clarity on this point.

Candor and Confidentiality

Every published ethnography of a nursing home contains some criticism of the institution under study. Specific points range from inadequate food, recreation activities, and privacy to low staff morale, the quality of care, the denial of death, the over-use of restraints, and the handling of finances. Works by Laird (1979), Kayser-Jones (1981), and Shield (1988) also note the theft of residents' possessions; Watson and Maxwell (1977) document racial tensions between residents and caregivers; and Vesperi (1987) details the institutional failure to rehabilitate people who could have been returned to their community.

Beyond the plethora of criticism, it is also worth noting what we do and do not know about the process by which such criticism gets articulated. Every ethnography cited protects the identity of the institutions and people discussed by giving them pseudonyms and by altering other details of their stories and attributes. The public gets to know what is wrong about unknown people and places. It is rarely mentioned whether the researchers have shared their negative assessments directly with the facilities where they worked. My own experience of passing on negative comments to staff at Elmwood Grove (another pseudonym) was itself naive, inadvertent, and disconcerting. It revealed, in a small way, the risks and problems of candor.

The common practice of critiquing pseudonymous nursing homes does conform to, and strike a balance between, two of anthropology's primary ethical precepts: confidentiality and truthfulness. The profession's code requires both the protection of people's "dignity and privacy . . . and sensitivities" and ethnographers' "positive responsibility to speak out publicly . . . on issues about which they possess professional expertise . . . [and thereby] contribute to the formation of informational grounds upon which public policy may be founded" (American Anthropological Association 1990). The first of these dictates is a moral obligation to the people with whom we work; the second is a commitment to the public we address. The institutions that ethnographers study, however, are corporate entities that fall between the two social categories of person and public, and so the ethnographer's responsibilities to the facilities are, at best, ambiguous. It would nevertheless be helpful to have more accounts of what happens when researchers give direct criticism to nursing homes, and reflections on whether fieldworkers consider such action to be an ethical imperative.

Reciprocity and Advocacy

The role of the ethnographer in a nursing home turns out to be a very active one. Kayser-Jones (1981), Powers (1988), and O'Brien (1989) as nurses, Henderson (1981), Vesperi (1987), and Diamond (1992) as nurse's aides, and Gubrium (1975) in his role as gerontologist, all did tasks and performed caregiving services for residents. So, presumably, did the graduate nurses who assisted Henry (1963), as did I and my students in our own capacity as volunteers and pet "therapists." Thus, the "participant" part of being nursing home participant observers has involved many researchers in direct, helpful engagement in people's lives.

While helpfulness is a form of reciprocity, it does not necessarily constitute advocacy. Several ethnographers, in fact, have noted that some of the most effective advocates for institutional residents are the family members who take an active role in their elderly relatives' lives, and who can, therefore, exercise leverage on their behalf (e.g., Gubrium 1975:89–99; Laird 1979:59; Shield 1988:59–60, 177; Savishinsky 1991:69–123). A number of researchers have nevertheless commented on the special requests that residents have made for assistance. Diamond remarks on how his provision of the extra food and aspirin that people requested involved him in breaking institutional rules (1992:91, 151–152, 195). Henry's students were asked to run errands and to do favors such as obtain glasses (1965:387–398). As noted before, my own experiences included requests to remove restraints, intercede with families, and deal with lawyers. Several researchers have also noted problems inherent in helpfulness itself. Diamond (1992:141), for example, encountered residents who resented being offered too much help, and both Powers (1988) and Shield (1988:176) remark on the staff dilemma of trying to give aid without promoting dependency. Gubrium also observed (1975:5) how Murray Manor's clientele did not distinguish between

different levels of staff. Consequently, when they made inappropriate requests for help to personnel, they felt resentful when workers did not or
could not comply. The very nature of helpfulness in the nursing home
setting is thus fraught with unexpected meanings and complications.

Inside and Outside

A number of ethnographers have stressed the importance of the outside
community with regard to the quality of what goes on inside institutions.
Kayser-Jones (1981), for example, praised the Scottish community for enhancing residents' lives at Scottsdale. Shield (1988:18–20, 114–121), on the
other hand, expressed disappointment in how disengaged members of the
local Jewish community were from their co-religionists at Franklin Nursing
Home.

What has gone unremarked in most nursing home ethnographies, however, is how the researchers themselves have negotiated the boundary
between the inside and the outside. This is a notable omission because some
ethnographers have apparently studied facilities in their own or nearby
communities. They have had to make decisions about the kinds of ties to
maintain with staff and relatives, and how involved to stay with the
institution's residents and personnel after the research itself is over. Such
decisions reflect not just practical considerations, but ethical ones as well;
they express a moral viewpoint on how durable or disposable human
relationships are, and whether research warrants a suspension or re-affir-
mation of the social bounds that characterize everyday life. Just as Erving
Goffman (1961) once stressed the "moral career" of people who enter and
live inside total institutions, we need greater consideration of the "moral
career" of the ethnographers who study them.

CONCLUSION

On a personal as well as a pragmatic level, fieldwork is often a balancing
act. Ethnographers weigh their individual wishes against their scholarly
interests; they counterpoint their own needs for privacy and personal space
with their desire for engagement in public life and intimacy with those who
once were strangers. Fieldwork tensions also extend to the ethical plane,
where compelling but conflicting precepts are often at play. In the nursing
home setting, dilemmas arise around such areas as rules, roles, relationships, and reporting. The specific ethical strains considered here have
centered on advocacy versus reciprocity, publicity versus privacy, informed
consent versus informal reality, candor versus confidentiality, and the problem of determining the "inside" versus the "outside" of the research itself.

Underlying these difficulties is another moral imperative felt by many
fieldworkers, the idea that for the time, effort, access, money, or information

that others have given them, they should do something useful with their data. The pet therapy project discussed here for example did, in fact, begin with an applied agenda (i.e., to evaluate the impact of a therapeutic innovation) and to make suggestions for improving the pet program's effectiveness. When the research expanded beyond this initial focus, it went on to examine the worldviews of residents, staff, and volunteers so that members of these three groups would be able to learn something about the way others saw and interacted with them. The insights my students and I gained about people's perceptions and feelings were shared with Elmwood's various constituencies by means of talks, publications, and a number of specific suggestions for enhancing the quality of life and work within the facility.

Turning the research in these practical directions of assessment, feedback, dialogue, and recommendation did not resolve the other ethical dilemmas that emerged. However, it did demonstrate that a willingness to consider these areas of ambiguity can enable individuals to become more conscious of their own values, needs, and assumptions. Full-length ethnographic accounts of nursing homes have included recommendations on how to improve such areas of institutional life as staff training, community and family involvement, responses to death, access to privacy, and the exercise of power by residents.[3] At Elmwood Grove, we found that an awareness of the cultural contradictions at work inside the nursing home was a vital step in helping people negotiate and learn how to live with these tensions. As insiders and outsiders, the lessons we were able to teach one another constituted another instance of reciprocity, and perhaps therein lies yet one more moral of the tale.

7

Ethics in the Nursing Home: Cases, Choices, and Issues

Renée Rose Shield

INTRODUCTION

Health care decision making in the United States has traditionally been the sole prerogative of the attending physician. In the last few decades, however, physicians have seen the emergence of the informed consumer, the civil rights movement, the feminist movement, and a burgeoning medical technology that has overwhelmed the capacity of practitioners to make simple, clear-cut health care decisions.

In this chapter, I discuss the complex nature of an ethics committee in a Jewish nursing home in the northeastern United States in the context of the emergence of the "bioethics" movement in this country. Observing the dynamics of the committee meetings reveals many of the tensions and conflicts that arise within the typical nursing home on a daily basis. I will trace the origins and development of this ethics committee within the facility. I will also discuss the kinds of activities in which it was engaged, how it grappled with ethical principles, practical considerations, and at times, the Jewish values underpinning it. Furthermore, suggestions will be made regarding the themes that these choices and behaviors represent.

Bioethics in general and ethics committees in nursing facilities, specifically, can be understood as uniquely Anglo-American constructions that dramatize characteristically American values. Ideas about autonomy, dependency, competency, sanctity of life, quality of life, and fairness are some of the issues contested in the ethics committee with vehemence. Daniel

Callahan has said, "Bioethics is a native-grown American product" (quoted in Jonsen 1993:S3). Its development shows an optimistic orientation to problem solving: gather a committee, encourage diversity of opinion, reach consensus, draw up policy, make guidelines and regulations, and meet again next week. The Ethics Committee at the Franklin Nursing Home worked hard to educate itself about moral complexity and how to reconcile difficult dilemmas within different kinds of competing polarities and antagonisms. It attempted to set direction in a murky environment and shine some illumination by which the institution could steer a tentative course.

Qualitative research methods and analysis are necessary to understand these values and ideas. In doing this work, I was allowed a glimpse into the uneasy chasm between the real and the ideal worlds of the nursing home. By observing and participating in an ethics committee that was formed to articulate and respect the wishes of frail old people in a medically oriented institution, I was able to witness the struggles of well-meaning individuals as they sought to understand and balance competing values. Some of these competing value issues included: how to or whether to "care for" nursing home residents when individual wishes clash, how to balance one resident's wishes against those of others, and how to guard the nursing home against liability. The qualitative nature of the work allowed "thick description" (Geertz 1973) of the world of nursing home decision making, without which we would be left with anemic numbers and outcomes of the decision, devoid of their contexts and fuller meanings.

BACKGROUND

In 1987, the Hastings Center published *Guidelines on the Termination of Life-Sustaining Treatment and the Care of the Dying* and provided specific policy recommendations for the formation of institutional ethics committees "or some other institutional mechanism for providing advice and education on ethical problems" in hospitals, nursing homes, hospices and other inpatient health care institutions (1987:101). The publication suggested that institutions should actively support the ethics committees and made recommendations about the composition of the committees to include diverse representation from inside and outside the institution. The guidelines further established the values of confidentiality, education, policy development, and prospective ongoing review of cases.

Ethics committees in nursing homes are a recent yet growing presence (Miller and Cugliari 1990). According to Olson et al., "Most long-term care institutions have followed their acute care colleagues and created ethics committees whose primary responsibilities are the provision of direct service and staff education" (1993:269). Most ethics committees in American nursing homes provide some staff education and conflict resolution processes in their activities. Ethics committees in nursing homes often concern themselves with issues different from those addressed by hospital ethics committees.

Nursing home ethics committees deliberate on issues having to do with life and death—for example, how to respect a dying person's wishes, how to ascertain an incompetent dying person's wishes, and how to reconcile differences between the family and the nursing home resident on end-of-life issues. The committee's greater potential for usefulness, however, lies in untangling the daily ethical issues that arise in the nursing home. As Freeman notes, "Although bioethics committees are more commonly associated with difficult decisions around withholding and withdrawing medical treatment, the interdisciplinary composition offers a promising means for education, policy development, and consultation on many of the most pressing issues of autonomy and safety, such as the use of restraints, petitions for guardianship, adherence to the therapeutic diets, self-medication, and room assignment" (1990:301–302).

Jonsen (1993) has written:

Modern bioethicists react to medicine, medical technology, and health care services with peculiarly American concerns about the rights of individuals, fairness and equity in access to benefits, and secularized reflections about death, abortion, suffering, and aging. Additionally . . . the resolution of many of these problems had been peculiarly American, namely, the devising of regulations and guidelines . . . and the fashioning of the living will, to save us. . . . In an uniquely American style, we create a class of mediators to fashion a mean between the extremes (1993:S3–S4).

The nursing home represents a place in which obstacles to the cherished American ideals of independence and autonomy are numerous. The presence of chronic illness, functional decline, and diminished cognitive capacity in so many of the people who inhabit nursing homes provides a ripe environment for the paternalistic attitude characteristic of many of the caretakers. Acting in a person's perceived best interests often substitutes for the competing notion of respecting that person's autonomy. The legitimate concern for the welfare of these frail individuals is further compounded by the increasing burden of regulations and requirements with which the facility and the staff members must comply. Nursing home professionals labor under the stigma of distrust and wary concern in a society that pounces on news of abuse and neglect with vehement calls for greater vigilance and further regulation. In stark contrast to the hospital, which is presumed innocent until proven guilty, the nursing home is usually presumed guilty. Regulations have proliferated to prevent a wide range of abuse and neglectful practices, and administrators of nursing facilities struggle to avoid investigation. As a result, the tendency is often to treat, rather than to forgo treatment.

Further, in the nursing home there are many shades of gray within the notion of competency, and attempts to distinguish "competent" from "incompetent" residents are founded on subtly distinguished rather than clear psychophysiologic criteria that are embedded in social and environmental contexts. Furthermore, individuals are intermittently capable. Many demented nursing home residents are declared legally incompetent but manage to express their wishes and preferences clearly. Hard and fast rules to judge competency are lacking. This makes the use of advance directives difficult in the nursing home setting. According to Johnson, "Advance directives rely on an informed consent model of decision-making and usually require that a patient be categorized as either competent or incompetent. This bright line assumed to exist between capacity and incapacity is not reflected in the experience of nursing home providers. More frequently, the capacity or incapacity of an individual wavers over some period of time" (1991:S4).

The nursing home, furthermore, occupies a troubled place in the American consciousness. Not really a medical facility, and more decidedly not really a home, the nursing home is a place where a medically-oriented regime and an institutional routine hold sway. It is at the same time the long term residence of many of its inhabitants—usually their last. As such it encompasses relationships among staff members and residents and embodies various and complex meanings of "home." The ambiguous position of the nursing home makes it a particularly interesting entity in which to study the dynamics of how health care decisions are questioned, perceived, and constructed by the various parties involved.

EVOLUTION OF THE FRANKLIN NURSING HOME ETHICS COMMITTEE

The Franklin Nursing Home (pseudonym), located in a mid-sized city in the northeastern United States, has been described elsewhere (Shield 1988). Fieldwork in this Jewish nursing home was conducted over a 14-month period in the early 1980s. In the following years, the author continued a close association with the research site and between 1989 and 1993 participated as a member and then the chair of the ethics committee of the nursing home.

The ethics committee came about in a two-stage process. During the initial phase, a lengthy treatment and testing protocol for the nursing home residents was created. Once this protocol was completed, the group felt it necessary to continue as an ethics committee in order to oversee the implementation of the protocol within the nursing home. I became involved with the ethics committee in the second phase, after the protocol was finished. Meetings were held for approximately two hours every two months, and issues related to incorporating the protocol into the nursing home became the subject of the meetings. I took notes, and minutes were written on the meetings.

Phase 1

In 1988, the Franklin Nursing Home initiated a process to define how individual nursing home residents could exercise their rights to refuse or accept testing and treatment. A long tradition of resident care conferences had already established the practice of including residents in some arenas where health care decisions were made. However, it was also apparent that medical decisions were often fraught with difficult dilemmas: the wishes of nursing home residents were not always honored; the role of family members in mediating the desires of the nursing home resident was unclear; and the legal issues surrounding advance directives and terminating treatment made ethical issues of growing interest and concern.

Furthermore, the resident care conferences at Franklin were occasions for differing viewpoints among medical staff, nursing staff, social workers, family members, and other staff members to emerge. For example, after the medical director hospitalized a hitherto highly alert nursing home resident who had repeatedly expressed her wish not to be hospitalized "should the time come," he found himself defending his actions and intentions in a resident care conference (Shield 1988). Had he done the right thing? The resident was angry with him. He believed he had upheld high medical standards and that the resident had a good quality of life as a result. The social workers, professionally trained to be resident advocates, were horrified that the resident's expressed wishes had not been honored. Meanwhile, nurses in the conference room were aghast that the doctor's judgment was being questioned. Life was the value to be preserved and upheld!

Scenes such as this were increasingly common in the 1980s. Prodded by one staff member who believed that residents' end-of-life decisions were not being honored, the facility formed a committee to define ways to better preserve these wishes. The staff member felt that certain nursing home residents believed they were at the end of their lives and wished to be made comfortable in the nursing home. When an alleged medical emergency arose, she was troubled that such a resident was wrenched from the comfortable and familiar nursing home setting and sent to the hospital's emergency room for treatments and procedures that were often invasive and intrusive. She felt that staff members were not sensitive to the needs and wishes of these residents.

In contrast, another staff member believed that elderly people in nursing homes were too often untreated because they were considered "too old" to live. He felt he should counteract this tendency and ensure that more life (and quality of life) was available to them given properly timed and appropriate medical intervention.

The committee undertook the job of designing a protocol to chart how to preserve resident wishes in treatment and testing decisions, both in the nursing home and in the hospital. The committee was composed of the administrator, the medical director, the staff psychiatrist, the home's attor-

ney, the home's social worker, and the director of nurses. After a draft
document was produced, the committee incorporated the comments of a
prominent medical ethicist. The document went through numerous drafts
and was the subject of heated debates over wording and intent. The Introduction to the document begins:

The [Franklin Nursing] Home is committed to providing the highest quality of life
possible for its residents despite the presence of one or more serious chronic
illnesses. Sometimes, however, residents and their families, physicians, and the
Home's professional staff, have different ideas and expectations about how much
medical treatment is desirable. To ensure that your wishes are known, the Home
developed the attached document. This will help ensure that the extent of testing
and treatment is consistent with your expressed wishes as long as your wishes are
not illegal or unethical.

The document recommends that a resident complete an advance direc-
tive recognized in the state so that his or her wishes would be known before
an event which might render the resident incapable of communicating
them. It continues with a list of principles that include various rights and
responsibilities that frame the guidelines. For example:

"Each resident has the right to define for himself or herself the goals and limits of
    testing and treatment."
"The resident should be encouraged to consider the views of other concerned
    individuals."
"The physician has the responsibility to assess the competency of the resident in the
    decision-making process."
"The resident's physician, family, and staff should attempt to resolve disagreements
    in a professional manner."

The document continues with a discussion of capacity for health care
decision making (e.g., the resident is deemed capable unless judged incapable). If there is a question of the person's capacity, a team would decide
if the resident understands the nature of the health care choice, its consequences and alternatives, and would judge if the health care choice was
determined in "due and deliberate fashion" and could be maintained over
a period of time. A procedure for assessing a resident with questioned
capacity for health care decision making was also included.

The document also outlines the nursing home's position on cardio-pul-
monary resuscitation (CPR). After much debate, the group decided that the
nursing home would not routinely offer CPR because of the intensive
hospital follow-up required after its administration and the poor prognosis
that usually resulted when applied to older individuals with multiple
chronic conditions. Should the resident expressly wish to have CPR administered, he or she would have to sign a form indicating this explicit choice.

The heart of the document was a classification system whereby a resident was asked to designate a category that best suited him or her. This designation could be changed at any time by the resident. The choice would be reviewed by the physician at the usual time medical orders were reviewed (every few months), after a hospitalization, and/or after a major change in the person's overall condition. If the resident chose "Group A," or if the person did not make any choice, maximum therapeutic effort including hospitalization would be extended on the resident's behalf. To borrow from computer language, the default value (no designation) meant maximum therapeutic effort.

Designating "Group B" signified choosing to have individualized therapeutic effort within the nursing home. This choice meant that hospitalization would normally be excluded, but diagnostic evaluation in the hospital emergency room could be included after discussion with the resident and/or family. For example, if the resident agreed to hospital testing, and hospitalization was recommended after the tests were completed, the resident could then refuse the hospitalization. Residents could also choose "Group C," the least interventionary category. Residents in this group would not be hospitalized, and only those therapeutic and diagnostic measures that are intended to maintain comfort would be performed in the nursing home.

Phase 2

Documents further established the ethics committee "whose responsibilities include review and update of these protocols, conflict resolution, study of ethical issues, and development of ethical guidelines." The ethics committee was expanded to include a second physician, a second administrator, the chairperson of the board of trustees, three members of the nursing department, including a nursing assistant, a past or present resident's family member, a current nursing home resident, two rabbis, and three community representatives with backgrounds in ethics, religion, or social service. I became a member of the committee at this point as a community representative.

Armed with a document that had consumed countless hours of debate and gone through numerous edited versions, the administration of Franklin Nursing Home nevertheless understood that the crux of the quandaries, conflicts, and questions lay in the next step—the implementation of the protocol. Already minutely scrutinized and overseen, the nursing home exists in a politically and socially combustible environment. How would the protocol play out with frail new admissions, solicitous and ambivalent adult children, in a medicalized nursing facility, in a Jewish community, and in a litigious society? How would the different worldviews of varied professionals, each socialized to believe in subtly different goals and outcomes, mesh with one another? How could the nuances embedded in the protocol be taught and transmitted to the staff, residents, family members, and the public? Where might the disagreements arise? How would they be resolved?

The ethics committee would be a forum in which the new protocol would be tested and implemented. The ethical issues it raised would be discussed and policies and/or guidelines would be created in response. Problems in caring for the individual residents at the Franklin Nursing Home could be brought to the ethics committee for discussion and resolution. Ways to educate staff, family members, and residents would be designed and implemented. The ethics committee had its work cut out for it.

ISSUES BROUGHT TO THE ETHICS COMMITTEE: THE CASES

The cases were described with as many nuances and significant details as necessary to illuminate the individual situations and the dilemmas they presented. It was as if the ethics committee attempted by "thick description" (Geertz 1973) to understand the complex, real underbelly of the nursing facility. In accordance with Davis (1991), this thick description was used to help committee members understand in a truer way why the dilemmas were difficult, but also in a way that maintained the confidentiality of those individuals concerned in the cases. Focusing on the idiosyncratic elements of the case helped to humanize nursing home life, illuminate the disagreements, and facilitate empathic decision making.

Lapses in communication, insufficient education about the content and purposes of the protocol, inadequate knowledge of the residents and their wishes, and enduring conflicts in health care goals among staff members, family members, and residents were salient issues. How the professional staff relates to family members during the course of the medical crisis was considered critical. Committee members felt that there was an urgent need to train staff and perhaps even to provide scripts to guide them when calling family members in a medical emergency. Should the role of the nursing home staff include educating and preparing family members for the inevitable death of the resident?

An article by Dan Brock discussing possible circumstances when advance directives should be "trumped" or overridden might have had relevance to the committee. Brock notes that "stopping treatment might then be very briefly delayed to help the family accept the patient's death" (1991:S6). In addition, he states:

Because of reasonable fears about abuse by physicians or family members of any authority not to honor advance directives, some believe they should always be binding. A better alternative, I think, is to develop institutional and judicial procedures and safeguards to reduce the risk of abuse to tolerable levels. . . . Though advance directives may not be ethically binding in all cases, they should be honored in the vast majority, and should only be set aside after careful consideration.

Brock properly notes the discrepancy between the realities of work settings and commitments to "ideal" policies.

Should the family members in such cases have been better "prepared" for the resident's death? Whose responsibility was the preparation? The policy was operative; the resident had fulfilled her part. Yet when a medical emergency was perceived to be occurring, the nursing staff, physician, and family members reverted to crisis reaction. Their response was to medicalize and thus hospitalize the resident who had sought to die "at home," in the nursing facility.

Life and Death

According to Marshall (1992:51), "The intensity surrounding current bioethical debate—in both professional and public arenas—reflects a deep-seated ambivalence in the U.S. value system toward scientific developments and their implications for control over life and death." Many of the subjects discussed in the Franklin Nursing Home Ethics Committee involved life and death. Most of these issues revolved around how the new protocol was being implemented. First, it was found that introducing the protocol was difficult. For various reasons, many people did not complete the protocol documents. Social workers presented them to new admissions, but in recognizing how difficult the transition to institutional life was, often did not press for rapid decision. Some family members and residents did not want to complete the protocol and delayed the decision to do so. Overall, despite considerable effort to encourage residents to complete the protocol, usually between 25 and 35 percent of all residents did not have a protocol filled out at any one time.

Was the protocol helping individual residents die at the nursing home or in the hospital, as specified in the document? Many ethics committee meetings included a review of those nursing home residents who had been transferred to the hospital since the last meeting. The ethics committee sought to know if each hospitalized resident had filled out a treatment and testing protocol. If so, had the resident's designated choice been fulfilled? A review conducted in 1992 revealed that fully 17 percent of the residents who had been hospitalized in the previous two months had not had their wishes followed. If the resident had chosen not to be hospitalized but had been, what were the circumstances that explained the discrepancy between what the resident had explicitly chosen and the medical emergency that had led to the hospitalization?

One hospitalization review stimulated much debate. A resident had signed the protocol indicating a wish not to go to the hospital. This cognitively intact resident had often expressed her wishes not to be hospitalized in a medical emergency. However, during a nighttime medical crisis, a family member had been called by the nursing staff and was asked whether the resident should be hospitalized. The family member and the physician on call decided the resident should go to the hospital for treatment. Treatment was undertaken in the emergency room, and the resident died shortly thereafter in the hospital.

In the review discussion, it was unclear whether the nursing staff had conveyed to the family member that the resident had indicated her wish not to go to the hospital. It was further unclear whether the staff person knew of the resident's wish. The physician who had made the decision to hospitalize defended his choice and maintained that the family had the right to override the resident's wish in the crisis. Others in the group protested that the resident had made her wishes known explicitly to avoid the hospitalization that resulted in spite of her efforts. According to the minutes, "Apparently, what seems to happen is that the nurse calls the doctor, the doctor recommends that a resident be sent to the emergency room, and the resident is sent to the emergency room. It was pointed out that frequently the process is not followed, and no one talks with the resident." The committee also decided, "Even more important, the resident ought to be given a choice even before the nurse calls the physician. . . . The Home is trying to solve a process problem with a procedure and while a procedure can certainly help, it will not totally solve the problem."

Sexuality and Dementia

This case was presented as follows:

J.P. is a 79 year old who lived by herself after her husband died several years ago. Mild dementia developed, and after she was hospitalized for emphysema, she entered the nursing home. D.B. is 82 years old and entered the nursing home with his wife six months ago. She died four months ago. He has mild dementia. Recently, D.B. and J.P. became friendly and began to spend a lot of time together. J.P. became happier, started eating better, and became more social. Though D.B. was quite saddened by his wife's death, his friendship with J.P. has helped him become happier. They now sit together, go to activities together, hold hands, and kiss. They spend time together in J.P.'s room and sometimes lie down on her bed and hug and kiss. Sometimes they cover themselves with a blanket and it is unclear if they are clothed. Sometimes D.B. does not want to go back to his room after 8 p.m. The staff thinks that J.P.'s roommate seems bothered by his being in the room so much of the time, but she is actually unable to express herself. J.P.'s family is aware of this relationship and are pleased with how well she is doing. D.B.'s family does not really know of the relationship yet.

The ethics committee discussed this couple because members were concerned about several general and specific issues: the meaning of consent of either party given the presence of dementia; whether either of them should be "protected" and from whom; whether the family had "rights" to be informed about a parent's behaviors; whether the family should have the ability to make decisions about a parent's conduct; whether explicit or implicit staff squeamishness should have a bearing on residents' behaviors; whether this particular couple's behaviors were infringing on the female resident's roommate's rights to privacy and self-determination; whether the couple should be given a separate room together or encouraged to become married; whether any limits whatever should be placed on the couple; and whether the home had a responsibility to the Jewish community to ensure certain behaviors in the home and prohibit others.

Committee members spiritedly debated the issues raised by this situation. Individuals differed about whether the couple's children should be told and whether they had any rights to determine behavior. Though staff members believed that the family that did not know of the relationship might be skittish about it, it was agreed that the family should be educated and/or counseled to accept the parent's sexuality, difficult though it might be for them. The committee also reached consensus about the ability of both individuals to consent to the behaviors, since they both appeared to be happy and functioning better as a result of their involvement. However, staff members believed that the couple should not have a separate room. The most problematic aspect of the case was the objections of the roommate, whose rights to privacy seemed to be transgressed. Committee members agreed that the roommate's wishes should be meshed with those of the couple insofar as was possible in order to accommodate all involved. Staff members were encouraged to arrange for the male resident to have a single room in order to protect the female roommate's privacy.

It was also of interest that the sexuality of the residents was considered a loaded subject by the ethics committee—both for the family members and for the community. The ethics committee tried to understand and resolve the institution's role in acting for the resident, mediating between the resident and adult children, reconciling the rights of residents vis-à-vis one another, and keeping a nervous eye on the home's public relations, as well.

Refusal of Recommended Nursing Home Care

This case was presented as follows:

The resident is a female who weighs in excess of 250 lbs. and is the youngest resident in the Home. Her body has deserted her but her mind is still quite clear and acute. She is totally competent. She has some personality problems and poor judgment. She has severe and significant decubiti on her buttocks which are being addressed by changing her position six times on the day and evening shift and four times on the night shift. Because of this regimen, her decubiti have begun to respond and heal, but the resident wants the times she is turned reduced to four times during the evening shift since the turning is interfering with her sleep. She has been advised that to do so would run the risk of her skin breakdown recurring, and she understands that. She has even been told that she could get an infection and become quite ill and even die, and she accepts that as well.

The staff reported that they resented the extra time it took to tend to this resident. She was "difficult" and "resistant," and the arguing and conflict took time away from their care of other residents. The discussion examined the treatment alternatives. Was it clear that the resident understood the rationale for the recommended treatments? Was it possible the decubiti might heal without so many treatments and nighttime interruptions? Had the resident, physician, social worker, and nursing staff actually talked through some of the issues and alternatives with each other?

It was recommended that some concerted attempt at improved communication be tried with the resident first and foremost. Committee members acknowledged her wish to remain in control, and they understood that "doing battle" with her over her rights was counterproductive. While no one on the committee believed that a less rigorous plan would be successful in healing the ulcers, it was agreed that any competent resident had the right to decide for herself how aggressive the treatments would be, regardless of how difficult it might be for nursing staff, and even though her life might be compromised. The committee reminded itself that she had that right, and she could also change her mind over time.

A follow-up discussion took place at the next meeting. Surprisingly, for most committee members, the less rigorous treatment to which the staff had reluctantly assented had not compromised the healing of the decubitus ulcers. In following the resident's wishes, holding meetings between staff and the resident to improve communication, and modifying the treatment regimen, the ethics committee notes read, "The situation is much improved and she is doing well. The worst did not occur as had been anticipated and it may teach us that we may be wrong and the residents do have a point which we need to consider." Enhanced communication among staff also resulted from the increased education, which everyone found to be beneficial.

The Alcoholic Resident Who Wanted a Weekend Pass

A nursing assistant brought this issue to the attention of the ethics committee. A resident wanted to be discharged to her son's home for the Christmas holidays. The nursing assistant thought the resident, who had problems with alcohol in the past, would revert to drinking at home during holiday festivities. In addition, there were concerns among the staff that the son who would transport her and be responsible for her while at home was also believed to be an alcoholic. The physician had agreed that the resident should not be permitted to go home. The physician was not sure he could remain her physician if she acted against his wishes in this matter. Ethics committee members were concerned about the nursing home's liability should the son have an auto accident while transporting the resident. Where did the home's responsibility lie? Could the facility prevent the resident from leaving?

The committee decided that any competent resident has the right to leave for the weekend. Although it was suspected, no one was positive that the son in this case had a drinking problem. There was a recommendation that if the resident's physician felt strongly enough that his wishes were not followed, he should document in her chart that medical advice was given and understood. Whether he chose to remain her physician was considered a distinct matter.

Assisting a Resident to Move to an Unsafe Environment

A final case concerned a long term resident who had been unhappy at the Franklin Nursing Home throughout his residence there. Though he was functioning fairly well physically, the social worker believed he had terrible judgment and social skills. The man wanted to leave the nursing home and live in an apartment in what the staff considered to be an unsafe, high crime neighborhood. The issue turned on whether the resident could insist on staff help to assist his move outside the home. The resident was adamant about leaving, and he had maintained his interest in this plan for a long time.

While the social worker believed the resident had every right to make what she considered to be an unwise decision, she also believed that she was under no obligation to help him make what she thought was an unsafe move. She felt it was professionally and personally unethical to aid him in this manner. Committee members were divided. Some felt that staff members must help this resident make the phone calls and arrangements necessary to move. Others believed that if he needed so much basic help in planning the move, he was incapable of moving and should not be assisted. When he had lived in the community, he had alienated staff at various social service agencies who knew him well. Some members of the ethics committee were also concerned about the nursing home's liability in the matter.

It was decided that the resident had the right to make this decision and to act on it. Furthermore, it was incumbent upon the nursing home to assist him in making the move as safely and fully as possible. When the nursing home's position was explained to the resident, he and his social worker planned the move together. A staff member drove the resident to the neighborhood where he wished to move to familiarize him with it. The result of this drive was that the resident postponed his intention to leave for a short time, and then indefinitely. In revisiting this issue several times over the following year, the committee noted with interest that the resident seemed to have reconciled himself to living in the nursing home. As the minutes of the ethics committee noted: "It was identified as a good example of when you give a resident the opportunity to make choices, often he/she does not exercise that opportunity." It was also instructive to staff members to remember that resident choices were to be followed.

CONCLUSIONS

The nursing home is an intriguing landscape in which ethical dilemmas find fertile soil. Conflicts are played out between the nursing home as "quasi-hospital" and as "home." The autonomy of the individual is pitted at times against powerful staff members, concerned family members, and the constraints of a bureaucratic institution. Furthermore, the individual resident's rights have to contend with the rights of the other residents. Also, paternalism can masquerade as beneficence, and autonomy can be code for dismissing responsibility for someone with whom one disagrees. Litigiousness shadows the nursing home. Adult children are torn between oversolicitousness and detachment. Respecting a person's wishes often means negating one's desire to help or one's sense of proper behavior. The members of the ethics committee themselves seemed constantly to be re-learning the distinction between their wishes and those of the residents, those whose rights the committee was established to maintain.

A critical gerontological perspective (Luborsky 1994) requires us to reflect on the meaning of the ethics committee within the nursing home. The institution of the ethics committee reveals the cultural belief that the typical nursing home resident would have little voice and few rights were it not for the rules and policies of protocol. The lengthy discussions and the elaborate policy guidelines exist to protect the frail individual, who would be without protection otherwise. The ethics committee also attests to how powerful the institution and the medical model continue to be.

In addition, the discussions in the ethics committee reveal the gulf between written policy and actual behaviors. The ethics committee attempts a rough catch-up to the messy, blurry activities on the floors of the nursing home. It assumes the power of the medicalized routine, and it attempts to squeeze out room for individual autonomy by means of intricate policy. It does not reflect the reality of residents who make decisions in relationship with family members (Kapp 1991), staff members, and physicians. What usually happens in the middle of the night when a resident is short of breath and the nurse on duty is new is that the doctor is called and all stops are out to save or prolong the life of the resident. The document in the chart that eloquently defines the treatment preferences of the resident, whose right to have his wishes met is protected by law, is of secondary

concern. The ethics committee activities reveal how vast the gap can sometimes be between daytime protocol and nighttime realities.

Decisions within the nursing home rely upon and reflect relationships,
and where relationships do not exist or are rent, there are problems. For all
the claims to respect resident "autonomy," which implies an atomistic
independence and separation, residents are embedded in webs of inter-
twining connections. This reality is particularly suitable to analysis using
"thick description" discourse. Some residents are meshed within their
family systems; others rely upon relationships developed within the
institution. Some have the complexities of both. The ethics committee
discussions frequently revealed where relationships broke down or communications failed. Suggestions for more explicit policy and more education usually resulted. In general, individual actors assumed that what they
did was correct and right, but they did not often stop to ask whether others,
especially the residents, shared their assumptions. As Kayser-Jones (1990)
has noted in relation to the use of naso-gastric feeding tubes in nursing
homes, communication among nursing home staff, physicians, patients,
and their families is often lacking, and procedures such as these are often
done for the convenience of staff members. The ethics committee of the
Franklin Nursing Home forced a pause upon all kinds of unexamined
routines, and the pause provided a way to ponder, be critical of, and weigh
those reflexive routines.

Interestingly, certain issues had to be reviewed time and again in the
committee. As if to belie the residents' purported right to autonomy, the
members of the ethics committee rediscovered and rearticulated the residents' right to autonomy. The belief often contrasted with the value of
beneficence, which underlay the reason for the existence of the institution.
When a resident's decision seemed unwise, the immediate reaction was first
to prevent it, then to reflect and allow it. Each time the committee reasserted
a resident's rights, it seemed to struggle against the implications of residents' rights. Ambivalence was striking. It is further revealing that at no
time were the residents in question asked to meet with the ethics committee.
At the same time, no other staff members involved in the ethical issues that
were discussed were asked to attend, either.

The committee's existence reflected the power and resistance of the
medical model that frames the nursing home, even as the nursing home
underwent the transition that questions that medical model [see Henderson, this volume]. As it sought to review real cases of real people within
problematic relationships, it revealed the complexly textured life of the
nursing home. It demonstrated in its ruminations that "[while] conflict
resolution is an important aspect of ethics consultations, it is precisely
within this context that a transformation of the patient-physician relationship can occur . . . [by focusing on the] . . . caring dimensions of healing
rather than the biomedical facts about disease" (Marshall 1992:55). The

daily details of nursing home life contain difficult dilemmas and everyday dramas of life and death. The ethics committee examined some of these and thereby helped to illuminate them.

8

The Head Nurse as Key Informant: How Beliefs and Institutional Pressures Can Structure Dementia Care

Athena McLean and Margaret Perkinson

INTRODUCTION

When an elderly person moves into a nursing home, she expects to face some changes in her life—a different physical setting, unfamiliar community of residents, a perpetually present staff, and perhaps less contact with family. What she may not expect are the less apparent conditions that can have a dramatic impact. Among these are the regimentation imposed by the bureaucratic organization, the interpretation and response of the staff to bureaucratic constraints, and the even less visible pressures that influence the way the staff interprets and structures its approach to caregiving.

Those residents suffering from some form of senile dementia may experience that impact even more severely because of the special nature of their problems and, some would argue, the accommodations necessitated by their illness. Dementia involves a progressive deterioration of cognitive functioning, including loss of memory of one's past and about elements of one's identity. This condition has been referred to as a progressive loss of self (Cohen and Eisdorfer 1986; Sabat and Harre 1992; and Scheibe 1989).

For those affected, a move to an unfamiliar setting occupied by strangers, separate from those with whom the elders share a meaningful history, can further contribute to their confusion and to questions about their identity. The adjustment of these residents may be particularly affected by the ways the staff accommodate to the idiosyncracies of their condition in the related context of their personal history.

Although researchers are finding encouraging evidence that accommodating to a resident (e.g., tuning in to a resident's toileting pattern to inhibit the development of incontinence) will positively alter or slow down the illness course (Kitwood and Bredin 1992), evidence is far from conclusive. The extent to which such accommodations would markedly improve the quality of a resident's life is also open to debate, despite the enormous importance many family members place on this (Bowers 1988; Schwartz and Vogel 1990; Schuttlesworth, Rubin, and Duffy 1982). The uncertainty about the impact of personalized accommodations to illness course and to quality of life allows clinical staff to exercise tremendous latitude in interpreting vital, from less vital, needs of these residents and in determining whether and how to respond to special requests from families.

Nursing home placement for elders with some form of dementia as the primary diagnosis is largely made to meet the ongoing needs of the elder, except for complications resulting from falls or medical conditions that may materialize after admission. Depending on the stage of the dementia, nursing home care consists primarily of varying degrees of assisting the elder with activities of daily living, such as dressing, bathing, and as the disease progresses, feeding and toileting as well. Many family members hope basic care in the new setting will also support a high quality of life and encourage autonomy and the preservation of their relative's personal identity.

Despite the family's hopes, the structure of care in a formal bureaucratic setting may create challenges to providing the kind of care families desire. The organization of care delivery in nursing homes, as Litwak has elaborated (1985), tends to be highly routinized, efficient, hierarchical, and impersonal, leading to dissatisfaction in those caregivers who aspire toward providing more personalized care (Bowers and Becker 1992).

While working within the constraints of bureaucratic settings, however, staff can exercise considerable flexibility in the way they organize their work and choose to respond to residents' needs. This is true both of supervisory nursing staff on the unit (the head nurse and the charge nurse) and of the nursing assistants (NAs). It is the head nurse on the floor, however, who is responsible for creating expectations with regard to quality, content, amount, and the nature of work to be peformed. If head nurses are flexible in supervisory style, NAs can exercise more freedom in carrying out their work; where head nurses are rigid, NAs are forced to conform to stricter guidelines about what they can do and how much time they can devote to a resident. The head nurse, then, is a key figure for shaping the caregiving environment of the unit and NAs' approach to their work.

Several studies have explored how the organization and management of the nursing staff shape the quality of nursing home care (Halibar 1982; Mullins et al. 1988; Stryuker 1982). In one such study it was shown that the impact of the management on the organization of care may be modified by the impact of lower level staff on the operations of a unit (Henderson 1981). More recently, another study (Bowers and Becker 1992) explored the perspectives of NAs concerning their work, their approaches to organizing it, and their perceptions about organizational constraints on the quality of care they felt able to provide (see also Foner 1994a). However, the study revealed little about how supervisors affected the work of NAs, except indirectly in terms of supervisors' evaluations of the work style each NA had developed. Given the accountability of NAs to the head nurse on the unit and her importance as the chief organizing force for delivery of care on that unit, the lack of studies exploring the perspective of the head nurse is surprising. The way in which her beliefs about "good enough" care and care delivery are assimilated and translated by her staff into the everyday practices of caregiving are crucial to the experience of residents on the receiving end of the caregiving chain.

The purpose of this chapter is to describe how the head nurse of one dementia unit of a nursing home conceptualized her professional health care mission and to explore the multiple contextual pressures that helped to shape the management style and approach she developed to accomplish it. We found that her understanding of the basic health care requirements that the institution must provide, as well as the special needs of the residents on her unit, influenced her own beliefs about the care needs she and her staff must provide. Moreover, her particular interpretation of the bureaucratic constraints imposed by her institution in light of her own place within it affected the managerial approach she assumed in structuring care delivery on her unit. An additional intent of this chapter is to share the process of conducting an ethnography, from the initial encounter in the field through an analysis of the data.[1]

THE STUDY

Setting

The study was conducted in a 40-bed special care unit in a nonprofit 500-bed nursing home complex on the urban East Coast. The nursing home itself was designed as a large biomedical complex containing ten nursing home units, several comprehensive geriatric clinics, plus a hospital to accommodate emergency medical crises. The nursing home was recognized in the community as a strong medical resource and attracted many families because of its rich and varied biomedical facilities. Many of its staff were also associated with a nearby hospital. The elders' easy access to the latter facility was influential in attracting many families to this particular nursing home.

Staffing of the Unit

Typically, the principal staff person on the nursing home units was the head nurse, a registered nurse from the day shift (7 A.M. to 3 P.M.), also known as the "7-to-3" shift. She organized the delivery of care on the unit, was responsible for administering routine treatment and sometimes medicine, brought suspicious medical concerns to the attention of the medical staff (physicians and physician assistants), and completed all required documentation about the resident and treatment. "Treatments" are physician-ordered procedures requiring licensed skills, such as catheter care, decubiti care, or tending other lesions or wounds.

During the day shift, the care manager, a licensed practical nurse, generally administered medication and assisted the head nurse in providing treatment, managing the unit, and documenting treatment. There was no registered nurse in charge for the other two shifts (3 P.M. to 11 P.M. and 11 P.M. to 7 A.M.) or on weekends, so the care manager was solely in charge during those times. In addition, care managers from the "7-to-3" shift assumed responsibilities of the head nurse in her absence (for example, during illness, vacation, or after leaving her job). Although head nurses and care managers in charge of nursing home units each approached their work and organized the labor of their staff somewhat differently, each head nurse tended to establish rules about accommodations to care that were generally applied by all shifts in their interactions with family members.

Nursing assistants carried out all the routine patient care, such as assisting with dressing, transfer from bed to chair, basic grooming, feeding, changing bed linens, and other assistive tasks. They had the most "hands on" contact with the resident and often brought medical problems to the attention of the head or the charge nurse. Nursing assistants ranged in number from only two on the night shift to as many as six during the day. A bathing assistant was also hired for one day a week for six hours to bathe the residents. Diverse other staff who had regular contact with the residents included the activities and music therapists and staff who provided religious services. Each of these individuals worked with residents at least once per week.

Most medical problems discovered by the nursing staff were referred to the physician assistant (PA), who came to the floor daily to investigate problems, provide special treatments, write prescriptions, offer recommendations, and make referrals to specialists. Of medical providers, the PA had the greatest amount of time dealing with particular medical concerns. Also, a psychiatrist came to the unit once a week to address referrals and consider medication changes. The visit could last as long as two or three hours. Finally, a physician came to the unit at the end of the day shift to briefly review charts and sign off on the PA's recommendations. This visit rarely exceeded 30 minutes. Although the physician probably spent the least time on the unit of all medical personnel, and thus was the least familiar with residents' problems in a comprehensive way, families usually preferred to go to her or him with requests or concerns, often to the irritation of the other staff.

The Residents on the Unit

The residents on this unit, as a whole, represented the most severely impaired dementia patients in the nursing home. Most of the residents were too cognitively impaired to be administered standardized cognitive assessments. In addition, most of these residents displayed disturbed behaviors, such as noisiness, repetitiveness, and/or inwardly or outwardly directed aggressive behaviors. Of the 40 residents, 32 were female. They ranged in age from 66 to 95, with 86.5 as the median age. Twenty-three were in their 80s, twelve in their 90s, and only five were in their 60s or 70s.

METHODOLOGY

The methodology was ethnographic, based on the approach to field work initially formalized by Malinowski (1961 [1922]), and later codified and elaborated by many others (for example, Agar 1980, 1986; Van Maanen 1988; Hammersley and Atkinson 1983; cf. Hughes 1992). It incorporated participant observation (the engagement and close observation of a supposedly different culture) (Keith 1988), a close relationship with a "key informant" (Morse 1991) who helped the ethnographer "interpret" the culture, detailed recording of observations, and both informal and semi-structured ethnographic interviewing (cf. Spradley 1979; Mischler 1986; Rubinstein 1988) of nursing staff.

Historically, participant observation was used to discover the culture of the "primitive" and nonwestern "other" (Marcus and Fischer 1986; Clifford and Marcus 1986). It has since become the hallmark of anthropological research and has expanded to the study of a wide variety of contexts in western society, including classical studies of medical institutional settings (cf. Goffman 1961; Estroff 1981; Rhodes 1991), studies of nursing home life (Shield 1988; Savishinsky 1991; Gubrium 1975), and other qualitative gerontological studies (Myerhoff 1978; Reinharz and Rowles 1988; Gubrium and Sankar 1994).

In studying these local contexts, anthropologists typically do not live among the people they study, as they did in their study of cultures far from home, but return home at the end of their work day. Similarly, the first author, who conducted the field research for this study, did not reside on the nursing home unit, but returned home at the end of her work day, which varied from evening to early morning.

The Head Nurse: The Key Informant to the Study

Since the purpose of the study was to learn the beliefs and social pressures that shaped the head nurse's approach to organizing dementia care on her unit, the head nurse was the natural choice for the "key informant" (Morse 1991). We expected that her perspective about the nature of dementia and her experience of multiple institutional, unit specific, and other pressures would further shape her supervisory style and structure for providing care.

Each unit of the nursing home was supposed to be run by a head nurse, who was a registered nurse (R.N.) and responsible for coordinating the care on the unit, with her assistant, a licensed practical nurse (L.P.N.), who managed that care. On this unit, however, the key informant "head nurse" had been occupying this position only as a "fill in" until a permanent head could be secured. She was, in fact, the "acting head nurse" and held an L.P.N. degree originally qualifying her as the unit's care manager. She was made the "acting head" after the previous head nurse resigned. This was eight months before the researcher began the study. During that time, this acting head nurse trained an R.N. for the position, but the latter left after three months. She remained the acting head for five more months until another R.N. was hired for the position. After training this new person, she resumed her previous position as the care manager. For most of the time that she was acting head nurse, another nurse, also an L.P.N., helped her out with regular nursing routines.

Families who were acquainted with the acting head nurse from the time she was the care manager regretted how the new position "tied her down" with desk work that removed her from floor contact with the residents. They liked her manner of interacting with and caring for residents and also felt that she could do a better job of supervising her staff from a perspective on the floor, rather than from behind a desk.

The acting head nurse (who will simply be identified as the "head nurse" in the remaining text) in fact expressed considerable concern and empathy for the residents on her unit. On several occasions, she referred to herself as their "advocate," sometimes even against their own families. She also expressed empathy with them for all that they had lost in leaving their homes to move into a nursing home.

Methodology

I (the first author) conducted ethnographic research over a nine-month period. I visited the unit several weeks before beginning research there to ensure that it was an appropriate research site, to become acquainted with the staff, and to learn if there were any potential problems that would interfere with research there. Subsequently, I met with a key administrator to describe my research plan and to elicit support and suggestions for facilitating the research without overburdening the caregiving staff with research demands. The administrator then introduced me to the Assistant Director of Nursing (ADON). The ADON officially introduced me to the unit, reaffirming the administration's support and encouraging staff support.

This study, though focused on the day shift nurse and her staff, was part of a larger project in which the ethnographer was investigating behavioral disturbances of the residents and the contexts in which they occurred, evolved, and/or subsided. Families of residents on the unit were all informed of the study by letter, including information for contacting the researcher about any questions.

The approval from the administration allowed entry to conduct the research. However, because of existing employee/administration tensions, it also raised some questions of the actual role of the ethnographer. In this case the strong perception by the NAs of their subordinate position within the administrative hierarchy fueled their concern about the ethnographer as a possible representative of power (the administration) who might threaten their position. It also immediately raised the important issues of the actual power differential between the researcher and subjects (cf. Tourigny 1994:178–179; Clough 1992:131–136; Clifford 1986). My earlier visit—an introductory strategy other researchers have recommended (cf. Kahana, Kahana, and Riley 1988)—served favorably to weaken suspicions about my association with the administration.

My ethnographic observations covered all shifts, although most of the time spent in the field occurred during the day (7A.M. to 3P.M.) shift and extended a couple of hours into the 3P.M. to 11P.M. shift. For several weeks, I came to the unit before the 7A.M to 3.P.M. shift to observe the early morning care routines of the nursing assistants. During this time, I also observed the transitional staff meeting between the two charge nurses from the night and day shifts and the subsequent staff meeting in which the head nurse familiarized the 7A.M. to 3P.M. staff with the status of residents, alerting them to pay special attention to unusual conditions. Many days I stayed late into the second shift, through the transitional meeting between the charge nurses on the two shifts. I also stayed through the 11 P.M. to 7 A.M. shift on three occasions. On two occasions, I spent 24 consecutive hours on the unit, napping on a lounge chair as needed, in order to experience the unit as a whole, with variations, during one complete day. This unbroken day allowed for a fuller immersion into the nursing home unit than on days when I spent only hours there.

During my nine months on the unit, I spent time talking with the entire staff (from housekeepers to professional medical staff), as well as families, companions hired by the families, and where still possible, the residents. All comments relevant to floor life, interactions with family, caregiving, and work organization were documented in a daily journal, which constituted the field notes.

Whenever possible, notes were taken immediately after a conversation ended in order to allow for the most accurate and clear retention of details. For similar reasons, observations were documented as soon after the event as possible. If this was not possible because of the need to focus on other issues, I jotted a short (sometimes single phrase) outline of the issues I wished to elaborate on later in my written notes. These were then completed on the unit or at my office. Daily notes, however, were not conceptualized as documenting isolated events. Rather, as much continuity as possible was incorporated into the note taking process by my ongoing reflections about the linkages between current and previous observations (cf. Atkinson 1992).

During the several initial months of the study, the detailed notes that were kept in the journal were dictated and audiorecorded on a daily basis. At the same time, incomplete notes or outlines of notes I could not complete because of the need to attend to competing activities (e.g., observations of new family/staff interactions, making an introduction with a family member, catching up on a previous conversation with an NA who had a few free moments to chat) were also elaborated on during dictation for audio-recording at this time. The audiotapes were then transcribed and made available on both hard copy and computer diskettes for later review. Because of limited funding, transcription of audiorecordings was no longer possible after the first few months, and hand-written notes or occasionally typed notes became the sole recording source of observational data. In making recordings of observations, I attempted to leave nothing to the imagination. Notes were taken not as if they would be used solely by me, because that could have left implicit many contextual understandings. Rather, they were taken as much as possible from the perspective of a naive observer who assumed nothing. This was to allow a full and explicit record of my observations as I constructed the text (cf. Atkinson 1992:471) and would be usable by other researchers on the project. It also provided a concrete check on particularities of events, which often become transformed in memory.

In addition to this narrative data, semi-structured interviews were conducted with the NAs from all shifts to acquire a flavor for differences in the delivery and organization of care across shifts. Nevertheless, consistent with the focus of the study on the organization of care during the day shift, the primary sources of data for this paper were the head nurse and the nursing assistants from the 7 A.M. to 3 P.M. shift.

I explained to the staff and families that while the general focus of the study was on the behavioral disturbances of the residents on the unit, the research concerns went beyond these to a larger investigation of the various contexts in which residents' behavioral disturbances were observed. I explained how this meant studying everything that might possibly affect a resident's behavior. I attempted further to describe how the research would begin with intense observations of the disturbed behavior and adjacent events, including the family's involvement or interaction with the resident, but would also explore the institutional context. As the study progressed, I tried to explain that this meant examining the institutional setting in which care was administered; the way care was organized on the unit; the perceptions, complaints and concerns families and residents voiced about that care; and the constraints the caregiving staff faced in conducting their work. Finally, I explained my interest in learning about dementia, both from the professional perspectives of the staff and from the family. While thus explaining that I would be very curious, or "nosey," I also made it clear to everyone who spoke with me that their comments would be confidential.

As part of this study, I conducted semi-structured, confidential interviews with the NAs, using an interview guide with space provided for the narrative response. The interview questions were generated from questions I developed empirically from observations and from earlier conversations with some of the NAs. The interview explored the way NAs structure their work and cooperate with each other to complete it, their priorities in caregiving, and the constraints under which they worked. They were also asked about their communication with families, the kinds of interventions they have used with disturbed residents, and their views about the most effective interventions.

Consistent with the emergent "open-ended" approach of the ethnographic interview (cf. Hughes 1992:443–444), I felt free to deviate from the guide and explore relevant issues that emerged. In fact, I often found that the interview form proved an impediment to conversation. On a few occasions as I prepared to write an informant's comments, the NA asked, "Do you have to write this on the form?" When I said "No" and put my pen down, the conversation began to flow. Later, I did note the event and related issues in my journal.

Because of the enormously busy schedule of the NAs, interviews were covered during brief periods when they found the time to take a short break. They guarded their regular break times and lunch periods because of the strenuous nature of their work, so, except on rare occasions, other periods were sought to conduct these interviews, often in piecemeal fashion. I continued to chat regularly with the NAs as they worked, or I would observe their delivery of care, possibly asking a question. At other times, they might call me over to show me something of potential interest.

The head nurse—the person responsible for organizing the unit's approach to care—was the key informant for the study. She too was assured confidentiality. Everything she said that was viewed as relevant to her approach to structuring care was elaborately documented in my daily field notes. These included information about the head nurse's priorities in caregiving, her rationale for these, communications to her staff, and constraints that limited care provision. Anything the head nurse said about the dementia process was also documented in detail in my notes. Finally, I noted verbal exchanges between the nurse and families over their relatives' care. Of particular interest were the nurses' assessments of families' views about their relatives' condition, and of their special requests and concerns.

For the larger study of behavioral disturbances, I would move from place to place on the unit as dictated by occurrences that caught my attention (e.g., a fight between two residents, a musical activity, or the entrance of a family member). The head nurse, however, spent much of her time behind the nurses' station, completing paper work. Thus, to gain information relevant to this study, I would spend long periods of time behind the nurses' station, reviewing chart work or conducting floor observations, as I conversed with the head nurse, the latter's time permitting. Sometimes I would ask questions that emerged from observations of a resident, the family, or the conduct of nursing assistants. At other times, I might query the nurse about official care expectations or ask more information about a comment she might have made about those expectations. At still other times, I would discuss with the head nurse points of information about the dementia process, based on the head nurse's understanding of it from years of exposure to residents with this disorder.

Although the head nurse had considerable paper work, she agreed to answer any of my questions while she completed her own work, unless she felt her participation would compromise the quality of her work. In such cases, or if the questions raised were too demanding of her available time, the head nurse offered to set aside time during a later period to elaborate on her responses. She always kept her promise to make herself available.

There were other contexts that also proved useful for gaining an understanding about the head nurse's views on dementia care. These included the weekly care conferences (cf. Shield 1988: 61–65) in which several residents were discussed on a rotating basis with the social worker, activities therapist, nutritionist, and medical professional. By open invitation, I attended these, as I did many of the staff meetings the nurse held with the NAs, and occasionally, with administrative staff. Comments by the head nurse and others during these meetings often provided the basis for further questions to the nurse. Thus, my ethnographic approach for learning about the head nurse's perspectives on care and about the institutional culture in which it was provided approximated one of student (the ethnographer) with teacher (the nurse)—one form of the informant/anthropologist relationship. Over time, I attempted to acquaint myself with all family visitors, identifying myself as a researcher and attempting to separate myself from the clinical staff. Many of them appreciated my interest in their family member and would often come up to me on their own to offer a comment, make an observation, or ask to talk privately. In this way I learned much about their views, concerns, and wishes.

Whenever a tense interaction occurred between the head nurse or other staff member and the family, I would listen and take notes about the issues. After the interaction ended, I would then approach the family, introducing myself if necessary, to learn about their concerns and the nature of the encounter.

The first time that this happened, I observed the nurse's raised eyebrows as I was approaching the family. After completing my conversation with the family, I made a point to explain to the head nurse that I was interested in learning the family's perspective as well. However, I would also talk with the head nurse about the encounter in an effort to gain her perspective about the issues, the validity of the family's response, and her views about accommodating the family.

Glitches in the Research Process

Despite considerable support from the nursing assistants, head nurse, and families, the research did have its glitches. For example, the close proximity of myself and head nurse, often seated together and talking behind the nurses' station together, initially inhibited some family members from talking openly with me. I explained that I was not part of the clinical staff and that I felt the family's perspectives about care were valuable. Only one woman remained mildly hesitant in talking openly with me. As families learned that I too had a parent with dementia, they seemed to share their thoughts with me even more openly.

For the first couple of months, the NAs wondered whether I was a spy for the administration. The relationship between NAs and the administration was becoming tense due to an impending strike, and my sudden appearance raised questions. The staff had experienced researchers before; they had even completed questionnaires for them. However, they had never experienced an anthropologist's perpetual probing. My curiosity, it seemed to them, went beyond the more limited structured research to which they were accustomed and it piqued their suspicion that I had been hired by the administration to evaluate their work. In such situations, an awareness of power differentials becomes sharpened, revealing the lack of balance within the ethnographic situation (cf. Tourigny 1994:178–179; Clough 1992:131–136; Clifford 1986).

Just as they were becoming convinced that I was indeed not working for the administration, an event occurred that once again challenged my security. One NA was asked to file a report on her involvement with a resident who had allegedly been abused. When I asked if I could see it, the NA was reluctant to share it. The sensitivity of the situation apparently had rekindled her suspicion. I was concerned that she might rally support against the research because she had seniority and enjoyed relative power among the other staff.

Despite this experience, the NAs continued to share their thoughts. By the time I was halfway into the study, one NA actually expressed appreciation for having been taken seriously and having apparently valued her perspective. She noted that being regarded as an authority of care, rather than being always at the lowest end of the medical hierarchy, was a refreshing contrast. Such an experience of reciprocal gain is extremely satisfying in field research (cf. Reinharz and Rowles 1988:8–9), where the potential for one-sided gain by the researcher looms ever too large, as the "new," or critical, ethnographers have warned (cf. Clough 1992; Marcus and Fischer 1992; Clifford and Marcus 1986).

The head nurse was the one who related the NA's renewed suspicion to me, perhaps as a way of communicating her own. In the conversation that followed and my expression of concern, however, it seemed as if the head nurse had allayed her doubts. A few days earlier, the head nurse's main assistant was also beginning to ask questions about what an anthropologist "really does." Similarly, during this time I sensed some tension with the head nurse when asking questions that did not specifically relate to a behavioral disturbance, such as a query about an administrative procedure (e.g., "How do you go about getting lost dentures replaced?"). At these times, I would reiterate the importance of the institutional context in which behaviors occur. By the time the nurse began to share her views about several administrators and their policies, several months into the study, I felt assured that the nurse indeed trusted me.

Although the tension with the head nurse diminished after this encounter, I detected some annoyance on occasions when I asked questions that challenged the nurse's belief system about dementia. These were instances when I took seriously a resident's complaint. In one case, the head nurse just smiled with raised eyebrows, noncommittedly.

In another case, the head nurse suggested I was seeing things the way families often do in attributing "unreasonable" credence to the resident's remark. I experienced this comment with particular sensitivity because I felt accused by the nurse, who knew that one of my parents resided in a special care unit. In retrospect, the head nurse's observation/allegation had disturbed me because it rang so true. I had to admit to myself that my experience as a family member enabled me, in fact, to understand families' perspectives about dementia and its care more easily than the staff's, since I experienced the families' life world myself. Such, however, is the nature of ethnographic research; there is no escaping the fact that ethnographers always bring their own life beliefs, history, and values to the field as they study others with different life experiences (cf. Silverman 1988). Our task is, in spite of our differences, to penetrate the life worlds of those others we study, as they penetrate ours.

FINDINGS

Ethnography is an ongoing process, engaging the ethnographer reflexively in a private discourse throughout, rather than waiting until "data collection" has ended (cf. Eckert 1988). Initially, I reviewed all the notes (the narrative data) to select material relevant to the study. My memory helped lead me to particular material, but I perused all field notes for possible missed insights. I then selected passages relevant to the head nurse's beliefs about dementia, her approach to organizing of care on the unit, her description about institutional and related pressures, and her perspective both on the operations of the institution and on the families' expectations. Notes taken from conversations and interviews with the nurses and NAs, from discussions with families, and about observations that might lend insight about the nurse's perspective were also pulled for review. These included the NAs' understandings about care priorities and the special requests they could or could not accommodate.

The relevant passages were then analyzed for their thematic content and consistencies (cf. Luborsky 1994). We (McLean and Perkinson) divided the data and independently reviewed and roughly categorized themes that emerged. Elaborate discussion followed, with considerable exchange in identifying key components of the head nurse's beliefs and approach to care provision. This dialectical process helped to heighten our level of agreement and to refine the categories we had initially formed.

It is important to note that an approach that uses selected data in this way, though useful to the task defined, can lend itself to a decontextualized, segmental approach (Atkinson 1992). To avoid the potential pitfalls of this approach and to preserve the holism of the enterprise (Noblit and Engel 1991), I maintained an intimate reference to the narrative data throughout this process. This helped avoid decontextualization of the narrative passages and also served to corroborate, challenge, and/or clarify findings.

The data were analyzed to determine the head nurse's beliefs about senile dementia and the related care needs of residents with this disorder. The head nurse's comments about dementia, reasoning about accommodating or not accommodating to special requests, and her criteria for judging families as "realistic" or "unrealistic" revealed some of the assumptions and conceptual frameworks that shaped her perspective about dementia care and helped her to establish care priorities.

The narrative data were examined to determine the various pressures that the nurse may have experienced in providing for her residents' care needs. Her history on the unit, her position of power within the nursing home, and the typical bureaucratic constraints she had experienced were all examined. Finally, we examined the criteria that the head nurse had identified with quality care. The analysis revealed a value hierarchy of care priorities that defined her criteria for care within the constraints of a bureaucratic economy of care.

The sections below will discuss the following sets of findings: the head nurse's beliefs, that is, her assumptions and conceptual frameworks for understanding dementia and dementia care; the nurse's peculiar professional history on her unit and position in the institution; and the bureaucratic constraints that limited the care options she could allow her staff to provide. These sets of findings identify the ideological, historical, and structural contexts—the institutional backdrop—within which the nurse organized the delivery of care on her unit. The last section will elaborate on the head nurse's value hierarchy of care as the intersection of these beliefs, experiences, and constraints.

The Head Nurse's Beliefs Concerning Dementia

From her professional training and years of experience working in different nursing homes with extremely difficult dementia residents, the nurse came to adopt a set of pessimistic assumptions about dementia through the lens of a medical model, linked to an image of a diseased brain. Her nurse's training, acquired during the 1970s, also attuned her more to acute care issues than to ongoing long term care needs.

Given this training and clinical exposure, the strong medical model under which this nursing home operated—in contrast to the social model adopted by many other homes—made sense to her and sharpened her focus on disease. The particular unit she headed housed the most extremely behaviorally disturbed residents of the nursing home—those individuals for whom a rehabilitation potential was viewed as slim. From repeated years of exposure to such severely disturbed persons, she came to adopt a fatalistic view about the general trajectory of dementia. She came to see dementia as a progressive and intractable disease that destroys the cognitive functioning of its victims—a prognosis and perspective she applied to all residents with that diagnosis. Despite her tendencies to see the residents on her unit as persons with desire and intent, her competing powerful disease lens generally led to her explaining their behavior in the reductionist, dehumanizing terms of disease process.

Yet, she revealed contradictory elements in her concern for the residents' well-being. She seemed to hover, as many nurses have in similar settings (Hyman, Bulkin, and Woog 1993), between an appreciation of their right to freedom and their right to protection. For example, she empathized that residents have given up so much in coming to the nursing home, that their wishes should be honored whenever possible, even over those of their family, if necessary. Yet at other times, she could not overcome her proclivity to protect residents even if that meant totally disregarding their preferences. This strong sense of protectiveness similarly came to dominate over her competing inclination to support autonomy in her approach to providing for dementia care.

Her comments about "unrealistic" families further elucidated her conceptual framework concerning dementia. Unrealistic families were those who saw their relative's problem as immediate and localized and thus correctable by immediate and localized environmental accommodation. These families, for example, would insist on replacing dentures in order to reduce their relative's agitation about a pureed diet which the resident considered unpalatable ("Pureed food is delicious!" insisted the nutritionist). From her view, the problem went far beyond this immediate concern. It was, in fact, beyond anything the families —or anyone else—could do to make a difference.

In addition, the nurse distrusted many families' judgments about their relatives' needs because she felt they were denying the severity of their relatives' dementia and that they based their views on their memory of how their relatives "used to be." The nurse also distrusted the view of some families concerning psychotropic medication because the family member lacked the medical training she viewed necessary to form any legitimate opinion or spent insufficient time with their relative in the nursing home environment to know how they tended to act over a prolonged period. Families, she was convinced, were also out of touch with residents' needs because they were often operating out of their own guilt, rather than out of genuine concern for, or ability to objectively judge, their needs. This was, she stated, because she was able to see residents as they are, whereas families were invested in maintaining a view of residents as they *used to be*.

On the other hand, she at times could empathize with families, and admit that she might behave similarly if she were in their shoes. The head nurse, however, insisted that she and her staff see more of the resident than does the family, so are thus in a better position to judge his needs. For example, the nurse thought the insistence of some families on replacing their relative's dentures was foolish when the resident would not cooperate with the dentist. It seemed to her also as a poor use of her staff's limited time to take him to multiple dental appointments, because of his inability to cooperate for long, just to get the mold completed. In addition, her experience was that residents with dementia often remove their dentures and lose them. To spend all the energy to get a pair made just to have them lost seemed wasteful and senseless to the head nurse.

The head nurse also regarded families' quality of life concerns, especially with the more cognitively impaired residents, as specious. She argued that these concerns, like the ones families raised about human dignity, reflected the family's notion of life quality, not the residents'. The head nurse's fatalistic disease model and pessimistic assumption about the value of environmental manipulation shaped the priorities she outlined in her hierarchy of care. Since, according to this view, so little can be done to change the trajectory of disease, "good enough" nursing care for dementia should focus on basic custodial and medical needs.

The Historical and Institutional Contexts of Her Position as "Acting Head Nurse"

Although she was charged with additional responsibilities as the "acting head nurse" of the unit, she did not perceive that the administration invested her with authority, and there were no material signs to mark her different from before. Her salary was not changed, and she was not given the additional time and clerical help that other unit heads received to complete their paper work. It seemed to other unit staff that the administration took advantage of her powerlessness and began also to transfer ("dump," in their words) behaviorally difficult residents from other floors. Many of the staff felt these residents were both atypical and "inappropriate" for the unit, given their higher level of cognitive functioning. Yet, unlike her predecessor, the head nurse accepted them without question. The head nurse accepted the additional responsibilities of her temporary position, but did not challenge, nor seemed to resent, her apparent lack of authority. She had always hoped to become an R.N. some day and did seem to enjoy her additional responsibilities, however.

The current head nurse, serving in an "acting" capacity during the study, had worked on the unit for six years. She had been trained originally as the manager by the previous head nurse—an extremely "tough" and "no nonsense" nurse. As one family member put it, "Lillian was very strong; under her, the NAs did exactly as they were told." Many families also felt that the NAs were more responsive to residents' needs when the former head nurse was heading the unit, and that things had become more lax with no one on the floor to offer "hands on" supervision. The NAs themselves remembered the former head as either "much too tough" or "tough, but fair." The former head nurse and the current "acting" head nurse had been a good management team and ran the unit as a "tight ship," bound by the institution's rules and expectations.

The acting head nurse retained Lillian's strong sense of responsibility, institutional obligation, and impatience with incompetence. However, unlike Lillian, she did not wield power with the administration or her staff. In addition, working under Lillian, she did not have to appear overtly tough with the NAs under her management, because Lillian was the "tough parent" to whom they felt accountable.

After Lillian left, this pattern was hard to break. Given her clerical support with paper work, Lillian had been able to spend considerably more time on the floor than the current head nurse, who received no assistance. Thus, floor supervision of the NAs became drastically reduced.

The current head nurse was respectful of institutional rules and policies, but critical of nursing home unit heads and NAs who were not. In addition, her style for communicating dissatisfaction was linked to her sense of institutional propriety. When one of the NAs under her supervision did something wrong, however, she did not openly challenge her, as Lillian would have done. She either bit her lip in silent annoyance or explained to the NA, sometimes in a disdainful tone, that she was violating the expectations of "her job." Some of the NAs claimed they were offended by this approach, because it expressed a depersonalized and moralistic appeal to authority. One NA compared it unfavorably to the more personal comment from yet a different supervisor, "Oh come on, it's not that bad, now. Is it?" Another NA—the senior NA on the unit—felt singled out in being asked to extend herself more because of her seniority. She disliked the moral tone the acting head nurse invoked in saying she had expected more of her.

With her literal interpretation of the institution's rules, she sometimes came across to her staff as an apologist to the administration. For example, when staff complained they needed an additional NA on the unit to handle the work load, she immediately discounted the idea on the basis of the administration's financial crunch—invalidating the staff's own needs. She also was careful not to reveal any information with families that might jeopardize their positive views of the nursing home. Her protective stance toward the nursing home and rather rigid interpretation of its rules may have helped to overcompensate for her inexperience and perceived lack of authority in her new role.

The acting head's history of working on the unit in a different capacity made it difficult to establish herself as a strong authority in her new, temporary status. Adopting a disengaged managerial style that appealed to institutional rules and morality only served to alienate a staff who already felt considerable tensions with the administration. Her tight interpretation of institutional rules, however, lent itself to a clearly defined hierarchy of care that delineated expectations for her staff.

Bureaucratic Constraints on the Nursing Staff

The bureaucratic constraints within which the nursing staff operated imposed a very demanding economy of care on its units to ensure that the fundamental needs of its more than 500 residents would be met. These constraints made staff reluctant to respond to special requests for nonroutine care. Under such a tight economy, special care requests could be provided only if they did not threaten the completion of the more fundamental routine care needs of other residents. The additional burden of paper work, without the clerical support other head nurses enjoyed, further limited the amount of nonroutine needs the head nurse felt she could "afford" to address.

For example, the bath attendant was required to handle eight frequently immobile and/or uncooperative elderly residents within three and three-quarter hours. This included undressing them, examining their skin, bathing, and redressing them. If she should exceed that time limit in the process of responding to special requests, she could be penalized for her inefficiency and eventually be terminated from employment. This constraint, so familiar to the head nurse yet invisible to families, drastically limited staff's ability to offer the individualized attention that families wanted.

Thus the formal organization of care delivery in the nursing home was structured, as Litwak described (1985), according to a detached division of labor that was impersonal, hierarchical, rule-governed, and instrumentally motivated (e.g., performed for payment). Although such routinization and lack of attention to individual difference could be experienced as humiliating and dehumanizing to residents, the nurse was convinced that this was not the case, since most of the residents on the unit were too impaired, in her view, to realize the difference. Rather, it was their family members, she felt, who projected their own feelings of humiliation at the situation onto their relatives. This occurred when they raised the issue of human dignity in response to staff refusal to satisfy special requests.

The Care Hierarchy: The Head Nurse's Criteria for Quality Care

In such a demanding bureaucratic system, neglecting to carry out prescribed care routines with a resident would lead to reprimand, suspension without pay, and even termination; not bothering to search for the resident's glasses, however, would not endanger the nursing assistant's job. Working within such a system required that some practical choices be made, not for the welfare of the resident, but for the protection of the caregiver.

In order to help structure care choices for 40 residents within the institutional constraints of staff and time limitations, and to avoid the system's wrath, the head nurse developed a general care hierarchy, based on her beliefs about "good enough" care. This hierarchy prioritized care needs according to their perceived importance to all residents. This was not an explicit, concrete, documented hierarchy as such. Rather it was an implicit operational one, inferred from repeated observations and extensive discussions with the nurse as to those concerns that demanded differential attention over the course of a nursing staff's day. This care hierarchy established staff's criteria for quality care delivery.

First and foremost on the hierarchy was custodial care (cleaning, feeding, toileting), protection (restraining a resident to prevent falls when unattended), and medical attention to urgent or apparent problems (e.g., trying to recover respiration, cleaning an open sore). Second was medical attention to more ambiguous, apparently less serious problems identified solely on the basis of complaints by residents whose dementia challenged their reliability. Third on this hierarchy of care was the placement, repair, and ordering of prosthetic devices such as hearing aides. Last on the staff's hierarchy were individualized nonroutine efforts to minimize agitation or respond to a nonroutine request by a resident or family member. Nonroutine requests were concerned with improving the resident's quality of life (e.g., trying out a mechanical device to improve a resident's experience with bathing). The higher up the hierarchy that a care request appeared, the greater the likelihood that staff would respond to it.

In contrast to families' care emphasis on individualized quality of life (cf. Bowers 1988), the nurse and her staff were most concerned with the pragmatic routine care of the body. This had been inscribed in the very definition of their work. Each nursing assistant was responsible for completing a list of *bodywork* tasks, which they referred to as activities of daily living (the ADLs) for the residents in her group, and was required to document each task on the patient/resident's chart as she completed it. Starkly absent from this list was any reference to feelings or affective well-being [see Henderson, this volume].

Several behavioral dynamics were involved in operationalizing the care hierarchy. The head nurse spoke about care priorities during daily staff meetings, especially when someone in her staff had used poor judgment in ordering her care. Any time a family member requested something that was not routine, she informed the NA to refer the person directly to her, so she could explain to them what her staff could and could not do. Finally, she communicated her annoyance to NAs who failed to operationalize her hierarchy as she conceptualized it. In these ways, the NAs were socialized to the expectations of the care hierarchy.

Staffing patterns also reinforce the care hierarchy. During the day shift, only five nursing assistants were available to meet the care needs of 40 residents. Even fewer were available on other shifts. A unit-specific nonformalized protocol had been developed to implement the principles of the care hierarchy. This enabled the staff to more effectively economize their time to finish the required ADLs and to guide nursing assistants in deciding how and when to help residents and their families. For example, it prohibited responding to requests during meal times—even for toileting—until all residents had already been fed.

The rules of this informal protocol extended to families as well. For example, families were supposed to request help only from their attending NA. Also, by restricting dressing to once daily, it prohibited families from making such requests as well. Families learned about this operational protocol the first time they transgressed it. Whenever a family made a nonroutine request (e.g., to try a new dress on their family member), the nursing assistant informed them of the rule and referred them to the head nurse. She reinforced this practice, often agreeing to accommodate the family "just this once" as long as they understood this was an exception.

DISCUSSION

Working within a bureaucratic system that imposed objective staffing and time constraints on care provision, the head nurse felt she could ensure the completion of only the minimal routine care requirements of her residents. In dementia care, tremendous variation exists from facility to facility, and from unit to unit, in considerations given to residents' needs beyond the custodial. Institutions differ in their philosophies from the most radical social model to the heaviest medical approach, like the facility in the study.

This study focused on the way in which care delivery on a dementia unit is further mediated by the head nurse, who is responsible for organizing it. In studying this process, I examined the nurse's beliefs about dementia as they entered into her construction of good care, her work history on the unit as that affected her supervisory approach, and the institutional constraints within which she had to structure the delivery of care.

The amount of flexibility a head nurse allows herself in interpreting institutional rules to organize care delivery, however, is by no means uniform. The rigidity the head nurse adopted in interpreting, and becoming constrained by, institutional pressures was related to her inexperience as a head, the temporary and uncertain nature of the position, and the pattern of her prior relationship with her staff as the "easy" parent. Adopting a rigid reliance on regulation and authority allowed her to safeguard her own uncertain position and provided a basis, no matter how alienating, for dealing with her staff. Her hierarchy of care provided the basis for "good enough" dementia care, based on her understanding about dementia and its needs, within a care economy based on her interpretation of the constraints imposed by the institution. This hierarchy helped assure her that none of the residents' most fundamental needs would be neglected.

This is necessarily a partial description, based on partial considerations of the head nurse's clinical beliefs and interpretation of, and response to, institutional pressures (cf. Clifford 1986). It is also partial in being based upon field notes that were restricted to the institutional context and produced as the text of a single ethnographer, who described and interpreted her observations from a uniquely personal and historical lens. Moreover, it is partial because it is based on my unique intersubjectivities with each of my informants, with the various self-representations each brings to a discourse (Ewing 1990; see also Rosenwald and Ochberg 1992:1), and the unique emergent narrative productions those intersubjectivities afford.

It is this complex character of human engagement that allows—or disallows/hinders—productive discourse, while always constraining it as partial. This is not to discount, invalidate, or minimize it. It is simply to insist on qualifying the limits of ethnographic investigation.

Many issues emerged, or were suggestive, in the ethnographic data and my subjective experience that reflected the complex interplay between the work setting and events outside the work setting, such as personal history and current life events. For example, how did the head nurse's life at home, church, or other noninstitutional contexts help shape her belief systems that penetrated into the nursing home context, like her respect for and literal interpretation of institutional rules and her appeal to morality and institutional authority in supervising her staff?

What other ideologies, beyond those that affected her beliefs about dementia, affected her provision for its care? For example, the head nurse maintained a strong egalitarian ethic in the way she parceled out the provision of care. She found family members who demanded special treatment for their relative particularly offensive. Yet, some of their concerns may have been valid, rather than based on desire or privilege. Was she able to make these distinctions within her powerful egalitarian practice ethic?

How did the particular ethnic differences between the head nurse, who was African-American, and the residents and families, who were mainly Jewish, and the strength of their ethnic identities intersect to further influence the nurse's willingness to accommodate their out-of-the-ordinary requests?

How did my experience as a family member of a close relative with senile dementia limit—or extend—my ability to understand the perspective of the nurse, who assumed a different care ideology than mine? While some researchers would call this "bias," it is of course a particular, but different, bias from that of another researcher who might have shared the nurse's dementia care perspective. Again, the relevant issue is how this particular bias worked to reveal the care hierarchy described. For example, did my rigidity in reading from the field notes about the nurse's interpretation of rules come from the way I perceived the nurse's personality, given our different life experiences? Probably not, since despite those differences, I really listened to and respected the nurse's comments.

Describing such a bare-bones hierarchy of care runs the risk of seeming somewhat demeaning of the head nurse, and minimizing her enormous job of providing care for the 40 residents on her floor. This is certainly not the intent here. Her work, like that of her NAs, is extremely difficult and demanding. It requires resourcefulness, energy, and intelligence, and it is undervalued. To concretize and generalize her values in dementia care within a hierarchy can be seen in her response to her perceived pressures. She was not fixedly committed to following her value hierarchy, but it captured her overall approach to coping with the multiple constraints of a long term care economy.

The head nurse's fatalistic view about dementia resulted in a standard care practice that relegated some care needs (person preserving, quality of life related) less important than others (those involving body work). Working as she was in a heavily medicalized nursing home setting, this approach was philosophically and economically compatible with the home's. Her inability to exercise administrative authority, however, resulted in the admission of more cognitively intact residents to her unit. Yet, care was organized on this unit in a way that special accommodations were minimized. The unit's inability to address the personal needs of these more intact residents limited their quality of life.

Perhaps, however, the concern about not meeting residents' special needs should be even greater when the dementia process is well under way. Perhaps it is then that the most energy should be extended to preserve personhood, especially when the body may still be in good health (Kitwood and Bredin 1992). But, perhaps this approach represents the ethnographer's bias.

Part II

Staff/Resident Life

9

Assessing Types of Residential Accommodations for the Elderly: Liminality and Communitas

Barbara Hornum

This chapter is an attempt to bring some of the perspectives of general anthropological theory to bear on gerontological research. As an anthropologist who studies aging, I have been using the participant-observation methodology for over a decade in a variety of residential settings for the elderly in the United States and in the United Kingdom. The research has focused on the housing and social needs of older individuals as they have shifted to housing types suitable to changes in health and other circumstances (Hornum 1982, 1986, 1987). With each change—from independent living to purpose-built accommodations to nursing homes—it has been obvious that there has been decreasing independence, both physical and psychological.

In instances where the choice to move has been made voluntarily, it has also been obvious that the trade-off of such independence has been perceived as bringing worthwhile rewards. There are benefits, such as increased care, safety, and security, and the opportunities for establishing new friendships as earlier statuses and contacts are altered. Structural and cultural variables have been studied by myself and by others (Clark 1972; Garner and Mercer 1982). My current research into life care communities and New Towns has, however, indicated that there is a need to explore the actual living patterns in terms of a theoretical framework that can help clarify the process of transition or passage into the last stage of the life cycle. This reiterates the concerns expressed by Hornum and Glascock (1989) with regard to the need for anthropological gerontologists to test anthropological theories as well as those from psychology and sociology, thereby bringing an important component to gerontological analysis. New Towns in both Great Britain and the United States are planned communities in which the elderly have a wide range of housing options available to them. Such settings facilitate exploring issues related to choice and transitions.

The theory of liminality first expounded by Arnold van Gennep (1960) and elaborated and expanded by Victor Turner (1969) seems most appropriate to assess changes in place, social position, and age. Van Gennep identified these rites of passage as marking the shift of place, state, social positions, and age. Each rite of passage is, in turn, marked by three phases: separation (preliminal), margin or threshold (liminal), and aggregation or incorporation (postliminal). In the first phase, the individual is separated from a known aspect of the social structure and from accompanying cultural norms. In the second stage, the liminal, the individual is in a phase of ambiguity. Should the final stage be attained, the individual is once again able to move with some degree of certainty, both structurally and culturally.

When older people change residence, they are doing far more than altering the housing stock in which they live. They are entering van Gennep's phase of separation by detaching themselves from previous positions in the social structure and from correlated cultural conditions. They are moving into a new phase of experience. It is a phase for which there has been little preparation, at least in western and modernized societies.

As a result of the vagueness about what the social roles of life ought to be in the United States and other urban, industrialized societies when older people move into the second stage of transition, the liminal stage, there are few successful role models or institutionalized and official rituals to guide people across the "threshold." As a result, older people are confronted with the relative unknown and with guidelines that are ambiguous at best. Human beings have a desire for stability, however, and they push for clarification of their rights and obligations to others. They also strive for clarity of norms that they and their new contacts can follow.

It may well be that some of the tensions in interpersonal relationships that exist in different types of accommodations for the elderly stem from the "trial and error" learning that follows the attempts to create structure and norms out of the unknown. As they shift into new sets of relationships within new housing patterns, the elderly clearly move into what we can call new communities in the structural sense. Whether they also can shift into what Turner has called "communitas," a modality of social structure distinct from an area of common living," is less clear (Turner 1969:96). Turner distinguishes among three types of communitas:

1. existential or spontaneous communitas, the direct, immediate, and total confrontation of human identities which tends to make those experiencing it think of mankind as a homogeneous, unstructured and free community; 2. normative

communitas, where, under the influence of time, the need to mobilize and organize resources to keep the members of a group alive and thriving, and the necessity for social control among those members in pursuance of these and other collective goals, the original existential communitas is organized into a perduring social system . . . ; and 3. ideological communitas, which is a label one can apply to a variety of utopian models or blueprints of societies believed by their authors to exemplify or supply the optimal conditions for existential communitas (Turner 1974:169).

My research among residents of varied housing for the elderly suggests that they are able to attain Turner's normative communitas, although they do not apparently have either ideological or existential communitas. The past has changed; the future is unknown, and to some extent, unknowable. There is only the "now" in which to live, and this "now" becomes even more critical precisely because it is occurring at the end of the life cycle. It is sharing this particular bond of age, which has both secular and mystical qualities, that brings the elderly together in age-segregated housing. The equality of aging provides a common denominator among people who may have experienced very different statuses earlier in their lives.

In western societies, where age grades do not officially exist, there are fewer clear-cut markers to help people shift to new stages in the life cycle. The earlier states are gone, but there are sparse and often only structurally meaningless rituals to assist in the preparation for the new. There are limited life cycle events that can be used to help people move from the liminal. There are some publicly celebrated rituals to mark the end of childhood, such as confirmation and the bar and bas mitzvah, but these do not mark an actual shift into the legal state of adulthood.

This lack of obvious and meaningful rites that truly prepare for the shift from one state to another is particularly true for the elderly. Even the point at which someone becomes old has been individualized. It is not actual age, but retirement from certain types of activities, along with physical signs, that define for each person when he or she has crossed this particular threshold. Earlier thresholds are at least marked by ceremonies that are publicly understood and publicly accepted; birth, puberty, and marriage all have special ceremonies that clarify the leaving of one state and the incorporation of the next in a predictable event chain. With the exception of some tightly knit communities that have resisted modernization, such as the Amish, this is not the case for the elderly (Hostetler 1993).

Individuals who are aging in place are largely left to make their own interpretations, which may be an extremely isolating and anxiety-producing condition. It is my contention that moving into age-segregated housing actually facilitates and clarifies the steps necessary to achieve normative communitas and that this takes place almost uniformly despite the absence of ideological factors and formalized rituals. To explore the contradictions between this uniformity and the absence of design, it is necessary next to look at different types of residential facilities.

The primary emphasis for this chapter will be the life care community; my research includes a care center and a nursing home in the United States and two nursing homes in Great Britain. For comparative purposes when discussing liminality and communitas, there will also be some discussion of other types of purpose-built housing, sheltered accommodations, and assisted living arrangements in both the United States and Great Britain.

METHODS

My research at Sumner Hill, the life care community in the United States, was the most intensive. It took place over a two-year period and involved visiting the site one to two days per week. During those days I worked with five key informants intensively and interacted with other residents and staff on a regular basis. I participated in at least one meal per day in the common dining room and would also spend several hours in one of the lounges, talking informally and observing interactions and activities. Data were collected using observations and structured interviews with residents and staff at all sites. There was some variation in length of time spent at sites; the other sites involved shorter time durations ranging from several days to two weeks. At these sites, structured interviews with selected residents and staff were used in conjunction with observations. The names used for specific accommodations have been changed to provide anonymity.

SUMNER HILL, PHILADELPHIA

My study of Sumner Hill, a life-care community, took place in the early 1980s and revealed some interesting data related to dependency fears. Many people then residing at Sumner Hill had selected a life-care community because they were afraid of losing their independence and becoming burdens to their children. They also wanted the option of selecting a living arrangement that would include a continuum of care, beginning with relatively independent living in self-contained apartments and conceivably ending with skilled nursing in the attached skilled care facility, a quasi-nursing home. People expressed a belief that they could then stay in control of their lives because they would have provided for most contingencies. At the same time, they generally avoided the skilled care area and preferred to maximize their social distance from its full-time residents. They were uncomfortable with such visible reminders of long term, non-reversible physical and mental incapacity.

Moving to a life-care community involved turning some decisions over to the professional management staff of that community. These decisions included the daily operations of Sumner Hill, such as the required daily communal meal, the choice of decorations in group areas, and some of the general property rules. Residents frequently complained about the meals and were often irritated by what they termed "management interference" in their lives. Despite an active Residents' Association, it was obvious that many of the residents were uncomfortable with no longer having total control over their living arrangements. As with many life-care communities in the United States, Sumner Hill attracted a population of elderly who had been managers or professionals in earlier phases of their lives. As such, they had exercised high degrees of autonomy in decision making and activity planning. Their residential change had reduced this autonomy, and there had been no real preparation for the new state of dependency. In Turner's typology, they were in the transitional, or liminal, stage.

Over time, the residents of Sumner Hill began to build their own symbolic and ritual behavior. Some of it certainly was designed to reassure themselves that they were still essentially capable of caring for themselves in terms of the types of statuses and roles they had filled in earlier phases of their lives. Other behaviors became part of the norms at Sumner Hill and thus served to bind people together into a shared sense of community. For example, an unspoken dress code operated for the public areas, the lounges, dining room, and commissary. It was appropriate to dress in street clothes when coming into these areas. This clothing might be casual, but not loungewear. It might be expensive, but this was not as necessary as the overall appearance of being well-groomed. It was expected that people would change their clothing for dinner if they were eating that meal in the common dining room. Negative comments were made to those residents who came down for their mail or to the small convenience store in housedresses. While the dining room was open for lunch, that meal was optional; dinner was the required meal for all residents. There were two sittings for this meal, at 5:00 P.M. and at 6:00 P.M. While many of those at the earlier sitting were the frailer elderly, they nevertheless dressed for dinner.

Other patterned behavior centered on mail time. All of the residents were aware of the approximate daily time for mail delivery. One of the areas that I used to observe and where I used to talk informally was a seating area in the wide hallway opposite the mailboxes and the convenience store. It was clearly customary for residents to gather in the small waiting area by the mailboxes about half an hour before the mail was delivered and placed in the boxes. Information exchanges and gossip accompanied the waiting time. Unless residents were ill, they came to get their own mail. Small pleasantries made this a social occasion and part of the regular daily routine. In fact, the larger, more formal lounges were seldom used on a regular basis. The routine of mail delivery, and the routine of the daily visit to the commissary, located in the same area, were focal points for interpersonal interactions. The rules, if such they can be called, were passed on by the "elders," those who were among the first to enter Sumner Hill. What had perhaps begun as random behaviors quickly became institutionalized and expected. Participation in these new norms was necessary for acceptance; it was used to mark "belonging" at Sumner Hill. Failure to comply elicited not only negative reactions such as verbal commentary but also avoidance. As a result, the linked care center was seen by the apartment residents as part of the physical and technical community but not as part of the social and interactional community.

At the time of my research at Sumner Hill only twelve of the rooms in the care center were occupied by former apartment residents on a permanent basis. Four of these had spouses who remained in the apartment complex. The other eight were too incapacitated, either mentally or physically, to stay in their apartments on their own. A fluctuating number of beds were used by apartment residents who were recuperating after hospitalization or from relatively minor ailments like colds. The remaining beds were filled by older people from the wider suburban community who needed a temporary place to convalesce. As the life care community ages, the anticipation is that nearly all of the beds will be occupied by former and present apartment dwellers. There are no provisions at Sumner Hill for intermediate care. Thus, those residents who needed some assistence in activities of daily living and wished to remain in their apartments utilize aides hired privately. There was ambivalence about using the care center, as respondents indicated that while its presence provided a sense of choice about future needs, its actual usage signaled a real loss of control and evoked a host of negative images about dependency (Hornum 1986).

My research expanded from Sumner Hill to other areas of the United States, to the United Kingdom, and to other types of housing for the elderly. In the course of this fieldwork it became apparent that the behavioral patterns observed at Sumner Hill were generic and cut across status divisions of class and ethnicity.

MARKWELL CARE CENTER, RESTON, VA

Markwell Care Center primarily provides care for people who require sustained medical and nursing supervision, with some assisted living accommodation for those who require help on a modified basis. It is a private facility affiliated with a larger hospital system. The building complex is bright and cheerful, with an arrangement of wings and annexes that enables the provision of units to meet the residents' needs for skilled and intermediate care, assisted living, transitional care, and long term assistance for those with Alzheimer's. There are also small lounges, larger common rooms, and a bright and airy common dining facility. A team approach to care giving personalizes the assistance: teams include nurses, nursing assistants, physicians, social workers, and recreation and rehabilitation therapists. On my site visits in 1993, I interviewed the director of the Home for Adults (Assisted Living) and the social worker. With their cooperation, nine residents were selected for intensive interviews: five were in the nursing home, four in the

Home for Adults. In addition, I spent time observing activities and interactions and talking informally with other residents.

Two of the residents in the nursing home area were in private rooms, three in semi-private rooms. The rooms were all equipped with hospital beds, dressers, and chairs. The occupants also had some space for personal items to decorate walls and surfaces. The corner rooms were more attractive than others because there were additional windows and more opportunities for individualized arrangement of furniture. All of the residents used highly prized items to individualize their space. In one of the semi-private rooms, a woman of 81 had used a net hammock over her bed and a shelf on the wall at the side of her bed for her extensive collection of stuffed animals. Others had brought favorite pictures and displayed these prominently.

All of those in the nursing home were women. Their abilities and inclinations to participate in activities, which ranged from bingo, Scrabble, and cards to trips to the Reston Town Center, varied widely and were correlated primarily to health and secondarily to preexisting patterns of sociability. While meals could be brought to their rooms when necessitated by health problems, all generally took their meals in the dining room and tended to share mealtimes with friends they had made at Markwell. The more active helped deliver mail to people's rooms and appeared to enjoy the sense of service this provided. Four of the five women had children in the vicinity who came once a week to visit and usually would take them out for a meal, typically on Sunday. One was more isolated; her closest relative was a niece who visited a bit less frequently. The level of personal grooming among these women was high, although dress was more casual than at Sumner Hill.

Acceptance of what had been a major change in lifestyle was clear, although all indicated that the choice of a nursing home had not been theirs but, rather, had resulted from the intervention of family and medical personnel. State of health rather than chronological age had precipitated the move—the age range was 69 to 93. In three instances the move was sudden, following a hospital stay. For these individuals the transition was more abrupt. It is also noteworthy that these individuals had semi-private rooms and thus continued to experience upheavals as roommates left. Two of the women had had eight roommates during a four- to five-year period. This obviously made it harder to come to a sense of "ownership," although they did mark out their territory with personal belongings.

The control expressed in the selection of living arrangements by those at Sumner Hill was simply not possible at Markwell. One of the women was very concerned about this and voiced a great deal of anxiety over her future. She had worked as a civil servant, and prior to coming to Markwell she had lived in a bungalow for 52 years. At 81, after over half a century of independence and a lifestyle that included caring for many pets, she woke unable to walk. The doctors told her she could never live alone again, and she was brought to Markwell directly after her hospital stay. She had been there for five years when I met her. The trauma that marked her sudden loss of mobility and her need to relinquish her beloved pets were major topics of her conversation. Yet, she felt that Markwell was her home, and she wanted to believe that the room she occupied was hers—the place where she would stay for the rest of her life.

Unfortunately, this was not necessarily true, and at the time of our formal interview she was in a state of high anxiety. This resident had paid for her care out of savings for three years. During that time she was able to continue to pay for her room at Markwell despite frequent hospital stays. Eventually, she used up all of her savings and went on Medicaid. Future hospital stays of over ten days would result in her inability to hold her room at Markwell, as Medicaid would not pay for both. If the room were to be lost, she could not even be certain of an opening at Markwell, let alone being able to return to the same room. Her fear of losing her "place" led her to state several times that she would rather die. Her level of vulnerability to being relocated again made her feel in "limbo." The staff could do little to assuage her fears, as they, too, were bound by the rules of Medicaid.

While the other four women did not appear to have the same degree of anxiety, they had also experienced major shifts in independence and autonomy. Others now made decisions for them in all but minor areas of life. They liked Markwell for its friendliness and its caring staff. It had become a familiar setting and they valued that, but they had not had any formal preparation for the loss of their independence and their sustained dependence on others. Nonetheless, there had been some experiential preparation for three of those in the nursing home, a type of scaling down of activities. One person was on a ventilator in the special care unit of the nursing home. She had experienced both an extended hospital stay and some time in a nursing home in another city. Her recognition of and resignation to her increased health impairment had culminated in acceptance and enjoyment of small pleasures, such as being able to bird-watch from her windows. Two of the other women had been in purpose-built housing. One had lived in an apartment arrangement that required one common meal and involved age segregation; the other woman had also been in a purpose-built apartment and subsequently in assisted living. In both these instances, the women had responded to their increased need for ongoing assistance and had played a part in the decision making that had brought them to Markwell [see Groger, this volume].

In the Home for Adults, the assisted living section of Markwell, I interviewed two men and two women, ranging in age from 76 to 98. While these residents needed some assistance with activities of daily living, they required minimal nursing care and were able to live independently. All the residents in assisted living took three meals in the common dining room.

These meals were a major part of their daily social contact and provided opportunities for some networking.

In this unit, each individual occupied a large single room with a private bath. They could bring more of their furniture from earlier residences. One of the males had previously lived for two years in a condominium apartment in a building for seniors. Although he was not in need of major medical assistance, his blindness did mean that he spent much time in his room.

The second male had cared for his wife during her illness and came to Markwell after she died. He felt lonely and believed he needed more care then he could get in his cooperative apartment in Washington, D.C. Despite his having made friends at Markwell, he kept his cooperative apartment, although he indicated that he did not plan to return to it. Apparently, this provided him with some sense of connection to his previous lifestyle. He perceived himself as an observer of activities and interactions at Markwell but still maintained some detachment. He returned to D.C. frequently on day trips with his son, who lived locally. At several points in the interview he expressed loneliness and wished that more people from his prior life would visit him at Markwell. Thus, despite the fact that he had been at Markwell for one and a half years, he still seemed to have feelings of dislocation.

The two women I interviewed had come into assisted living to be closer to relatives and to receive more help with activities of daily living, such as bathing and meals. The latter provided a major source of social contact. Both indicated that they tried to eat with their friends on a regular basis. The existence of the common dining hours three times a day was very important to them, and even after meals they apparently lingered in the dining room to socialize. At Markwell, none of the rooms provide facilities for cooking, and so the pattern of inviting people in for coffee could not develop. When I walked around the assisted living area, room doors were generally closed. People did not easily visit with one another in their rooms, which were bedrooms no matter how they were furnished. People socialized either in the main areas like the dining room or in some of the small lounges on their wings.

The residents of Markwell's Home for Adults were not as dependent on others for as wide a range of care as those in the nursing home, yet there were a whole range of activities and decisions that they had had to relinquish. Others planned their meals, arranged which social activities would be available on a regular and special occasion basis and, indeed, determined who their neighbors would be. They had more privacy than those in the care center and could surround themselves with a few more reminders of prior residences. Whenever possible, they returned to their earlier communities for religious services and visits with friends and family. At the same time, they were linked to the nursing home by design and interaction. However reluctantly, they recognized that they might have to move to the nursing home if they needed increased medical care.

HIGH TREES, RESTON, VA

High Trees, in another section of the new town, is designated as an "Assisted Living Retirement Community." While not connected to a nursing home, it does provide levels of increased care that can bridge the ability to live independently and the need for constant medical supervision. Most importantly, it offers opportunities for adjustment to increasing loss of autonomy and acceptance of a loss of decision making over some lifestyle arrangements. The facility at High Trees provides three types of residential options. There are studio arrangements, which consist of one large bed-sitting area with a private bath; one-bedroom units with a living room, bedroom, and bath; and suites, which are two-bedroom units with a shared living room and bath. A suite may be occupied by a couple but may also be occupied by two unrelated individuals. This last is the least expensive living option. None of the living arrangements include kitchens, although some residents can have small refrigerators and microwaves in their apartments. The monthly rental fees include a wide range of services, including assistance with taking prescription drugs; nursing assistance with bathing, dressing, and grooming; emergency call service in baths and bedrooms; and three required daily meals. Weekly laundering of bed and bath linens and weekly housekeeping are also provided.

High Trees has a wellness program and a number of social and recreational programs. Options available at additional cost include physical therapy and an intensive personal care program. Although they are not inexpensive, individuals can use such services to avoid shifting to a nursing home setting. Some of the people I interviewed at Markwell had come from High Trees only after a major medical problem left them in need of sustained medical supervision. Even this may not require a move, however, as one floor at High Trees has been established with a nurses' station, and those who need increasing levels of care may move to that floor if space is available. The atmosphere at High Trees is very attractive and much less institutional than a nursing home. The individual units can be decorated as any private apartment might be and personalized to the taste of the residents.

With the assistance of the administrator, I was able to select and interview four residents. One was a 93-year-old woman who had lived at High Trees for six years, the last three months on the more supervised third floor. She had difficulty in walking; she came to High Trees because of an increased need for housekeeping, meals, and general care. This respondent is not able to get out much on her own, but when her health permits she does participate in activities, chiefly those that are craft-related.

A second respondent, a woman of 91, had lived at High Trees for two years. She had had several falls prior to her arrival, and her family was concerned about her living alone. The decision to come to High Trees was made in conjunction with her family and was influenced by the availability of a walk-in shower and other types of assistance in the activities of daily living. Although her son now lives in another state, she wishes to stay at High Trees because it is "nicer than a nursing home," her option were she to move, and because she has good friends at High Trees. She had some negative comments about the meals and the requirement to use a specific company for drugs and would have preferred more autonomy in making choices in these areas. Nonetheless, she was generally satisfied with her ability to decorate her unit with her own furniture and antiques and with memorabilia, which enabled her to feel that she was in her own place. She also expressed her enjoyment of some of the available activities like bridge, bingo, various crafts, and baking for the bake sale. Much of her time is spent on writing articles on a variety of subjects, many of which have been published.

The third woman, age 89, had come to High Trees two years earlier from an apartment in Florida after fracturing her pelvis in a fall. Following a hospital stay and an effort to live at home with the help of aides, she moved to Reston to be closer to her grandchildren. Her level of satisfaction with the living arrangements and the social interactions was very high, and she indicated that she wanted to remain at High Trees "till she dies." The assistance provided enables her to get around to meals and to a few other common activities, and the physical setting enables her to enjoy the scenery. While physically frail, she felt that there were still small pleasures she could enjoy at High Trees and more privacy than she would have in a conventional nursing home.

The last person, a woman of 82, was interviewed in the summer of 1993 and had only been at High Trees for three months. With her background as a psychiatric social worker and family therapist, she indicated that she had given much thought to how and where she wished to live if and when she became increasingly frail. She had researched various assisted living accommodations and had visited some of these. She liked both High Trees and Reston. Following cataract surgery and a fall, she made the decision that she needed more care than was available in her Washington condominium. When a one-bedroom unit became available, she made the move. She saw High Trees as enabling her to maintain independence from her children, which was very important to her. In addition, the ability to replicate her earlier apartment, although on a smaller scale, was important to her. She wanted space sufficient for an elaborate bedroom suite with a double bed and a bookcase-lined living room. The required three daily meals were also seen as desirable. In fact, she rejected offers from her family to provide her with a refrigerator and microwave, stating that she had "no desire to do any cooking ever again." She did not see this as a loss, but as a release from something she "had done too much of." It was very important to this respondent to have her books and her music collection. She felt that the available activities programs were not as intellectually stimulating as she desired.

The residents I interviewed at High Trees expressed more satisfaction with their living arrangements than those I had interviewed at Markwell. They had apparently exercised more control in their selection of living arrangements and had been able to retain more of the symbols of prior life experiences. In this they matched the residents of Sumner Hill. However, they had also relinquished control over many daily activity choices more overtly and had apparently come to terms with this and the changes in status it implied. Their new state of being was perceived as normal and appropriate to their age and health. Both the residents of Sumner Hill and those at High Trees enjoyed a comfortable economic situation and felt more in charge of making general control decisions. They did not feel vulnerable to the cost containments of Medicaid.

NEW TOWNS IN SCOTLAND

In August and September, 1993, I revisited accommodations for the elderly in the New Town of Irvine, Scotland and at Glenrothes, Scotland. The patterns for applying for admission to residential and sheltered housing within the public schemes are established through the joint reviews of the social work department, housing officers, and health officers. A tripartite assessment is done based on need and then coupled with a review of what is available. While bungalows with some special features are available to the elderly, my focus during the 1993 research was on sheltered housing, similar to what we would call assisted living, and on residential homes, similar to our nursing homes. There is much emphasis on providing contacts between the residents and the wider community through the use of volunteers from the community who help plan and coordinate activities for the elderly. These individuals, often involved in a well-organized voluntary association called Age Concern, act as links back to the community and can prevent feelings of isolation for the elderly, who have made major housing shifts. In addition, there are auxiliary services such as Home Helps, which provide personal assistance with several of the activities of daily living. The political as well as the social agenda currently looks to keep people in their own homes through case management. When this is not possible, sheltered housing with a warden system and monitoring is perceived as better than full-scale residential care.

I interviewed two of the residents at one sheltered housing scheme in Glenrothes. In both instances, they had physical conditions that would likely have resulted in nursing home placement in the United States. The woman, who was in her late 70s, had moved to sheltered housing two years earlier after a stroke that left her partially paralyzed and unable to move about outside. The man, also in his 70s, was a paraplegic and confined to a wheelchair. Both of these residents lived in bed-sitting rooms with their own kitchens and with private bathrooms. The rooms were arranged and furnished to look as non-institutional as possible. Both residents had many small objects that they had collected during earlier life experiences. They were responsible for their own meals but received assistance with personal care. The warden or deputy warden visited daily. Each apartment was equipped with sensors to monitor who was up and moving.

The level of satisfaction was high, despite the severe mobility impairments of both residents. They enjoyed being able to contribute to their own care and felt that they were still relatively independent as a result. Obviously, neither could have functioned as well without assistance in bathing, shopping, and other tasks. They both stated with pride that they enjoyed planning their meals and taking care of their apartments. In the large communal areas inside and out, they were also able to socialize. While this sheltered housing arrangement had many similarities to High Trees in the United States, the presence of kitchens in the units and the encouragement given the residents to continue to make as many decisions as possible for themselves presented major differences.

In Irvine, a similar arrangement existed in the two housing complexes I visited. One of these combined sheltered housing with a residential home; the other was a new sheltered housing arrangement, one which had received many design awards. Here, too, the wardens interacted with volunteers from Age Concern and with community care teams composed of social workers and occupational therapists. Many people shared lunch in the large dining room at the linked accommodation, including residents of the residential home, some of those from the sheltered apartments, older people who came in for day care, and those elderly from the local community who belonged to a lunch club, as well as staff and visitors. The meal choices were attractively prepared and presented.

Irvine Development Corporation has fostered a concept of integration that appears to have a positive impact on the elderly. They are able to maintain sustained contacts with others and do not seem to perceive themselves as isolated. Unlike the residents of nursing homes in the United States, those in residential care in Scotland did not seem to have been socialized to "learned helplessness." The combination of the ideology of the planners of the accommodations and the structuring of these accommodations to maximize the circumstances of autonomy was well designed to foster positive acceptance of some of the limitations of increased physical frailty.

CONCLUSION

While normative communitas might not have been reached, it seemed nascent in the Scottish setting. In the United States, on the other hand, it appears only marginally in the assisted living complex. For different reasons, the transitional stage of liminality was more of an end in itself in the nursing homes and in the apartments of the life care community. In the nursing homes, there was such a drastic loss of decision making over a broad spectrum of activities of daily living that resignation was the most typical state of mind. In the life care community the need to tie "wellness" to surface symbols such as dress and not being in need of assistance created ambiguity and ambivalence about being old. In none of the settings, in either nation, were there clear-cut "rites of passage" for being old. Yet the existence of social policy in Scotland that both articulated and tried to actualize the connections between people's pasts, presents, and futures was of importance in facilitating satisfactory psychosocial adjustment.

It appears that acknowledging both the continuities and distinctiveness of reaching the status of elderhood enables the individual to reduce some of the equivocality that now exists. When society also officially recognizes the distinctive needs of moving into this stage of the life cycle, it can assist in policy development that can maximize the adjustment of the individual. As the example of Irvine highlights, the elderly are more satisfied with their lives when they can continue to see connections to earlier life states as well as having "new" resources available for their current needs. Further, some overt recognition of the various changes that accompany growing old may lead, if not to formal rites of passage, to conscious preparation for new social roles.

Those involved in caregiving, whether families or staff at various long term care facilities, would also benefit from open dialogue about the emotional as well as the physical needs of those to whom they provide care. When older people shift responsibility to others for certain decision making areas, such as menu planning and choice of neighbors, as they do when they move to age-segregated living arrangements, we need to recognize that this creates confusion. There can be a discrepancy between some of the core values of U.S. society concerning independence and individualism and the realities of increasing frailty. This is not only confusing for the elderly, but also for those who interact with them. If care givers are confused, they may not be able to be as supportive as they would, ideally, wish to be. Establishing rituals that acknowledge the different aspects of the new status would benefit everyone.

For the larger society, clarifying the meanings of being old could be beneficial in moderating some of the dialogue about generational conflicts, whether the topic is Social Security or the perceived need to competitively divide resources between the very young and the very old. If we see ourselves as moving naturally through different stages and thresholds, then we are less apt to separate ourselves into "I" and "other."

10

Relatives as Trouble: Nursing Home Aides and Patients' Families

Nancy Foner

Patients' family members are an ongoing part of the American nursing home scene. Contrary to popular opinion, studies show that most American families do not "dump" their relatives in nursing homes and ignore them (Johnson and Grant 1985). Many family members try to continue their caregiving role after their spouse or parent is institutionalized, and visiting by family members is common. Not surprisingly, research documents that this contact has positive effects for residents' psychosocial well-being (Greene and Monahan 1982) and can even improve the quality of family relationships (Smith and Bengston 1979).

In her study of a New England nursing home, Shield (1988:59–60) sums up the positive role of actively involved family members: they are arbiters, promulgators, and nurturers. Shield describes how family members provide such valuable services as doing errands and ensuring that clothing is properly mended and cleaned. By interceding on residents' behalf and talking to social workers or administrators about specific matters, such as overheated rooms, they can protect their relatives (see also Savishinsky 1991). They also soften institutional existence by bringing home-made or special foods residents prefer.

If involved family members are a decided benefit for patients, they are more problematic for nursing aides, the main caregivers in nursing homes. My own in-depth field research in a New York City nursing home, specifically focusing on nursing aides, shows that patients' families often bring added pressures and difficulties for workers. "Their family makes things worse for us," said one nursing aide, and most others I knew would heartily agree.

Nursing home aides, like other "people workers" in human care or service organizations, must not only cope with demands from clients or patients but with demands from clients' or patients' families as well. In nursing homes, patients' relatives bring with them their own sets of pressures and complaints—kin as critics, in Goffman's (1961) phrase. What is clear is that to understand the role of relatives in the nursing home we have to widen our field of vision and consider the impact of family members on staff—as well as on patients.

FIELDWORK IN THE NURSING HOME

For eight months, in 1988 to 1989, I immersed myself in the life of the Crescent Nursing Home, a 200-bed nonprofit skilled nursing facility in New York City. The name of the facility, like all personal names used here, is a pseudonym. I spent nearly all my time on the five patient floors, in the world of the nursing aides.[1]

Getting a start in the nursing home was not difficult, thanks to the cooperation of the administration. A week before I arrived, a letter from me was placed in every nursing aide's pay envelope explaining that I was an anthropologist who wanted to learn about their experiences. On my second day, the union delegate introduced me to aides on each floor, assuring them that I was not working for the state or the administration and giving me a chance to answer questions about the project.

In my "official" role as a volunteer, I performed a wide range of chores that allowed me to observe and get to know aides throughout the nursing home. Among my tasks were wheeling patients to activities, making beds, helping patients eat at mealtimes, surveying personal items in patient rooms, straightening up supply closets, and organizing patient records.

From the very beginning, I was concerned that aides accept my presence and my role, agree to talk to me, and allow me to watch them work. Some initially suspected I was an administration spy. A few continued to be wary throughout my stay. I tried to dispel the aides' fears in various ways: talking to them and explaining my research, being endorsed by popular union delegates, even giving copies of my book on Jamaica (Foner 1973) to several Jamaican aides to prove my academic credentials. I ate meals and took breaks with aides in their staff dining room. On the patient floors, I spent most of my time helping, talking to, and sympathizing with aides and nurses. Indeed, as the fieldwork progressed, I spent a lot of time simply watching aides as they did their jobs; a few allowed me to follow them around, pen and notebook in hand, recording what they did for the entire shift.

At first, I gravitated to the Jamaican workers, especially at mealtimes. Given my previous research among Jamaicans, both in Jamaica and abroad, I felt comfortable with them, and they, too, were intrigued by someone who had spent time on the island (Foner 1973, 1978, 1987). It turned out that I knew the Jamaican politician-relative of one aide, and one of the dietitians had actually spent several months as a teacher-trainee in the village I had studied in Jamaica. After a month or so, however, I was equally at home having meals with groups of black American, Hispanic, and Haitian workers. Over the course of many months, I developed close ties with many aides of different ethnic backgrounds.

After a while, I became a kind of fixture of nursing home life. Aides got used to my being around and accepted, or at least generously tolerated, my presence. In addition to participant observation, I carried out semistructured interviews with 34 aides, some interviews done formally in one sitting, others completed in several sessions at meals and breaks and in snatches on the job. Although nursing aides were the focus of my interest, I spent time with and formally interviewed administrative staff, social workers, and nurses. I became close to several alert patients who were willing to share their views with me. I listened to complaints of patients' relatives and talked at length with several outside the nursing home. With patients, I sat in on resident council meetings. With patients' relatives, I attended family council sessions.

This kind of in-depth fieldwork is, of course, the anthropologist's trademark. Its great virtue is the intimacy that develops with members of the community over an extended period of time. Participant observation allows us to view people "with their hair down," to learn things that they might want to keep outsiders from knowing, and to see whether people actually live up to the norms and values they say they follow. Through fieldwork, we can begin to appreciate the complexities of everyday experiences that quantitative studies relying on questionnaires simply cannot capture. Using fieldwork material, we can get a sense of the texture and feel of everyday life in nursing homes, something that quantitative studies rarely permit. What I found was that by talking with and listening to aides, day after day, I heard their views and worries and learned how they reacted to concrete situations on the job. As I observed them over an extended period, I was able to see the way they coped with pressures at work and how they got on with different groups in the nursing home, including patients' relatives.

While anthropologists remain committed to the participant-observation method, there has, of late, been much soul-searching in the discipline. Clifford Geertz refers to this as "epistemological hypochondria" concerning "how one can know that anything one says about other forms of life is as a matter of fact so" (Geertz 1988:71). Some postmodern critics feel anthropology is in crisis because, as Margery Wolf sums up, "we have claimed an authority that does not exist, told truths that are only partial, and (mis)represented an Other that conceals the construction of the Other by an invisible anthropological Self" (1992:136).

The response to these concerns, as Sherry Ortner (1984:143) suggests, is that we can only try to know "the other." She writes: "It is our capacity, largely developed in fieldwork, to take the perspective of the folk on the shore, that allows us to learn anything at all—even in our own culture—beyond what we already know." My own research offers a glimpse—inevitably filtered through the nature of my participation and interpretations—of the complex nature of nursing home life. What I have tried to do is search for patterns of behavior and consistencies in attitudes and meanings at the same time as I attempt to give a sense of the complexities that are an inherent part of social life in any institution or community (cf. Wolf 1992:129).

CRESCENT NURSING HOME: SETTING THE CONTEXT

The Crescent Nursing Home dates back to the early period of nursing home expansion in the 1950s. Beginning as a profit-making enterprise, it changed ownership several times and finally became a nonprofit facility in the 1970s. The nursing home is something of an anomaly in its gentrified neighborhood, located amid expensive apartment buildings and trendy boutiques and restaurants; many passersby who fail to notice the sign on the main avenue doubtless assume it is simply another old building recently converted to cooperative apartments.

Any in-depth study of one particular nursing home inevitably must deal with the question of how "typical" it is. Crescent shares many features with nursing homes around the country, but it is also a product of its local environment. Indeed, nursing homes in New York City are quite different from the "average" U.S. facility in a number of respects.

From a nation-wide perspective, Crescent is large (200 beds) and unusual in its nonprofit status; three quarters of the nation's nursing homes are profit-making enterprises and most have fewer than 100 beds (Strahan 1987). In New York City, where nursing homes are much larger and more frequently nonprofit, Crescent is less unusual. Occupancy rates are high everywhere—99 percent at the Crescent Nursing Home and well over 90 percent in almost every state (Institute of Medicine 1986).

By national and city-wide standards, Crescent is clearly an above average facility. Indeed, since substandard facilities are unlikely to welcome curious researchers, social scientists needing a nursing home's approval for intensive fieldwork projects are bound to study the better institutions.

Crescent patients fit the national profile in many ways: typically female, widowed, and white (see Hing 1989). Most Crescent residents, male and female alike, have no spouse, usually because of death but sometimes on account of divorce. Quite a few never married at all and have no children, either. Several have outlived their children, while the surviving children of others often live far away. Sometimes a caretaking daughter is too ill herself to continue looking after her parent. A great many residents are so infirm and incapacitated, with such complex medical needs, that caring for them at home involves enormous physical, emotional, and financial stresses that children (or surviving spouses) cannot handle.

Few Crescent patients are private paying—only 6 percent in contrast to a third in the nation, the low figure probably due to its location in an inner city area and its far from luxurious physical plant. Most patients' care is covered by government programs, mainly Medicaid. Although now in severely reduced financial circumstances, most patients were formerly middle or lower-middle class citizens. Most had lived in the local neighborhood, moving there when apartments were affordable for those with average means. Their occupations were diverse, ranging from beauticians and secretaries to musicians and teachers, and a few had been fairly prominent university professors and professionals.

Crescent patients are extremely ill and dependent. Although the most common ailments, diseases of the circulatory system and mental disorders, are those most prevalent in nursing homes throughout the United States, Crescent residents are more incapacitated than average. This is mainly due to New York's Medicaid reimbursement system, which gives nursing homes in the state financial incentives to accept heavy care patients; even nonprofit facilities like Crescent must consider reimbursement rates in admissions policies in order to maintain adequate funding (see Foner 1994a). There were few patients with whom I could carry on a regular conversation because most were too confused or too weak and ill. Hardly any can walk on their own or even with a walker; most cannot eat without assistance; and nearly all are incontinent. Nearly two-thirds are diagnosed as having at least one mental disorder.

Nursing aides at Crescent, like those throughout the country, are overwhelmingly female. All are black and Hispanic, hardly unusual in New York facilities and a pattern that is becoming more common in other large cities as the number of minority aides continues to grow. Crescent aides reflect the special ethnic composition of the city's minority population, affected by the large influx of Caribbean immigrants in recent years (Foner 1987). Black West Indians predominate among aides at Crescent, with especially large numbers of Jamaicans. There are also quite a few black Americans and Dominicans, and a smattering of Guyanese, Haitians, Puerto Ricans, and Central Americans.

Like most New York City nursing homes, Crescent is unionized. This helps explain why aides' wages and benefits are relatively good compared to those for other low-skilled jobs available to women in the city—and why the annual turnover rate among Crescent aides is so low, only 5 percent in 1987 and 1988. (During my research, Crescent aides earned $10.30 an hour for a 36 1/4 hour week, with an added 10 percent for night and evening shift workers.) Elsewhere in the country, nursing homes are less likely to be unionized, and wages and working conditions are much worse (Quinlan 1988; see also Diamond 1992). Turnover rates among nursing home aides in the nation are also notoriously high, in the 40 to 75 percent range annually (Waxman, Carner, and Berkenstock 1984).

AIDES AT WORK: THE CAREGIVING JOB

On the job, aides are involved in a full range of patient care. As Johnson and Grant (1985) sum up, aides "lift patients out of bed, wash them, brush their teeth, bathe them, groom them, make their beds, change their soiled linen, clean up after them, dress them, escort them to the dining room, help feed them." Toileting patients involves taking them to the bathroom, offering a bedpan, or most often, changing their incontinence briefs. Bedfast patients must be turned and positioned every two hours. There is regular paperwork too, such as recording vital signs and regular bowel movements. When I was at Crescent, most on-staff aides were permanently assigned a specific section of their floor, with specific patients, whom they looked after day after day—in some cases, for many years. (There were five patient floors, each with 40 patients.) On the day shift, aides typically had eight to ten patients apiece; on the evening shift, they had ten to fourteen.

As this description begins to suggest, nursing aide work is physically straining and emotionally wearing. There is the sheer physical effort of lifting and bathing fragile and often immobile patients. Many patients are bitter and hostile, often because they are so confused. Patients may yell and scream while aides try to wash and dress them or help them eat. Some actively resist, while others, usually through no fault of their own, undo work aides have already completed. Throughout the day, residents understandably make constant demands, and patients suffering from dementia frequently cry, plead, and moan. On top of this, there is abuse from residents, ranging from angry comments to actual physical violence. "Curse you, scratch you, bite you," is how one aide I knew summed it up. There are insults, name-calling, swearing, and even threats of blackmail. Aides have to swallow racial abuse as well.

Despite the relentless emotional and physical demands of the job, most Crescent aides are not the villains so frequently portrayed in the literature. In fact, most are neither monsters nor saints (see Foner 1994a, 1994b). Only a small minority are consistently cruel, like Ms. Riley, [2] an aide I knew well. If looks could kill, hers would, and she often yelled in loud and angry tones. "You better shut up or I'll fix your ass. Eat your food," she screamed at a patient who was slow to eat. She glared at another resident and barked, "You bastard." At the other extreme, a few aides never seem to raise their voices and are always gentle and affectionate. When Ms. Roy smiled to greet a resident, a real warmth came through. She carefully listened to and cared about what residents had to say, and never spoke to them in a condescending or harsh manner. "They need affection," she said about patients. "Yesterday, I was going to see Mr. Rose and I gave him a big hug and he just clung to me. I said to myself, how long is it since that man hug somebody?"

Although not as compassionate as Ms. Roy, most aides are generally considerate and conscientious caregivers. Admittedly, most, on occasion, lose their tempers and behave in ways that would come across as mean to an outside observer. Yet most aides, most of the time, are friendly and helpful to residents and listen and respond to residents in a kind, or at least not unkind, way. Indeed, many establish relations with residents that both they and the patients find gratifying. As far as I could tell, race had little, if any, effect on actual patient care in individual cases. From my observations, racial and ethnic similarity between patients and aides did not lead to better relations with patients or more sympathetic care. Interestingly, hardly any of the black or Hispanic patients were aides' special favorites.

PATIENTS' FAMILIES: AIDES' REACTIONS

Against this background, we return to the heart of the matter: aides and patients' families. Whatever the time of day or early evening, there were always family members at Crescent. Although many visit once a week or less, a sizable number are regulars, coming almost every day, some for a few hours and some for even longer. During my research, there were about 20 regular family visitors on the day shift and about the same number in the early evening. In fact, many families had sought out the Crescent Nursing Home precisely because it was near their homes and they could visit often. Although most regulars lived in the neighborhood, a few traveled long distances every day (in several cases, more than an hour and a half each way) to see their parent or spouse.

The regulars not only provide residents with companionship and support—soothing and reassuring the anxious, depressed, and confused—but also watch over them and monitor care. In addition, they perform some basic bed and body work. Many fed their spouses or parents lunch or dinner. Often, they helped residents get dressed and cleaned up after them. Some brought residents downstairs to the main dining room and, on nice days, to the rooftop deck. They organized clothes and occasionally did all the laundry. And there were lots of little chores or comforts they provided, like pouring a glass of water when their relative was thirsty or fetching items for the bedridden.

Given this kind of involvement and help, one might expect aides to be pleased when patients' relatives visit frequently and assume some of their work burden such as feeding and sorting laundry. Quantitative studies, using checklists to gather ratings from nursing staff and family concerning who should do various tasks, also point in this direction. For the most part, relatives and staff agree on who should do what (Rubin and Shuttlesworth 1983; Schwartz and Vogel 1990).

Yet far from being grateful to family visitors, I found that nursing aides tended to be annoyed, occasionally deeply angry, with them. The general view is that actively involved relatives are another source of pressure on the job.

It is not that family members are thought to be infringing on tasks that aides claim as their own. Indeed, aides generally take for granted assistance that family members offer. Aides have come to expect that certain regulars will do specific jobs, like helping with meals, and they build such assistance into their own schedules. When these relatives do not show up, aides are irritated since now their routines are upset and they have what they perceive to be added work.

Consider the case of Mr. Rubin. Despite his own serious health problems, including a bad back and a heart condition, he came every day to feed lunch to his wife, a woman in the late stages of Alzheimer's disease. On some days, she seemed unable to recognize him, though generally he had a calming effect on her. When Mr. Rubin fed his wife, she ate much better than when aides tried to do it; he sat next to her, in the hall, coaxing her slowly and patiently to eat spoonful by spoonful. Occasionally, when he did not turn up, aides' normal routine was disrupted in that they had one more, very difficult, person to feed. They understood that Mr. Rubin was probably ill, but they were annoyed nonetheless.

Aides do in fact feel sorry for many relatives, like Mr. Rubin, who wear themselves out, physically and emotionally, by their daily visits. Some aides, moreover, get along well with family members and go out of their way to keep them up to date about the patients' conditions and to try to cheer them up despite the unhappy circumstances. What aides appreciate about family members is not material gifts or presents, which a few gave, but personal concern for them as people. Vanessa Clifton was clearly pleased that a number of residents' relatives sent her cards and letters when she was out sick for several months. What gratified Ms. Price was not that a resident's husband spent money on a book to help her study for the high school equivalency exam—he, too, spent his time by his wife's side study-ing for the exam—but that he sincerely wanted to assist her.

This said, however, the common view among aides is that patients' relatives interfere and make life more difficult for them.[3] This view is summed up well in a conversation I had with Ms. Price, an aide with four patients in her section who had family visitors who came virtually every day. When I once commented at lunch on the number of family visitors in her section, she assumed I was sympathizing with her and said, with enormous appreciation, "Thank you. You see the problems I have." Ever-present relatives, in short, spell trouble, and an aide with many in her section is considered unlucky. A couple of aides even mentioned patients' families as the biggest problem they had in doing their job.

A major reason for this is that patients' relatives are thought to be too demanding. "They feel," said one worker, "you never doing enough." Or as another put it, "Some of them don't want the mother home, but when they come to the nursing home, they want her perfect. But when you have 10 patients, you cannot give them that kind of care." A common complaint about regular family visitors is that they think their relative is the only patient. "I can't stand that woman," said Ms. James, referring to a resident's daughter. "She comes round saying, you have to reposition my mother *now*. I was busy with someone else."

Relatives may insist on a level of care that the aide would not normally provide. One resident's sister, who came every day, made an issue of the need to put her relative in pants instead of a dress, which other female residents wore. This made more work for the aide, who explained that putting pants on the resident was extremely difficult, much more difficult than a dress.

In general, relatives who are around make requests that residents themselves are not able or would not bother to express. Concerned with their relatives' welfare and often physically unable to cope with problems that arise, family members have a sense of urgency that aides do not share. A wet bed, a resident who has slipped down in a chair, food that has spilled on the floor—these, to aides, are the realities of nursing home life. If an aide is in the midst of bathing or cleaning a patient, she will not want to interrupt this procedure—which, after all, often means leaving the patient naked or in an uncomfortable position—to deal with what she regards as a minor and routine matter. When relatives ask her to see to their family member and abandon the task at hand, aides are irritated. That they must, moreover, suppress this annoyance and be polite adds to their difficulties.

Jean Hunt, viewed as an especially demanding relative, constantly put her mother's aide in this position. In her late 60s and in poor health herself, she came every day, rain or shine, to see her 98-year-old mother. Ms. Price, the aide, sympathized with Jean's problems—having to deal with her deep attachment to her mother, who was bound to die soon, and her own ailing health. Never once did I see Ms. Price express irritation or anger toward Jean. Ms. Price was always calm and polite, even when she was the object of Jean's outbursts. To me, however, Ms. Price complained about what a trial Jean was. There seemed to be an endless stream of requests—to clean up, remake the bed, change her mother—when Ms. Price was in the midst of tending to other patients. If Ms. Price did not respond immediately, Jean was visibly piqued and, later, often exploded.

If relatives are annoyed, there is always the possibility that they will take their complaints and demands to higher authorities, a distinct drawback from the aides' point of view. They may complain to social services and other higher-ups; at the least they might cause a nursing administrator or social worker to ask questions.

Family complaints and demands may be all the more irritating and carry added symbolic weight because they come from people of higher class and racial status. Most family visitors at Crescent are middle class and white; virtually all aides, working-class women of color. Social class and racial differences often reinforce, in subtle and unconscious ways, the relatives' sense that aides are there to serve them. For the aides' part, they may be especially sensitive to signs of condescension and superior attitudes and behavior from white, better-off visitors.

Whether regular visitors complain or not, aides feel that they spoil patients by lavishing attention on them and raising expectations of care. This is true of undemanding relatives as well as those with constant complaints. Take Mr. Rubin once again. In many ways, he was the ideal relative. Careful to cultivate good relations with his wife's aide, he hardly ever complained or asked for anything. He sat quietly with his wife, helping out with many tasks and even assisting other patients in her room. As much as aides liked him personally and sympathized with his situation, they saw him as causing problems: his constant presence spoiled his wife. By giving her the kind of attention they were unable to provide, he got her used to a relatively high level of care. When he left, she was, they felt, more difficult than before, whining and crying and inconsolable. And if he did not show up at all, she was especially hard to manage.

Of less importance, but still a factor, is that family members sometimes create problems for aides by interfering with care. In these cases, relatives are intruding on technical aspects of care that aides—and nurses—think are beyond relatives' purview. The general principle of task allotment is not an issue. As noted, aides readily accept relatives' help in such "technical" or instrumental tasks as feeding, bedmaking, and cleaning that are officially aides' duties. Aides view relatives' help as interference when it adds to their workload or contradicts nurse's orders, possibly harming patients and getting the aides into trouble.

Jean Hunt, the demanding daughter, provides a perfect example. Upset that her mother was physically restrained in bed, Jean often removed the restraints even though she was repeatedly told by the nurse in charge why they had to be in place. As a result, one afternoon, the old woman fell out of bed onto the floor. Luckily, she was not hurt, but obviously this was dangerous. What the aide focused on was having to lift the resident to put her back to bed: more heavy work.

On a different floor, nurses and aides suspected another demanding regular, Mrs. Adams, of causing her husband to slide down in his chair by trying, ineffectively and improperly, to reposition him and make him more comfortable. He was a heavy, paralyzed man suffering from severe dementia. Aides, once more, had to lift and move him to sit him up straight. This was an enormous strain since Mr. Adams was so heavy and could not help. Nurses and aides also believed that Mrs. Adams imagined symptoms, like pains and headaches, that were not there; she demanded medication and immediate treatment for her husband that nursing staff were not allowed to give without a doctor's permission.

RELATIVES' GRIEVANCES

Family members, of course, have a long list of their own grievances. In interviews with family members in a Wisconsin nursing home, Bowers (1988) found them to be deeply upset by the staff's failure to provide protective, as opposed to purely technical, care. They were distressed when their relatives were treated in a demeaning or insulting way—made to feel like nuisances, difficult to care for, or that they had unreasonable requests—and when their relatives' emotional needs, personal preferences, and unique personal histories were ignored or overlooked (see also Duncan and Morgan 1994).

These are issues, too, for regular family visitors I met at the Crescent Nursing Home. What figured even more prominently in their complaints, however, at least in conversations with me and at family council meetings, is aides' failure to provide competent technical care and their lack of responsiveness to relatives' own requests and difficulties.

Over and over, family members pointed to failings in care: the husband who wore no special stockings when his wife arrived, though these had been ordered by the doctor; the ulcers on one man's grandmother, as well as roommates who were not being fed; the husband whose eating patterns were not checked properly, though he had serious eating difficulties, which once, before he came to Crescent, required him to be hospitalized for dehydration. Typically, family members blamed aides, the direct agents of care, for the problems. Lost laundry was a universal problem that most were resigned to. As one grandson said, "I take it as a factor of life that you lose all your clothing here."

Family members complained, too, about aides' unsympathetic attitudes to them and unhelpful, sometimes antagonistic, behavior. Family members are often overwhelmed, sometimes to the point of tears, by the helplessness entailed in asking staff busy with other priorities to attend to a relative's needs—something that drives home the fact that their relative's care is no longer in their hands. Often, they are humiliated and upset by having to plead with or cajole aides to get them to meet requests (Hooyman and Lustbader 1986:302). Understandably, family members are distressed when aides are not responsive, ignore requests, or show signs of hostility.

Mrs. Bernard was especially vocal in her criticisms at one family council meeting I attended. Her characterization of aides was blunt: "When you ask them something, they never answer." She went on, "A patient in my husband's room threw a tray with food all over the room and over my husband's bed. So I didn't want to leave it like that. I asked for a broom and the aide tells me where to get it. I have a bad back, she didn't even offer to help. In my opinion they're underworked and overpaid." That Mrs. Bernard was expressing the anger and frustrations of many other family members was clear in that other relatives at the meeting all nodded in agreement.

Like others, Mrs. Bernard was annoyed that her requests and instructions were often disregarded. "I left a laundry bag to put dirty laundry in every day," she told the crowd at the meeting. "I explained it to the aides and left a big sign. What do you think? I come and the laundry is not in the bag." Around the room, the family members were abuzz with comments like "She's bringing up all our points," and "It's true." A frail old woman chimed in, "I come every night to feed my mother who is visually impaired and they expect me to put a bib on her, to prop her up, and I really cannot do this. It is very hard for me."

Perhaps one of the most interesting cases is Mrs. Adams, one of the "demanding regulars" already mentioned. She wrestled with the political dilemma of criticizing black workers, whose causes she and her husband championed. Mr. Adams had been a well-known figure on the political Left, to which both he and his wife devoted their lives and for which they made many sacrifices. She was deeply upset over the inadequate care she felt her husband received, and she had nothing but criticism for his nursing aide. Her feeling was that aides, as union members, should be better workers than nonunion employees.

Ill herself (she had suffered from a stroke a few years before), it was more than she could bear to come day after day and see instructions ignored or her husband left in an unhealthy state. Having bought undershirts to keep him warm, she arrived to find that his room was cold and he had no undershirt on. Despite the doctor's recommendations, aides continued to use small incontinence briefs that gave her husband a rash or, alternatively, left him in open briefs that resulted in a wet bed. She thought he was uncomfortable in his chair and not positioned properly and even suspected that a cut he got one evening, that needed stitches, was due to negligent care in the shower. On top of all this, when she made any comment, the aide, a feisty West Indian who was one of the least sensitive aides in the nursing home, often snapped at her.

At a family council meeting she summed up her frustrations: "If the nursing aide is not functioning properly, they come to me and say he's a problem. I say I know he's a problem, I was looking after him at home for years, I couldn't do it anymore. That's why he's here. They're union workers, paid union wages, and if they don't work, they should go." In response, all the relatives in the room enthusiastically clapped and cheered.

Usually, relatives keep such complaints to themselves, and it is only in private conversations, well out of the earshot of staff, that they express their views. Even at family council meetings, most relatives are diplomatic in the way they couch their dissatisfactions. Many were only spurred on to air their views at one meeting by the angry comments of Mrs. Bernard and Mrs. Adams, who were seen as bold to be so honest and vocal. Even Mrs. Adams told me, "Of course, I wouldn't say anything to the aide." Family members do not want to antagonize aides, which might result in worse treatment for relatives and more uncomfortable visits for themselves. Some fear that if they complain directly to the aide, or if word of complaints gets back to higher-ups, their relatives will suffer retaliation. Others come to have a sense of hopelessness: that whatever they do, nothing will change anyway.

To say that relatives have complaints does not, of course, necessarily mean that their relationships with aides are continually conflict-ridden or even seriously strained. Typically, regulars develop a tolerable working relationship with their relatives' aides. Just as there are sources of irritation on both sides that develop day after day, so, too, there are times when they chat about the patient and even work together to help him or her. Usually, they become accustomed to each other, and a level of cordiality is maintained. Often, their relationship extends to asking about each other's health and family. Many family members had, in fact, become attached to their relatives' aides and were seriously troubled when the administration brought up a proposal to rotate aides among patients.

Relatives who have extremely hostile relations with an aide are unusual. In fact, when tensions become too serious, the social service department generally intervenes, sometimes because the aide herself has complained of insults or difficult relations. In such cases, social workers talk with family members about the problem, with the hope of making them sensitive to aides' feelings. As a last resort, arrangements are made to switch aides so that relatives can start out on a new footing.

CONCLUSION

No matter how much they might want to do so, nursing aides cannot escape from patients' relatives. Understandably, spouses and children who visit try to continue their caregiving and protective role in the institutional setting. While this is a blessing for patients, it creates additional pressures and demands for nursing aides. Although aides may like and even become fond of certain family members, aides' general view is that regular family visitors are a source of trouble.

One of the benefits of in-depth fieldwork is that it can capture the complexities, strains, and contradictions involved in daily life in nursing homes. Just as it reveals certain tensions and difficulties, so, too, can it point to some policy suggestions. Clearly, on a case by case basis, social workers can work with especially troublesome family members to sensitize them to the needs and problems of aides. For their part, aides can and should be encouraged, informally and through in-service training programs and sessions with social workers, to be sensitive to family members' concerns and needs. Yet, even if successful, these kinds of interventions will not eliminate the potential for strain.

There are, in short, some basic dilemmas when it comes to relations between nursing home aides and patients' families. What emerges from my account is that the very nature of institutional care, with aides responsible for many patients, is bound to create frustrations for interested relatives even in the best nursing homes—and aides, as the direct caregivers, are the likely targets. For aides, relatives' frequent presence, in itself, is likely to lead to a certain amount of interference and escalation of care demands. Patients' relatives, in short, come with the job. This chapter shows, above all, that they need to be included in any thorough-going analysis of nursing home life and work.

11

From the Inside Out: The World of the Institutionalized Elderly

Bethel Ann Powers

THE ETHNOGRAPHIC APPROACH

How can we begin to understand the world of the institutionalized elderly as seen from the inside out? For several years I observed and interviewed residents of a 212-bed health-related facility housed within a county-operated long term care institution that also is licensed to provide acute and skilled levels of care. I found that elderly people's stories about how they became institutionalized are highly personal. Some, like Teresa, report making a thoughtful choice:

I did it because I didn't dare stay home alone any longer. . . . I didn't want to fall and not be able to get to the phone. . . . Now I feel safe . . . (but) it was a big decision . . . to give up everything, knowing this might be my home for as long as I'm alive. . . . So that was a trauma alone.

Others, like Brenda, report that they entered against their will:

I didn't want to come. My daughter-in-law sent the ambulance after me. . . . Said I wasn't eating the way I should eat. . . . And I wouldn't get in the ambulance . . . and then my son came (and) put me in the ambulance. . . . They say I gotta eat. Sometimes I can't eat what's here. I don't like it. I don't like the food. I like to be someplace where you can see somebody cooking the food.

Despite individual differences, however, common elements in the stories that I have heard include the difficulty of the decision and the characterization of a nursing home as "the end of the line" where one becomes separated from the familiarities of home and life outside the walls.

Ethnographic fieldwork in nursing homes poses some challenges. The first issue for me, as a gerontological nurse anthropologist, was one of "making the familiar strange and the strange familiar." George and Louise Spindler (1982) used this terminology to describe their experiences of studying schooling, both within and outside of their own culture. Since I had worked in other health care facilities and entered the field with my own understanding of nursing practice and institutional systems, I had to make a conscious effort to overcome my familiarity with the type of setting. This involved attempts to take nothing for granted in writing preliminary fieldnotes. I immersed myself in observing and recording many details of everyday life that I realized might or might not be of importance later on, since at the beginning of a project everything in the field is viewed as a potential source of data. The discipline of fieldnote writing—at this and later, more focused stages of the research—was helpful in controlling tendencies to make assumptions based on prior knowledge. I concentrated on listening, asking sometimes naive questions, and observing ordinary activities in the setting to try to create for myself a new sense of familiarity, this time with the informants' view of their world. In addition, I tried to imagine myself in their circumstances, and I searched my fieldnotes and transcribed interviews for evidence of "blindspots" and researcher bias. Finally, in communicating the results of this research, I am once again faced with, as Wolcott put it, "making the obvious obvious (or, more kindly, making the familiar strange) because, quite literally, [the task of the ethnographer] is to describe what everybody already knows" (1985:193). In this case, most people in American society already have beliefs and conceptions about what nursing home life is like, beliefs that are often accompanied by some kind of personal experience. But, "of course," Wolcott continues, "no one individual, ethnographer included, ever knows it all or understands it all."

Another issue involved assessment of residents for participation in the focused phase of the study. Here, interviews elicited descriptions of residents' personal social networks, that is, all direct contacts that they had with people in and outside of the institution. Nursing staff were asked to help identify persons who could participate in research. From among those who could give legal consent and who met study criteria, there were 21 refusals and 69 acceptances. Inclusion criteria required informants to be 55 years of age or older and able to give reasonable and consistent responses to interview questions. They needed to be oriented to person and place, with memory intact enough to describe socialization patterns as structured by the interview. Human subjects' approval was granted, and signed consent was obtained from participants.

On the one hand, I feel assured that all informants understood that they were participating in a research project, knew what was involved in the interview, and willingly consented to participate. The risk to them, as in most interview research, was perceived as minimal. On the other hand, one cannot help but be mindful of the fact that nursing home residents are a type of "captive population" whose decisional capacities may be influenced by fear of reprisal for refusal to participate. Additionally, decisions to participate could be based on the strong desire of lonely people for companionship, often recognized as a benefit of such studies, but again calling into question the extent of voluntary consent. I am reminded of one recently bereaved man who physically detained me well beyond several interview sessions by seizing and holding my hand with almost painful force.

Fieldworkers in nursing homes need to be particularly alert to informants' possible motivations for participation, and they should make a special effort to honor their needs and protect their dignity. In other words, responsibility to show every consideration for the sensitivities and well-being of the informant far exceeds the formalities of written consent. Furthermore, in my research, visiting of a purely social nature occurred sometimes with non-participants so that they would not feel ignored, and in a few instances individuals who did not meet the inclusion criteria were interviewed because they wanted very badly to participate. (Their contributions were summarized in fieldnotes but not included in the network data.) Being attentive to the needs of non-participants during the interview phase of the study required extra time, but it was time well spent. The point is that compassion as well as procedural concerns should drive the data collection in this type of field situation where special care must be taken to avoid compromising people and to preserve individual integrity.

Informants were paid a nominal amount for their time and participation. Payment of study participants always raises questions about coercion. In this research, there were instances where the extra money was put to some use, but many individuals said that the payment would remain in their accounts because they had no pressing need for it. I think that most informants would have participated without payment. However, since the funding was available, it seemed only right to compensate people for their patience and effort in the interviews, which involved two or more tape-recorded sessions of about two hours each in length. In addition, I believe that payment also symbolized the importance of their contributions.

Keeping my roles as observer and nurse separate while conducting the research was another issue. I anticipated that problems could arise if study participants saw me primarily as a nurse. However, since I did not wear a uniform and was not a recognized staff member at the institution, there were few attempts by residents to use me as a care provider/consultant or go-between in matters related to health services. I do not know if staff members who informally volunteered comments and stories about their experiences saw me more as nurse or as researcher. Nursing staff sometimes encouraged me to visit or spend time with residents whose moods or behaviors were a source of concern, since visiting and spending time for any purpose was viewed as potentially therapeutic. They did not attempt to use me as an informant or contributor to the care plan, although there were times when our mutual concerns about the residents prompted some exchange.

An ongoing issue involves the choice of examples from the qualitative data base used to shape ethnographic description and to illustrate particular points in written reports and presentations of the research (Fischer 1994). I always use fictitious names and try to avoid certain informational details to maintain confidentiality. And, as time goes by, the likelihood that readers and listeners will be able to connect the descriptions and quotes to actual individuals lessens appreciably. However, I have had individuals familiar with the institution in which I conducted the research approach me after a presentation to respond to a particular example with the assertion: "I know *exactly* who you were talking about." They then have supplied the name of someone who never was a participant in my study, and I have had to convince them that they were mistaken. Even though I feel assured that participants' real identities remain protected, decisions about what and how much of their experiences and verbatim accounts to disclose at any time makes me thoughtful. I believe that this is a common concern in the reporting of ethnographic research, which relies so heavily on the richness of detail that participants provide about their lives.

SOCIAL NETWORK MAPPING

Sixty-nine residents participated in the research. There were 37 women and 32 men, with a range in age from 55 to 95 and a mean of 73 years. I asked participants to identify people with whom they had contact in each of four sectors: (1) other residents, (2) institution staff, (3) kin, and (4) outside non-kin friends and acquaintances. Questions were framed around each sector of interaction, and additional memory assistance was given by focusing on residents' known spheres of activity. For example: "Can you tell me about the people you see in the dining room?" "When you go to play bingo, whom do you go with? Who do you see when you get there?" The lists were further expanded by asking about certain types of circumstances. For example: "When you need some extra money, who will lend you some?" "Who cheers you up when you're feeling blue?" A network diagram was drawn, and residents were encouraged at various points to think about whether anyone had been left out. Detailed comparable data on each network member included when, where, how, and how often contact took place; the sorts of things that people talked about and did for one another (for example, conversation, advice, food, shopping, errands); and which network members knew and interacted with other network members. Only after the extent and behavioral aspects of the networks were obtained were questions asked about the subjective importance of network ties. Consequently, the networks were not limited to subjectively important people or friends. A conversational, in-depth interviewing style was used to expand the qualitative data base. Discussions centered around interactions within networks and other systematically collected information about participants' lives before institutionalization, recent changes in networks, current routines and reactions to institutional life, and how residents perceived themselves to be doing in general and with regard to their health status. This network profile approach was developed by Sokolovsky (1980), who has applied it to the study of elderly living in inner-city hotels and to the homeless on skid row (Cohen and Sokolovsky 1989; Sokolovsky and Cohen 1983).

A form was developed (tailored to the site by using knowledge gained from the prior period of extensive participant observation) to ensure that certain minimal data would be gathered on all networks regardless of conversational directions pursued in the interviews or the order in which network sectors were discussed. Efforts were made to reduce methodological limitations of self report data by validating information through repeat questioning and observation, having more than one interview session, and structuring interviews, as described above, in as positive and concrete a manner as possible.

Taped interviews were transcribed, and transcripts were reduced to a series of index cards containing one bit of content each. This allowed for easier sorting by topic and the creation of categories of information. Analysis of collected network data involved description and comparison on an item-by-item basis of (1) interactional characteristics of networks (interactional content, frequency and intensity of interactions, multiplexity—whether the tie provided one or more types of resource—and directionality—whether the resource exchange tended to be reciprocal or whether resources tended to flow in only one direction), and (2) structural characteristics of networks (size, clustering and interconnectedness of network members). Comparison of networks on the basis of density (proportion of members of a network known to one another) and clustering (extent to which a participant's personal network seemed to be focused around particular groupings of people) involved the diagraming of each network with the participant in the center and names of network members positioned around. Lines were drawn between members who had some communication with each other.

PATTERNS OF ADJUSTMENT TO NURSING HOME LIFE

The finding that there is no uniform pattern of adjustment to nursing home life is consistent with reports of other researchers who have remarked upon the highly individualized adaptations of elderly people to other types of living arrangements (Cohen and Sokolovsky 1989; Keith 1982; Rubinstein 1986; Rubinstein, Kilbride, and Nagy 1992; Sokolovsky and Cohen 1983). Individual adjustments reflect varying abilities to access social support and to shape personal networks. [See also Groger's discussion in this volume about differences in elderly people's decisions about long term care arrangements.]

Social Support

Although they are distinct conceptual entities, social support and social networks often are linked in the literature. Social support is broadly defined in terms of resources provided by other persons that are thought to contribute positively to an individual's health and well-being. Social networks are complex sets of interpersonal ties that in personal networks connect network members to a focal individual and to each other. Network analysis is of interest to some social support theorists because it can identify patterns of social interaction that may affect the flow of resources to the focal individual. However, it is misleading to refer to constellations of personal relationships as "social support networks," since the presence or absence of social ties is not in itself an indicator of social support. To assess social support one needs to know the meaning that network relationships and activities have for individuals.

In the process of discussing personal network relationships, residents compared themselves to other residents, and they judged how well they were coping with institutional life on the basis of perceived support. The closeness of institutional living presents endless opportunities for comparison. Residents often compared their health with that of others whom they perceived as worse off. Comparison of a "downward" nature has been described in social psychology and gerontological literature as a defensive action to preserve self-esteem (Hakmiller 1966; Hochschild 1973; Powers 1988a; Wills 1981). Here are selected examples from interview transcripts, preceded by speakers' sex and age:

Male (85): My leg. That's the only thing that's holding me back. I feel good. And when I look around . . . I'm not sick. Believe me, some of these men and ladies around here . . . I'm not sick. I don't wanta brag, but I wouldn't wanta be the way some of these people are that hafta be here.

Male (58): I push their wheelchairs back to their rooms after activities. It makes me feel as though they're jealous of me, that I can walk. It's a strong feeling that I have.

Social comparison also involved noticing and commenting upon personal appearance—grooming, hair, clothing—and whether or not one was recognized and included in informal visiting and conversations among residents and institution staff. To be known and accepted, attractive to others, and loved gave residents confidence and self-assurance. Other forms of support to self-esteem derived from status positions associated with (1) control of information in gossip circles; (2) commanding favors and service from other residents; or (3) securing a paying job within the institution, such as running errands, helping in the library, distributing newspapers, or answering telephones (Powers 1988b). Supportive flow of resources through social network ties most commonly involved the following types of exchanges: informal conversation, personal services, assistance with activities of daily living, cheering up when blue, advice, food, gifts, social outings, shopping, money, aid when sick, laundry, clothing, and eating out. A little more than half (54 percent) of the total number of recorded exchanges between participants and network members were dependent (i.e., resource directed from network members to respondents), and 70 percent of this type of material and emotional support came from ties to kin and friends outside of the institution. Recorded transactions within networks of a reciprocal (33 percent) or instrumental/participant-generated (13 percent) nature occurred to a greater extent within the institution. The most common types of exchange among residents involved food, cigarettes, reading material, small money loans, errands, help with dressing, and visiting.

Some residents performed distinct services for one another. For example, one woman took in sewing and mending in exchange for money, services in kind, or small gifts:

Female (72): I don't pick up or deliver. They have to bring (clothes) to me and come and get them. . . . I (do) sleeves . . . false hems . . . sew up seams and cut things off . . . whatever they want. . . . I make bags for the backs of wheelchairs when patients want 'em.

Another resident regularly ministered to others by welcoming and orienting new residents, visiting the ill and sending them cards, greeting and asking about the health of her neighbors, and offering prayers for those who asked. She recounted the following about a friend whom she had been visiting in a room on another unit for seven years:

Female (78): When I first knew her . . . she'd lost one leg and she declared she'd never let them amputate the other one, but she had to, and then two years or so ago she had a stroke and can't talk. So, when I visit her, I have to do all the talking. And she understands quite well. I gave her a book a friend gave to me. It has beautiful pictures. . . . Usually when I go there, I pray with her. . . . I would like to visit more people than I do. . . . I'm sure I don't do as much as I should.

These findings about the direction and content of resource exchange within networks suggest that not only do outside ties continue to be important sources of support, but, also, there is a level of reciprocal and instrumental exchange between participants and network members that contrasts with the image of institutionalized people as being wholly dependent and unlikely or unable to extend themselves to others.

As noted previously, not all ties are supportive. The methods of network mapping were used to try to capture *all* direct relationships; consequently, some negative as well as positively perceived social ties were represented in the data. In addition, findings showed that there was not always agreement between institution staff and residents regarding the actual "supportiveness" of particular network members. For example, a resident said of a relative whom the staff had identified as highly supportive:

Male (73): Frank brought me a few packages of food around the holidays, but he's odd. He just comes up here and looks around, asks a few questions, and then he walks off. Maybe he stays 15 minutes. He hates these places. He don't care if I die. It's my mistake if I live and if I croak it's my fault.

Finally, findings suggest that presence or absence of support should not be judged on the basis of network size. A greater number of ties does not necessarily indicate access to more support. In this research, the participant with the largest network had the most superficial ties and frequently became overextended. For instance, he reported:

Male (76): Since I was told by my social worker that I'm in too many activities, I've tried to cut out what I could. I've stopped going to college, and I was thinking of giving up swimming, but the more I considered it the more I thought I needed that kind of exercise, so I'd like to continue the swimming . . . course I do have enough to keep me busy because the church has programs and trips; and then the Red Cross has trips and things during the summer; and the hospital itself has camping.

In contrast, some residents with smaller networks were more satisfied with the quality of relationships as well as with their ability to mobilize and manage receipt and reciprocation of resources.

Social Network Typology

Four types of networks were identified that differed in terms of size, clustering of ties in particular spheres, interconnectedness, and interactional characteristics. These types are called: (1) institution-centered, (2) small cluster, (3) kin-centered, and (4) balanced. They will be discussed in connection with the four sectors of network relationships that were explored in the research: (1) resident–kin, (2) resident–outside non-kin friends and acquaintances, (3)resident–resident, and (4) resident–staff.

The function of the typology in relation to empirical findings is heuristic; that is, like typologies in other network studies (Bott 1957; Brannen 1985; Wenger 1987, 1989), it facilitates discussion of alternative kinds of organizational patterns observed in the data. Such classifications are tentative and ideal in the sense that there is an accounting for how individual cases fit into typologies, but there may be ways in which certain ones do not completely conform.

Institution-Centered Networks

Institution-centered networks were among the smaller in total size with proportionally fewer outside as opposed to intra-institutional contacts. Ties were more often simple, consisting of one type of content, for example, informal conversation, shopping/errands, assistance with personal care, money loans, advice. Relationships were more frequently described as low intensity, that is, few network members rated as "very important" or identified as close friends and confidants. Of the 27 people (39 percent total sample) with this type of network, 20 (74 percent) were men. Many were self-proclaimed "loners" who developed their own routines that brought them into contact with individuals who could be used to meet needs for passing the time or to supply material goods and services with a minimal amount of emotional involvement. Relationships with kin and outside acquaintances were often nonexistent, tenuous, or strained. Yet, emotional attachment often persisted despite a lack of physical presence. One woman said:

Female (71): It's none of her (social worker's) business where my children are. I can't keep track of 'em. I have three. . . . I had to adopt one out when he was a baby. He don't come very often, but I don't hold that against him. And, I don't know where the other two are. I guess they all know I'm here. But if they don't come to see ya . . . They don't have to come. I don't say nothing; I just keep going.

The data suggest that most residents with this type of network placed high value on self-reliance and resisted bureaucratic control. Relationships with institution staff were casual and sometimes confrontational. There were, however, a smaller number of residents in this category who tried to use staff to fill a void brought about by the loss of formerly important people in their networks.

Informants tended to deny close ties with other residents, but they were not socially isolated. On the one hand, they talked with satisfaction about companionship with "buddies" that settled into familiar routines of small talk, sharing meals, meeting at an appointed time to pursue an activity, or sitting quietly together. Many maintained at least one confidant. On the other hand, most residents in institution-centered networks pointed out other residents, people whom they had identified as members of their personal networks, who were intensely disliked or towards whom residents felt a general indifference or antagonism. For example:

Male (77): Everyone I ever liked here died on me. . . . How am I going to get along with these guys? I come in here first. . . . I hit a guy in the elevator. Knocked some teeth out! The guy punched me first. Then I let him have it. . . . The good ones die like flies. . . . The bad ones like me don't. You gotta be angry to live.

Thus, in various ways, these residents expressed the value of self-sufficiency, creating limited opportunities for support and exchange of resources. However, the levels of intimacy and companionship experienced with those network members who were most accessible often were insufficient to overcome their sometimes acknowledged feelings of loneliness (Powers 1991).

Small Cluster Networks

Five residents (7 percent total sample) were involved in small cluster networks, which were most like institution-centered types. Their distinctiveness lay in the tendency of residents to form small, tightly knit, and fairly exclusive cliques within the larger networks of people with whom they came in contact. This focus on the "good friend" or "best friend" clusters appeared to serve as a buffer, insulating people from some of the movement and change in the larger institutional world of which they were a part.

For these residents, ties with kin and outside friends were warm, though contact was limited; institution staff and other residents were largely taken for granted. The focusing of energy within smaller friendship circles enhanced opportunities for reciprocity and support. Also, the pace of everyday life was generally slow and comfortable. For example:

Male (94): Frank and I kinda chum together. . . . We visit in each other's rooms and eat together. . . . He pushes my chair and we go off . . . have a beer . . . [visit] with the guys.

Female (67): I didn't have a social life at all before I came here. I lived at home. . . . I did housework every day. . . . (Now) we [roommate and self] get together and gab (but we) don't do much at all. I check the [activities] board, and we go to mass and parties. . . . We talk a lot together, and we go to meals together. . . . People don't come in here much. . . . Sara's [roommate's] daughter [who visits weekly] brings us things and helps out. My important ones are in heaven. And I don't know anybody (here) very well, but everybody's nice. . . . There's not too much to worry about.

The intimacy of residents' relationships did not prevent loneliness, but the loneliness was shared as well as the pain of inevitable losses along the way. Some of the best examples of companionship were in small cluster networks in which the identity of small groups or pairs of individuals was reinforced through established daily routines and small acts of kindness (Powers 1991).

Kin-Centered Networks

Kin-centered networks varied in total size, but, in many cases, kin ties equaled or exceeded institutional contacts, and residents had an average of four relatives who visited and communicated with them on a weekly or monthly basis. Of the 18 people (26 percent total sample) with this type of network, 11 were closely engaged in emotional ties to families, which made it difficult for them to accept new relationships and activities. Residents distanced themselves from the give and take of institutional life, and staff often expressed concern about those who stayed in their rooms and declined to engage with other residents. Residents in kin-centered networks, however, expressed contentment with their personal routines, asserting that they were doing what they liked to do. For them, occupying the time intervals between contacts with family members was the issue. Residents chose familiar pastimes (reading, television, knitting, napping), or simply sat apart from others and mentally dwelt upon and/or awaited reunion with kin (Powers 1992).

Seven of the residents in kin-centered networks were beginning to become disengaged or distanced from ties with family members. Several had begun to attend activities where they drifted in and out or sat alone. For example:

Male (76): The volunteers get a [poker] game going every week. I go for the coffee and doughnuts, and I play. And they have sing-alongs every Friday; I don't miss them. I know some of the oldtimers [songs] but not all of them. I go alone.

Others had begun to single out staff with whom they thought friendship might be possible. Sometimes there were attempts to transform resident-staff relationships into kin-type relationships, as follows:

Female (82): She [nurse] was like a little daughter to me. She'd talk to me just like a daughter and take me here, there, and everywhere. I love her, and she said [she loved me] too.

Residents with kin-centered networks differed among themselves in terms of their initial imperviousness to the institutional setting, degree of self-isolation from staff and other residents, and the amount of time that passed before they began to become involved in institutional activities, such as clubs, religious services, games and crafts, organized entertainment, trips, and other social events.

Balanced Networks

Balanced networks were the largest in total size, with network members distributed across resident, staff, kin, and outside friend sectors. There were multiple types of resource exchange, and greater interconnectedness among a wide range of contacts facilitated the flow of communication and support. Of the 19 people (28 percent total sample) with this type of network, 15 (79 percent) were women. The flow of resources among residents in balanced networks involved a variety of services, including material and physical assistance, emotional support, and friendship.

Residents in balanced networks were connected to the outside world at the same time that they were able to maintain close relationships with institution staff and other residents. Some residents made themselves available to assist staff with helping, advising, or comforting other residents. For example:

Female (71): Mrs. Poole [head nurse] asked me if I would go upstairs and see Pauline [resident]. She's sick and very unhappy. I thought it might cheer her up to think that I would bother to come up.

Many became selectively involved in friendships with other residents that satisfied needs to share experiences and to identify with and confide in another. They also involved each other and staff in webs of gossip and tattling. Trustworthiness was a quality often mentioned in connection with these resident friendships, as evidenced in the following quote:

Female (58): I'm very careful about everything because I don't want any more conflict. . . . Everything is so tight [here] it *squeaks*, and you say something, and someone misinterprets or misunderstands what you said. Then it comes back said in the wrong way. . . . There's a few you wouldn't dare tell [anything] 'cause they'd blab it all over . . . but they don't tell it right because they didn't hear it right, and it's a situation like that that can cause trouble. . . . I say very little [but] I can tell May most anything. We hang out together. She helps me out, and I help her out.

The same resident distinguished between friendliness toward residents with limited capacities to engage in relationships and situations that promoted more possibilities for friendship formation:

Female (58): It's a pretty equal deal. Some of them know what's going on. Some don't. They [staff] can only do so much with them. . . . You can talk and say things, but it doesn't stay with them. . . . You say: How are you? How are you feeling? . . . [and they'll say] Oh, pretty good. [You'll say] How's your day? And they'll say good or bad. And that's about as far as you can go. . . . In ten minutes time they won't even remember that you talked to them.

In the dining room you get a variety of people (from different residential units) whose minds are still pretty sharp, and there you can communicate quite a bit.

On the whole, residents in balanced networks engaged in institutional activities, although the level and nature of participation varied in accordance with individual interests.

PERCEPTIONS OF NURSING HOME LIFE

Every nursing home is different in terms of such objective features as location, design, resources, organizational make-up, policies, personnel, and residential mix. Also, at one time or another, we all have heard people describe and differentiate institutional settings on the basis of less tangible features associated with the "feel" of a place, its character, and its reputation. Yet, there is a sameness about institutional living that transcends such differences.

The nature of the communal experience represents a significant change for most people. The resident groups of which they become a part are not of their choosing and contain individuals whose habits, opinions, abilities, and interactional styles may be highly divergent. They encounter many annoyances with limited opportunities to distance themselves, and privacy is always at issue. In addition, there is mourning to be done over the loss of "home" and one's former life. Some nursing homes encourage residents to bring furniture and items from home to personalize their living spaces. There may also be visible effects of efforts to create and maintain attractive, comfortable, and stimulating environments. Nevertheless, residents will say repeatedly that "it's just not the same," echoing both sadness and a sometimes articulated sense of stigma related to "ending up" in a nursing home.

In my research, residents' perceptions of nursing home life often unfolded as stories, the substance of which was the ordinary trivialities associated with daily routines, individual worries and concerns, and residents' observations and insights about themselves and others. Common patterns representative of many accounts involved participants' struggles to retain a sense of personal freedom or autonomy at the same time that they sought to retain and/or regain connections with other people who could be relied upon in terms of both presence and support. Regardless of network type, residents' needs to achieve some sort of balance between personal attachment and autonomy were evident in the data. Several factors affected success in achieving such a balance. First, residents' personalities and social skills influenced the structure and function of their networks. So, for example, it is not surprising that the more gregarious and self-confident could maintain multiple relationships in balanced networks that tended to serve them well.

Second, ability to obtain resources and support through network linkages reflected past life experience. Therefore, some residents were more willing than others to seek and accept help. There were also differences in the conditions under which a resident might assume that help could be received, and preferred sources of assistance—selected friends, family members, or staff.

Changes in individual networks through loss of important relationships is a third factor related to successful balancing of residents' needs for attachment and autonomy. In this research, as in other studies that involve network typologies, there is evidence to suggest that some network types may develop out of other types in response to changes across individuals' life-spans. For example, the kin-centered network may be a transitional type out of which institution-centered, small cluster, or balanced networks evolve if residents become increasingly disengaged from kin ties as a result of diminished contact over time. Similarly, individuals could shift in any direction between having institution-centered, small cluster, or balanced networks in response to the effects of time, new opportunities for relationship formation, and loss of personal network members. Further study would be required to determine the likelihood and conditions under which some network types may evolve from others.

In summary, residents' perceptions of institutional culture were shaped by their experiences within different types of personal networks. Therefore, while it is possible to describe their perceptions of nursing home life in terms of their shared experience, it is also important to move beyond. The diversity of responses to the culture needs to be taken into account in evaluations of individual adjustment to the institutional setting, and the network typology offers a way to conceptualize diverse patterns of adjustment.

IMPLICATIONS FOR CLINICAL PRACTICE

Evaluation of residents' adjustments to institutional life tends to focus on compliance and agreement with the goals and motivations of staff. According to staff, the "well adjusted" person performs as much self-care as possible, reports needs and problems to staff, gets along with other residents, and participates in the social life of the institution. However, this view of adjustment does not accommodate many residents' attempts to deal with the setting. For example, staff insistence on self-care may be interpreted by some residents as rejection, at the same time that urging residents to report needs and problems may be in opposition to their desires for independence and privacy. Few residents in any network type reported that they could "get along" with everyone; networks contained their share of unwanted members. Finally, planned activities and social events can have different meanings for residents than they have for staff. The option to participate in the social life of the institution may be more important than participation per se.

What does this mean for clinical practice? The view from the inside out accepts and values difference. It is the homogenizing effect of institutions that belies the heterogeneity of residents by dealing with them in a fairly uniform manner. This makes it difficult for staff and residents alike to overcome prevailing notions about the meaning of "adjustment" in terms of how residents should behave and present themselves. The study reported here describes different ways in which individuals in institution-centered, small cluster, kin-centered, and balanced types of networks appeared to adjust to nursing home life. It also invites appreciation of variety in individuals' actions and concerns without labeling particular network types as more or less functional or socially acceptable. This way of thinking about differences expands narrow formulations of what constitutes a "good adjustment" by placing the emphasis on the way people are instead of the way it would be convenient for them to be.

On occasion, I have been asked what nursing home staff members think about the findings of this research, which I have shared. I have found that people who care for the institutionalized elderly often want to share their own experiences with residents of whom they were reminded by the anecdotes embedded in my reports. Allowing participants' voices to be heard through frequent use of direct quotations and personal accounts to illustrate a point is characteristic of the anthropologist's craft and of the ethnographer's commitment to the emic perspective, otherwise known as the insider's point of view. Sometimes these voices alone evoke a response. But the work of ethnography is not complete without the etic perspective, the researcher's outside interpretation of people's actions in the context of their particular situation. In this project, inferences about generalized patterns of adjustment to the nursing home setting were drawn from descriptions of residents' interaction in social networks. These, in turn, were contrasted with staff's idealized notion of personal adjustment that most easily accommodates to the constraints of a highly regimented institutional system. At this level of discussion, what nursing home employees seem to identify with most are descriptions of the system, that is, the cultural context. They recognize the nature of nursing home environments and the sorts of problems that residents have with them. From their own vantage points, they as well as residents must deal with routines, rules, and regulations. They react to residents' stories with murmurs of sympathy for the beleaguered and chuckles of support for the assertive residents who challenge the system. Though from another place and time, the stories are familiar to them. I am not aware of staff who have, as some people have supposed, viewed the researcher's interpretations and conclusions as criticism of themselves. However I feel compelled to respond briefly to these assumptions that fellow anthropologists and others outside of the health-related fields have voiced to me. Why should commentaries on residents' views and relationships be seen by some in terms of reprimanding nursing home staff?

I spoke earlier of the importance of separating the nurse and researcher roles for the purposes of conducting the research. I speak now both as nurse and anthropologist in the reporting of it. Nursing homes have received a lot of negative press over the years, in the professional literature as well as in the media. Some of it has been deserved, but that history tends to overshadow the efforts of caring professionals who seek to make a difference. The ones who take the time to talk to me about this research are the caring kind. Further, they do not identify tensions between the unique, human needs of individuals and the regulated, operational issues pertaining to systems as personal criticisms. They already know that (1) sometimes what we say we do about individualizing care and what we actually do within the health care system turn out to be different, and (2) sometimes we may take a position on how clients need to be to survive and do well in certain subsystems, such as nursing homes, even though it may serve some clients' needs better than others. Nursing home administrators and staff deal with dilemmas of residential life on a daily basis. However, it would be unfair and misleading to assume that the causes of and solutions to the problems of institutional living rest solely with them.

Residents together with the people in their networks, which include nursing home administrators and staff, must be perceived as partners in search of ways to improve the conditions of what, in any circumstance, is not an ideal situation. Nursing homes are not nice places in which to live. For residents, there is little privacy and personal space. One is forced to tolerate numerous annoyances, inconveniences, and impositions. Opportunities for autonomy are limited. It is easy to become bored and restless. For staff, nursing homes are not always nice places in which to work. Research of all types provides one avenue toward identifying approaches that may increase the satisfaction of those who live and work in nursing homes. Qualitative studies, such as nursing home ethnographies (Gubrium 1975, 1993; Kayser-Jones 1981; Laird 1979; Savishinsky 1991; Shield 1988), have the potential to clarify and help solve human dilemmas by providing both descriptive and analytical substance as well as opportunity for reflection.

Criteria have been developed that may be used to judge the quality of the work (Altheide and Johnson 1994; Guba and Lincoln 1981; Leininger 1994; Sandelowski 1986). Some evaluative criteria relate to ethnographic methods and reporting styles. *Contextualization*, for example, involves the portrayal of people's ideas, experiences, and the meanings that those have for them within their total environment. The cultural context in ethnographic work is what makes the data understandable. *Patterning* refers to recurring events, experiences, or lifeways (sometimes called themes) that are identifiable in the data across participants over time. *Confirmability* refers to the validity of accumulated evidence, obtained primarily through participant observation and interviews, that is used to support the researcher's interpretations. Researchers use varied approaches to confirm or validate evidence in the field, such as systematically repeating questions and restating ideas to which participants respond, verifying interpretations with participants, and using different data sources or different methods that serve the study purposes. *Credibility* and *transferability* are evaluative criteria that depend on reader/listener response to the report. For example, the research is credible when other people can recognize and relate to a situation on the basis of what the researcher has written about it. Transferability happens when the meanings, interpretations, and inferences from research findings can be transferred to other, similar environmental contexts and human situations. Colleagues who have engaged me in conversation about similarities of experience with other elderly people in different nursing homes provide important validation of the research [see also Vesperi, this volume]. The application to practice comes through intentional reflection upon and interpersonal dialogues about qualitative texts that produce insights about specific situations and aid in recognition of or increasing sensitization to issues in particular environments. Such activities, in turn, stimulate clinical problem solving.

I have spoken about the responses of two types of audiences for this research—professionals from health-related and non-health-related fields who are mainly nurses and anthropologists, respectively. But what of the residents themselves, and their families? I did not, in fact, report back directly to this group, though in the fieldwork interviews, I reflected with residents about my understandings of what they were teaching me about their world as a means of clarifying and validating information.

There is another group to be considered as well. A presentation of my research for an audience of mostly student nurses and their families focused on residents' experiences with the everyday dilemmas of nursing home life. Topics included the use of public and private space, reactions to rules and regulations, experiences with roommates and tablemates, obtaining and distributing goods and services, and dealing with issues of privileges and restraints. As I was leaving the auditorium, I heard someone say, "There she is," and soon I was being introduced to the parents and siblings of one of the students, who all expressed an eagerness to talk with me. "We're so excited," I was told. "We can hardly wait to get home and tell our mother [grandmother] what you said. She's been telling us all of these stories about what goes on in the nursing home where she is [in another state]. And, she will be so happy to know that the people in nursing homes here have the same stories. We think that sometimes she thinks we don't believe her. Well, we sure do believe her now! You don't know what it means to us. . . . We just wanted to thank you."

What does this response signify? The key is in the statement, " You don't know what this means to us." For narratives about what life is like in nursing homes contain subjective meanings that transcend particular circumstances. In other words, the stories from the research, though rooted in the experience of specific individuals, become, in the telling, a kind of communication that is not necessarily limited to one setting. Therefore, they can and do have meaning to an elderly nursing home resident and her family in another state, far removed from the residents I interviewed.

The products of ethnographic research may be used in a variety of ways. However, generally, the application of the results is of a conceptual nature. Earlier in this paper I commented that the ethnographer's task is one of describing what everybody already knows. But do we truly know it all? More importantly, how do we come to know what it is that we think we know? (Husserl 1965, 1970; Turner and Bruner 1986; Van Manen 1990). I reflect often on what I have learned from elderly institutionalized people. I also reflect on the family described above. They know some things about the experience from the inside out that are the essence of lessons yet to be learned about how nursing homes can become nicer places in which to live and work. Through the telling, acknowledging, and reflecting upon the experiences, we engage in moral activity that pushes us to move beyond descriptions of what nursing home life is to prescribe and actualize what it can and should be.

12

Continuities and Discontinuities in the Life Course: Experiences of Demented Persons in a Residential Alzheimer's Facility

Myrna Silverman and Carol McAllister

This chapter describes, in a qualitative way, the continuities and discontinuities in the lives of a group of demented persons now residing in a
residential Alzheimer's facility in the context of their experiences, social
roles, interests, and personalities. Also, it examines the use of the life-course
perspective on a population of institutionalized and demented older individuals. Last, it describes a qualitative system of data collection that enables
anthropologists and others to obtain life-course data on a population with
limited cognitive and communication skills.[1]
    "Fairhaven" is a 36-bed residential Alzheimer's facility licensed as a
personal care home which is designed for persons with mild to moderate
dementia. (The name of the facility and the names of all individuals are
pseudonyms. When the experiences of a single resident are used to illustrate more than one point, the resident's identity is further protected by
assigning a different name in each case example.) Fairhaven and its philosophy of care differ in several significant ways from most traditional nursing
homes or personal care homes in their treatment of demented persons. The
facility is organized into three separate houses that each contain twelve
beds, a small kitchen, dining room, living room, and outdoor patio. The
three houses are, in turn, connected to other common rooms and a wander-
ing path. Fairhaven provides an environment that has been designed to
better accommodate demented residents and allow for greater flexibility
and freedom of choice in their daily lives, a program that has been designed

to focus on the residents' individual needs and time schedules and to promote residents' independence and autonomy, including their participation in self-care, and a treatment regimen that discourages confinement of the resident and overuse of medications.

In July 1991, a multidisciplinary team of researchers led by Myrna Silverman, an anthropologist, and also representing neuropsychology, architecture, and health services research, was contracted to conduct an evaluation of this model of care. The goals of the evaluation were to assess the effectiveness of this approach as compared to care provided by a traditional nursing home. Realizing the difficulties of assessing the extent to which characteristics of autonomy and independence were expressed in a basically non-communicative population, we designed an evaluation that would incorporate the observational and interviewing skills of an anthropologist, in addition to the use of structured instruments designed to track changes in the behavior, function, and mental status of each of the 36 residents over a period of three years. We felt that the use of an ethnographic approach would allow us to better address research questions such as: How does dementia and institutionalization facilitate and limit the continuity of lifetime roles and expressions of self? To what extent does this specialized program and environment enable demented individuals to continue with patterns of activities and interests developed prior to the onset of the disease?

BACKGROUND

This study involves three bodies of literature: ethnographic research on nursing homes, qualitative or ethnographic studies of persons institutionalized with dementia, and studies using a life-course perspective in regard to aging and chronic illness.

Ethnographic studies of nursing home populations have become more common in the past few years. Studies such as Gubrium's (1975), Kayser-Jones's (1981), Tisdale's (1987), Shield's (1988), Savishinsky's (1991), Lidz, Fischer, and Arnold's (1992), and Diamond's (1992), have used standard ethnographic techniques to describe in general the environment and daily life of patients and staff in these settings. These studies have enriched the field of long term care by bringing to life the personalities, needs, constraints, and cross-cultural differences of patients and staff in these environments. Other studies have focused on specific problems in the nursing home environment by using the ethnographic method (Henderson 1981; Kayser-Jones 1981; Vesperi 1987; and Lidz, Fischer, and Arnold 1992) and point to the usefulness of this methodology for capturing sensitive information.

In contrast, studies of institutionalized demented persons are not common. Goffman's *Asylums* (1961) and Henry's *Pathway to Madness* (1971), while useful for the methodology, focus more on the theme of insanity and psychiatric problems and their treatment in an institution rather than on the "normality" of life in such facilities. It has been more typical, particularly in the field of gerontology, to study the effect of dementia on the caregiver (George and Gwyther 1986; Morycz 1985; Pratt, Schmall, Wright, and Cleland 1985; Orona 1990; Stephens, Kinney, and Ogrocki 1991). One recent study has addressed the perspective of the patient with Alzheimer's disease (Cotrell and Schulz 1993) and the need to direct our attention to the feelings, thoughts, and reactions of this population. In fact, studies of older adults and their perceptions of their lives have deliberately excluded this population from their sample in order to ensure the accuracy and comparability of the respondents. Research designed to study demented populations is generally conducted indirectly through surrogate respondents or through observational techniques that are non-interactive (Beck and Heacock 1988; Cohen-Mansfield, Werner, and Marx 1989; Orona 1990; Clark and Bowling 1990; Burgener, Jirovec, Murrell, and Barton 1992; Burgio et al. in press). We do not know of studies other than ours that have attempted to use both direct and indirect methods to describe and analyze the experiences of demented persons.

Similarly, studies using a life-course perspective on aging populations have focused more on the "normal" persons living in the community (Myerhoff 1978), although recently researchers have begun to examine the life-course perspective of persons experiencing a chronic illness (Becker 1993; Schulz and Rau 1985; Kaufman 1986; Rubinstein 1990; Robinson 1990; Gerhardt 1990; Conrad 1990). Disruption in the life course of an older person and the implications for enabling continuity or causing discontinuity is the theme of Becker's study (1993). Becker undertook a study of 100 stroke survivors in order to expand on Atchley's (1989) formal theory of continuity, which is based on the premise that middle-aged and older adults make adaptive choices in an attempt to preserve and maintain the internal and external structure of their lives. This study is an example of the discontinuities that occur among older people who are experiencing the effects of a critical medical problem. Through interviews with stroke survivors and participant observation of hospital rehabilitation wards and patient–practitioner interaction, Becker (1993:152) views stroke as a "profound disruption to their lives, destroying the fabric of predictable, everyday life." This study is certainly a marker in the field of studies of the aging and the life course. However, none of the respondents in the Becker study were cognitively impaired.

With the loss of memory and community residence experienced by the participants in Fairhaven, we might assume that opportunities for and the likelihood of continuity in the life course would be greatly diminished. The possibility of examining continuities and discontinuities in the life course of a demented population, particularly in a context which has been designed to foster continuity, provides the focus of this study. Complicating the situation is the extent to which the course of the disease affects a person's ability to continue activities experienced as worthwhile prior to the onset of the disease. The extent to which there is continuity in behavior among the demented residents may cause us to rethink some of the earliest concepts of the life course (Neugarten 1969, 1979), which suggest that continuity depends on memory and that memory aids in the interpretation of life so that continuity is fostered. Our study also provides insight into the impact of environmental and programmatic design on demented residents' abilities to maintain a degree of social continuity and sense of self. As far as we know, there have not been any studies examining the life-course transitions of persons with dementia, including those living in a residential care facility.

METHODS

Carol McAllister served as the ethnographer on this project. Ethnographic data collection was done by participant observation and interviews. Initially, systematic participant observation of daily life in Fairhaven was used, with a focus on the activity patterns of the residents as well as the overall workings of the facility. Such observation took place over different periods of the day and night, on both weekdays and weekends, and averaged 15 to 20 hours a week. Carol regularly joined in group activities planned for the residents, shared meals with residents in their dining rooms, and spent time informally socializing with residents either individually or in small groups. She also accompanied the residents on field trips and, when requested, helped them with their daily care. Such regular participation in their lives enabled her to become familiar with the residents and for them and the staff to adjust to her presence. Since there is an absence of specialized staff clothing or uniforms in this non-traditional facility, and since there are frequent visits to the facility by family and professionals, Carol's role as observer was relatively unobtrusive. In fact, she was generally able to blend into the group and was treated by residents as either a fellow resident or as a familiar visitor.

Such intensive participant observation allowed Carol to closely observe the way the residents themselves react to various aspects of Fairhaven's program as well as their relationships with each other and with the staff. Carol also found that she was able to establish some form of communication with most of the residents. Sometimes this consisted of largely nonverbal exchanges, while in other cases she could carry out extensive conversations with residents. Such informal talks became an important part of the research and contributed significantly to our understanding of resident experiences. In particular, these conversations or resident narratives provided insights into residents' own perspectives on both their past lives and their present situations.

Near the end of the first year of research, case studies of 8 of Fairhaven's 36 residents were designed in order to achieve a more in-depth understanding of the experiences of individuals. The selection of cases was based on differences in mental status as measured by Folstein's Mini-Mental Status Examination (MMSE) (1975). The cases were selected from clusters of high (15–24), medium (8–14), and low (0–7) scores on the MMSE, in combination with high or low levels of socioeconomic status and social supports. Factors such as gender, ethnicity, age, and general activity level were also taken into account in order to select a sample of individuals who represented the social diversity found in the Fairhaven facility.

The case studies attempted to describe each individual's personality and social roles before developing Alzheimer's disease, and how the disease affected his or her personality and behavior. Within the context of the residential Alzheimer's facility, the case study approach allowed an in-depth exploration of the daily experiences and patterns of activity of each of the eight residents. This included a description of the kinds of social interactions they engaged in with other residents, staff, and visitors; their use of the physical environment; and their participation in both formally organized programs and informal events that make up the rhythm of daily life at Fairhaven. Attention was paid to ways in which each resident continued to engage in activities or interests important in their earlier years and the vehicles through which they expressed personal preferences and a sense of personal history.

The case study format was also used to integrate data from other sources into the ethnographic research. This included structured tracking of the health of the residents and formal interviews of family caregivers being carried out by another researcher on the evaluation team. These family interviews were conducted first when the resident entered the facility, then again 6 and 18 months later. They were particularly useful in obtaining background history on the eight residents, and family members' assessment of ongoing changes in the residents' lives. Through an integration of these different sources of information, the case studies would provide a life history of eight of the residents, examine how the disease affected them, and produce a detailed analysis of their experiences while living at Fairhaven.

All of Carol's observations were recorded in a field notebook. Reports on these observations to other members of the research team provided the opportunity for comparison and verification, and the linking of other data sets to enrich the ethnographic interpretation. Additional information used to clarify and verify such direct observations included Carol's participation in care conferences reviewing the residents' care, informal discussions with staff, formal staff interviews concerning their work with residents, and informal conversations with family members. Such multiple data sources were particularly useful where controversial issues arose to aid in developing interpretation and conclusions. Occasional feedback reports by Carol to Fairhaven staff and administrators on her findings, and the opportunity for comment and critique of our interpretations and conclusions, has provided a reflexive and interactive system of data collection and analysis.

During our first two and a half years of ethnographic research at Fairhaven, we focused on three main themes. Our first goal was to gain an understanding of the general patterns of daily living in this residential Alzheimer's facility and how these relate to the overall organization of the facility. Second, we were interested in seeing to what degree a community formed among the residents and staff of Fairhaven, how such a community developed and changed, and the kinds of resident interactions and relationships this entailed. Third, we wanted to assess the extent to which residents could continue to maintain and express social roles that were important to them earlier in their lives and the degree of autonomy or independence they could achieve in the context of a residential care facility. While these themes are closely related, our focus in this article is on the extent to which the specialized program and environment of Fairhaven enables demented individuals to continue with patterns of activity and interests developed prior to the onset of the disease. Our primary concern here is with both the facilitation and the limitation of the continuity of lifetime roles and expression of self by the context of institutionalized living.

FINDINGS

Development of Social or Community Roles

The opportunity to express lifetime roles and self takes different forms, depending on the context of the living environment. For institutionalized persons, the development of a community within the institution may be a stimulus for the expression of these roles and the activities associated with them, much as this is the case in the non-institutionalized world.

On the basis of extensive periods of participant observation, we argue that to a large extent a community came into being at Fairhaven that exhibited both functional and affective dimensions. While at first this newly created community seemed relatively undifferentiated, an important change gradually occurred with the emergence of distinct social roles among several of the residents. A good example occurred in conjunction with the development of an informal network that drew together a number of the women. This network was centered around a group of residents who lived together in the most centrally located wing, or "house," of the Fairhaven facility. It particularly revolved around two individuals whom we will call Norah and Charlotte. Lasting over the course of several months, the network had a certain structure but also a fluidity so that others could join in as well. It is difficult to determine the relative importance of the location/space versus the personalities of the residents in fostering this social development. It is clear, however, that Charlotte provided a kind of emotional node for the network, while Norah was its initiator and director of activity. Charlotte's ability to verbally communicate was fairly limited, but she had a wonderfully empathetic set of visual expressions and body language. She also had a knack for showing interest in what others were doing or saying. For example, she would often wave her cane in someone's direction or at an object of mutual interest, smiling and raising her eyebrows at the same time.

In contrast, Norah acted as the boss. She actively and assertively initiated interactions with other residents, staff, visitors, and even outside medical staff. One day Carol heard her say to a doctor who had come to examine another resident, "Oh, you're a doctor, well I was a teacher." She then continued to demand his attention as she told him in detail about her years of teaching. Norah's role became particularly clear when she was away from Fairhaven for about a week during a stay in the hospital. Her "group" kept going into her room looking for her and was reported by a care attendant to be "lost" without her. On her return, Norah quickly reasserted her role of directing activities among this network of residents—especially trying to initiate and sustain their walking and eating together, joining in or leaving activities as a unit.

It seems likely that the roles played by Charlotte and Norah in the evolving Fairhaven community were related to their earlier family and community roles, thus indicating considerable continuity of personal identity. Charlotte was the mother in a large family that appeared to depend on her to play the primary serving and caregiving role. For example, one day Carol was eating lunch with Charlotte and Norah when Charlotte—in disjointed though fairly comprehensible phrases—began describing to Norah how she had to wait on her husband and accommodate him. Norah's reaction was critical, with a blunt suggestion that Charlotte should have asserted herself and told her husband to wait on himself. In a way, this is what Norah did at Fairhaven. Norah was a school teacher for most of her life and, it appears, a remarkably competent and active one. She showed Carol a scrapbook that had clippings from the newspaper reporting on her involvement in various innovative educational programs. While obviously an organizer and director throughout much of her life, she was also well liked by her young students (this was clear from other clippings and cards in the scrapbook). This was the case at Fairhaven, too; Norah was a popular as well as an insistent leader.

Other residents have developed more explicit caregiving or nurturing roles in the context of Fairhaven's emerging community. For instance, during her first year of residence, a woman whom we will call Martha played a central part in daily housekeeping. She helped set the table, serve the food, and clean up after meals. She especially liked to wash the dishes by hand, not just rinse and put them in the dishwasher as desired by staff. Martha also folded clothes, swept the floor, and at night shepherded everyone into (or out of) her house in preparation for bed. She was usually the last to go to bed, "locking the door behind her." In this and other ways she acted as a kind of gatekeeper for her house. While all of these activities converged with the staff-determined routine of daily living, Martha also initiated her own homemaking and nurturing activities. For example, one night she facilitated a kind of "pajama party" in the kitchen area of her house. As other residents, dressed in nightwear, gathered around her, Martha made peanut butter sandwiches and handed them out to each individual in turn. For several months, Martha also "adopted" another resident in a mutually dependent and supportive relationship, alternately referring to this woman as her daughter or her mother. When this resident died, Martha attempted to develop similar relationships with other residents. During a certain period, other residents even came to Martha for information and help about housekeeping matters, asking when meals would be served or inquiring about available food in the refrigerator between meals.

According to Martha's daughters and sisters, this role is a direct continuation of Martha's previous caregiving role in both her natal and her conjugal family. One of her daughters told Carol about her mother's propensity to be over-protective of her children, a tendency she has carried over into her relationship with other residents. Martha married at age fifteen and lived for a long time with her in-laws, raising her first five children in three rooms. Martha has commented to the ethnographer on how she has worked all her life and how housework was much harder in the past. She especially mentions having to frequently wash the walls, probably in an attempt to control the constant inflow of soot from the steel mills. She then often adds, "It doesn't pay to do all this work." Martha's daughter indicates that the main change in her mother since she developed Alzheimer's disease has been an increase in anxiety about matters such as checking many times to see that the doors are locked, showing concern about meals and sleeping arrangements, or sending her daughter home almost as soon as she arrives to visit because she is worried about her traveling after dark.

Through interviews with and informal comments from care attendants, as well as our own observations of staff behavior, we learned that their reactions to Martha's homemaking and nurturing role varied. Some of the care attendants easily accepted it and integrated it into their own work routine; others, however, expressed impatience at Martha's insistence on "taking over" various tasks. They then tried to put Martha off so the tasks were organized more for the convenience of staff. For several months, Martha's close relationship with another resident, mentioned above, caused considerable upheaval and conflict among the staff and between the staff, on the one hand, and Martha and her family, on the other. Some care attendants felt that Martha was controlling the behavior of this other resident to the degree that it was interfering with her care and contributing to her cognitive and functional decline. At times, staff even intervened to try to separate these two women and to block their own choice to spend time together.

There are, however, other cases where conflicts resulting from residents' assertion of former roles and personality traits have been more creatively handled and defused by the administrative and caregiving staff, as seen in the case of Sadie:

Beginning around Thanksgiving, Sadie began to exhibit much more agitated and anxious behavior. She was often upset, paced around the facility, and was very restless. This sometimes reached the point where she was wringing her hands, her hands and jaws were shaking, she was becoming red in the face, and breathing in a labored manner. . . . One issue that particularly upset Sadie concerned her money, or more generally, her access to resources and financial security.

Sadie was concerned about several things. The first was where her Social Security checks were going. One day she asked Carol if she received *her* Social Security checks at Fairhaven. Sadie indicated she had not received any checks since she had been living there and was worried about where they were being sent. Perhaps they were being sent to her home in a nearby town, but then how could she get them? She was then worried about whether she would have money at Fairhaven to pay for things she needed, including her room there. She also wanted to make sure she had enough money to get home later. In addition, Sadie thought that she had put $300 under her mattress but that someone had taken it because the money was no longer there. She raised these concerns over and over with Carol, staff, and other residents.

Sadie's anxieties about finances were handled in several ways. First, the staff tried to explain to her where her checks went, that everything at Fairhaven was already paid for, and that no one had stolen her money from under her mattress. Sadie, however, was not reassured and continued to press on these matters. During this period she was also seen by a psychiatrist, who ordered a change of medication. The staff became increasingly frustrated by Sadie's anxiety and constant questioning about these matters, which, however, would be very reasonable concerns in the "outside world." Finally, the office secretary wrote Sadie a fictitious letter from the president of her bank which explained that her checks are deposited there, that the $300 was also sent there, that the bank is taking care of all her financial concerns, and that some money has been sent to the Fairhaven office to be kept in their safe if she needs any small amounts of cash. Sadie was more reassured by this letter, which she now carries around with her most of the time, showing it to Carol, to staff, and to other residents. However, she was upset that the Fairhaven office had not told her before that they had money there for her. Sadie continues to be concerned about these matters but refers often to her letter, either reading it to herself or out loud to others, which seems to ease her anxieties somewhat.

Sadie's concern about money reflects not only a psychological tendency toward anxiety but also her previous role as financial manager for her family of fourteen, whom she effectively fed, clothed, and housed on her husband's modest salary as a carpenter. The same is true of Martha's zealous pursuit of housework and her protective and controlling behaviors toward other residents and toward her "house." In the case of Sadie, staff were able to develop a creative response that lessens the burden on them in dealing with resident anxiety while at the same time allowing Sadie to continue to feel that she is dealing with key concerns in her life, including that of managing money. In the case of Martha, the resolution has not been so positive. Perhaps this is because Martha's role continuity involves a number of interlocking dimensions, several of which come into conflict with the roles of staff themselves. Staff become frustrated when they perceive Martha interfering with their own housekeeping work or with their care of other residents. As a result, a power struggle developed between Martha and several of the staff. This, along with Martha's declining capacities, may help explain her gradual withdrawal from housekeeping roles and her more anxious responses to other residents in subsequent months.

Continuity of Specialized Skills and Interests

When we begin to address the question of how much residents are able to continue more specialized skills and interests, the picture becomes more problematic and complex than continuities in common social roles. Only a few residents continue to carry out activities related to their previous work roles or their life-long hobbies. This may be, in part, because they no longer remember the specific skills required in such activities, although competency in social interactions persists. It may also reflect a lack of opportunity in the organized program of Fairhaven to facilitate and encourage such activities and skills, especially when this would require adaptation to the residents' declining cognitive and functional abilities. The gardening program provides a good example of this dilemma.

The first spring and summer after the facility opened, Fairhaven had a gardening program in which the activities director and a small number of residents planted and cared for a very productive and beautiful garden. For the residents who actively participated in this program, primarily two individuals, it provided a sense of accomplishment and responsibility and kept alive a role they had enjoyed earlier in their lives. For one of these residents, a man who had been seriously depressed and alienated from the life of the facility for several months previous, the garden provided a vehicle to both shift his psychological state and to integrate him more into the existing social community. However, the majority of residents had little to do with the planting or upkeep of the garden. In large part, this was because they no longer had the cognitive skills to carry out the tasks of gardening in any kind of independent fashion or to responsibly care for a garden in an ongoing way. This is the case in spite of the fact that gardening had been an activity and interest of many of the residents before they developed Alzheimer's and moved to Fairhaven.

The next spring, however, the gardening program was reorganized so that more residents could participate. In particular, the activities director worked with a number of the more impaired residents on an individual basis, guiding them through the basic steps of seed planting and then caring for the growing seedlings. The emerging plants were also frequently brought into other group activities, such as the daily morning gathering, and used as materials to encourage reminiscing and awareness of one's immediate environment. This reorganization of the activities program allowed more residents to participate—at different levels and in different ways—in an activity or role that was important earlier in their lives. However, after the seedlings were transplanted into the outside garden, resident involvement again sharply declined. A way to effectively involve residents of different abilities in this activity in an ongoing and meaningful way has not yet been found.

While activities such as gardening may be important in maintaining or reactivating certain practical skills, they are equally important in the maintenance or reactivation of a sense of self and self-worth. Such activities and the practice of specialized skills also provide a context for remembering and recounting important aspects of residents' personal history. This is illustrated in the case study of Kate:

During her first year and a half at Fairhaven, Kate spent most of her time alternating between participation in organized group activities and doing things on her own. One of the things she did on her own was to crochet. This was quite significant, since Kate was the only resident at Fairhaven who engaged in such a craft activity on a regular basis and on her own initiative. While many of the other women were very skilled at crocheting, knitting, or doing embroidery before they moved to Fairhaven, no one except Kate continued these activities at Fairhaven. Using variegated yarn and one simple stitch—a double crochet—Kate produced rather large multi-colored afghans. She tended to work steadily, turning out several inches a day until she ran out of yarn, which she called "thread." The yarn was supplied by one of Kate's daughters and the afghans were then given as gifts to her children and grandchildren. At one point, there was a problem with Kate's "thread" which kept disappearing, probably into the rooms and closets of other residents. This was a source of frustration to both Kate and her daughters, who then asked the staff to keep the yarn for her. Kate also frequently laid down her crocheting and forgot where she put it. Then there was a scurry among staff to help her find it.

Kate's crocheting in and of itself was important. What is equally interesting and significant is the way the process of crocheting and the afghans she produced seemed to stimulate Kate's memories of earlier periods in her life. This is seen most clearly through the stories she told while she sat crocheting. Kate usually did her crocheting while sitting along the front windows or in other well-traveled corridors of the facility. Though she sometimes occupied other spaces while engaged in this activity, these were the most common. Kate did not necessarily seek out others when she sat down to crochet, but others frequently came and sat by her. They then ended up watching her, talking with her, or just sitting side-by-side silently enjoying each other's company. Whenever Carol sat down beside her, Kate usually began to talk, often about various events and people in her earlier life.

Kate's stories covered a range of subjects. She often began by talking about the afghans themselves—how she had made so many, first for her children and then for her grandchildren, or how her children and husband each liked to wrap up in their own afghan to lie around watching TV. Other residents, staff and visitors frequently admired her work and Kate then offered to make them afghans as well. Talking about her afghans often led Kate to other stories about her family. She talked about her children and her feelings about several of them moving so far away, especially to California. She talked about her daughter who died. Several times she has shown Carol this daughter's doll and large framed picture which are kept in her bedroom. Kate also showed Carol photographs of her other children and her husband. She talked about her husband's death and how she misses him.

Kate has also shared some very interesting details of her family history. For example, one day Carol encountered her standing in the entry-way of her house talking with a couple of care attendants about changes in women's work. While staff and residents at Fairhaven frequently interact, this was one of the few times they were observed in such extended conversation, mutually exchanging experiences and impressions from their personal lives. In the course of this conversation, Kate described the boarding house which her mother owned and managed in a nearby small town. A month or so later, when she was sitting crocheting along the front windows, Kate talked more about this boarding house, mostly in response to Carol's questions. At the same time, Kate described her father's work as a coal miner and her husband's as a carpenter. Hard work—her own and others—seems to be an important part of Kate's self-identity. At times, these stories became more personal and painful, such as when she talked about her father's drinking problem and abuse of her mother, and his finally taking a vow with the parish priest to give up alcohol. In a somewhat lighter vein, Kate has repeatedly described her father's initial negative reaction then subsequent acceptance of her choice of a husband outside their own ethnic group. She notes that her mother was always more supportive of her marital choice. As her mother commented, "At least you're of the same religion and he goes to church!" Ethnic differences enter in again as Kate describes her husband's nightly visits to a local club to talk with his buddies while slowly sipping a single beer. She indicates she went there only for dances, something she really liked to do. This helped in understanding how Kate developed her skills as a polka dancer, which she frequently displays during the dance-parties at Fairhaven.

Through both her crocheting and her storytelling prompted by the crocheting, Kate was connecting her present activities and sense of self to her family history and long-standing personal roles.

It is more difficult to assess the self-identity and experience of role continuity of those residents whose bent is not so much toward the caregiving and traditionally female roles that characterize daily life in Fairhaven. However, some of these individuals had strong professional identities that they continued to exert, although in a largely fantasized way. For example, Leonard was a practicing lawyer until shortly before his admission to Fairhaven. For most of the time he lived at this facility, he could be found going around looking for and trying to unlock his "office door." He likewise imagined himself going up and down elevators and writing and discussing briefs with his "clients" (i.e., the staff and other residents). Thomas, another Fairhaven resident, had been an obstetrician for most of his life. He regularly talked about going to professional meetings and often tried to structure his days around such commitments. He stated that he had reduced his practice to part-time while he continued to consult with visitors and volunteers whom he treated as his professional colleagues. Nellie worked as a secretary in several different cities in the U.S. She also appears to have spent considerable time traveling, including several trips abroad. Nellie frequently treats the facility as a neighborhood or urban village environment in which she systematically goes to various locations for meeting friends, drinking a cup of coffee, getting an ice cream, or even waiting for a bus. She later talks at length about what she saw and experienced on her travels.

In the case of these three residents, role continuity exists, but not through the maintenance of specific skills or through the recounting of life experiences brought to mind by activities actually involving those skills. Rather, the continuity consists of an *imagined* engagement in forms of work or activity that were central to the resident's previous life. While an institutional setting might provide opportunities for the continuation of home-based hobbies, such as crocheting or woodworking, it is more difficult to create opportunities for the continuation of actual professional roles or roles that require active use of a wider environment. In a non-demented population, such continuity might be fostered through opportunities to recount and pass on to others the knowledge and experiences acquired in a person's professional roles or travels. Among demented individuals a more typical response appears to be the continuation of such roles or activities in a fantasized way.

For example, among the three individuals described above, frequent expressions of frustration have been observed when either the physical environment or the behavior of others constrain the acting out of these imagined roles. Some of the other residents respond negatively when Leonard treats them as his clients. They become irritated and openly dismissive of his approach to them. This, in turn, generates frustration and sometimes anger on Leonard's part. For Nellie, frustration arises largely from the constraints of the physical environment—the bus doesn't come, the ice cream shop isn't where it is supposed to be, and she sometimes can't find either her friends waiting for her or her way home. The situation of Thomas is even more complex. His medical role involved caring for predominantly female patients. It probably also fostered an expectation that such patients would follow his advice and direction, and defer to his more specialized knowledge and experience. At Fairhaven, Thomas sometimes attempted to realize both the caring and control aspects of the doctor–patient relationship. However, in actuality the roles were reversed, in that younger female staff were both caring for him and also expecting him to at least cooperate with them, if not to follow their direction. The result was a considerable degree of conflict between Thomas and several of the care attendants. His frustration and anger were often expressed by explicitly negative characterizations of women, especially those responsible for his daily care.

Over the past year, Kate began to crochet less and less often until she completely ceased this activity and the patterns of socializing it involved. At the same time, her expressions of agitation, distress, and depression have intensified. The challenge here is for the Fairhaven staff and program to find alternative ways for Kate and residents like her to express themselves given their declining abilities to maintain long-standing hobbies. For residents like Leonard, Nellie, and Thomas, the challenge is even greater. It involves the development of environmental and programmatic features that accommodate the fantasized continuation of previous roles while at the same time reducing the frustrations involved when those roles cannot be fully realized.

Meeting these challenges will most likely require an increase in individualized programming, something that is difficult given common living space for 36 residents and limited staff. Some recent improvisations by the staff represent attempts to address this issue. For example, care attendants have offered baby dolls to a number of residents, several of whom responded with interest. While the use of dolls and other children's toys is controversial in the field of geriatric care, Fairhaven residents appear to use the dolls to reenact their roles of parenting and nurturing as well as soliciting attention and interest from others. For residents like Leonard, Nellie, and Thomas, opportunities to talk about their professions, the education involved in their training, and the travels such schooling and work took them on seem especially important. Carol found that it was during such conversations with her that these three individuals appeared both actively connected to their former lives and less frustrated about their present situation. The key, though, is to find ways to integrate such opportunities for individualized self-expression and continuity into the daily program of facilities like Fairhaven.

Sex, Race, and Social Continuity

A particularly interesting and complex form of role continuity involves resident expressions of sexual and racial or ethnic identities. It is now generally recognized that people continue to be sexual beings and may experience sexual desires and an identity as a sexual person throughout their lives. The loss of sexuality is not a characteristic of Alzheimer's disease. There is even some evidence that the disease may lead to increased sexual needs and drives. However, sexuality in American society is very much a social and cultural construction, surrounded by various prohibitions as well as encouragements. Much of the sociocultural aspects of sexuality may be lost or changed by the progressive cognitive impairment caused by Alzheimer's. This, in turn, may result in a release for the individual from certain longstanding taboos or inhibitions—such as sex outside of marriage or between individuals of the same gender—at the same time as it may create new social problems as people violate community sexual norms. Adding the context of institutionalized living, which provides new opportunities for the development of sexual relations but also entails its own set of taboos and barriers, creates additional levels of complexity.

Within the community context of Fairhaven, a number of residents developed close relationships with each other that involved a fair degree of both emotional and physical intimacy, if not an explicitly sexual dimension. Such intimacy included spending long hours together, helping with each other's care, expressing various forms of physical affection, and sometimes sharing sleeping quarters. In a few cases, residents developed relationships that were more explicitly sexual in nature. All of these relationships were mutually chosen and appeared to have positive meaning for the residents involved.

However, the reactions of staff and family members to these relationships were not consistently favorable. Three examples illustrate some of the problems that emerged. First, there is the case in which a relationship between two women which had a familial character was identified by some of the staff as sexual. This misperception on the part of staff resulted in part from their lack of awareness of diverse living patterns. For example, among working class families in an earlier period of American history, it was common for family members to share a bed. Some care attendants were very uncomfortable with this behavior and actively attempted to disrupt it and separate the women involved. The second example involves a case in which staff "discovered" two residents engaged in sexual intercourse. When family members were told about this relationship they became very upset, in part because their parent was involved with another resident who was still married. Active intervention by the family ended this relationship, leading to considerable distress on the part of the residents involved. Finally, there is a case in which the sexual activity of a resident became very aggressive and assertive. While there was no evidence that other residents were being forced into sexual activity against their will, staff felt this resident's "uncontrolled" sexuality was potentially harmful to others. This eventually resulted in the removal of this resident from the facility and placement in a more restrictive environment.

In all of these cases, there is a fundamental contradiction. On the one hand, as a result of both their dementia and the institutional arrangements in which they are living, several Fairhaven residents have found themselves able to engage more readily in self-chosen intimate and sexual relations. At the same time, their choices often result in misunderstandings, social disapproval, and attempted control by others. As a result, their sexual and intimate relationships, and thus their continued involvement in sexual and affectional roles, have the potential to generate considerable pain and lead to further restrictions on their lives.

There is a similar, though not identical, dynamic in relation to the racial or ethnic identities of the facility's residents. There is one African-American resident at Fairhaven, a person who moved into the facility more than a year after it opened. Among the white residents, several different ethnicities are represented.

First of all, we can note that ethnicity remains an important aspect of personal identity for many of the Fairhaven residents. In fact, our ethnographic research indicates that this may be one of the expressions of self that is most salient and longstanding in spite of significant memory loss. There are a number of residents who frequently make reference to their own ethnic background either directly or through talking about the kinds of foods they know how to cook, the ethnic music they like, the ethnic-derived activities they like to engage in, such as dancing polkas, or their "real" names in their ethnic cultures (e.g., Maria rather than Mary). A few residents look for opportunities to speak their mother tongue with visitors, staff, or other residents and become quite excited when they can do this. Several residents are also aware of the ethnicity of others and show interest in this aspect of their lives. A good example of this involved the African-American resident who, during a music program, actively encouraged another resident to join in on an Italian song, commenting, "That's your music." In a few cases, Carol has had extended conversations with residents about their ethnicity and their assessment of ethnic identity and relations among others.

Continuity of ethnic and racial identities, however, also exhibits a contradictory character. In some cases, Fairhaven residents seem released from common social prejudices and barriers. They can relate with greater ease and respect across racial and ethnic lines. This is particularly striking in regard to the ready acceptance and genuine valuing of the African-American resident by most of the white residents. Could this be due to both the effect of dementia in loosening cultural taboos and prejudices and also the community environment that characterizes life in this facility? In other cases, however, residents seem to have lost the social mechanisms and cultural codes that keep ethnic and racial hostilities somewhat under control, rather than having left behind the hostilities or prejudices themselves. For example, at least two of the white residents at Fairhaven have expressed overt hostility toward the African-American resident, one instance involving explicit racial slurs.

The case study of Maggie captures some of the contradictory dynamics involved in the persistence of ethnic identity:

Maggie's own ethnic background is Irish, while her husband was Slovak. She has a positive relationship with Martin, an African-American man, who is also a resident at Fairhaven. Martin and Maggie are quite friendly, enjoying each other's company and frequently exchanging greetings and comments. They have explicitly identified each other as friends. Maggie, in turn, often comments to Carol about how nice Martin is. She then usually adds a comment about his race—not an intentionally negative comment but one that indicates she is very aware of this difference between them. For example, one day she told Carol how she found the inside of Martin's hands, which are light compared to his dark brown complexion, very interesting. More recently, Maggie was pointing out a picture of Martin. She commented, "He's a very nice man. He can't help it that he's Black, can he?"

Carol hesitated, then said, "I don't think it's better to be white than to be Black." Maggie thought for a moment, agreed, and then began to talk about being Irish and Slovak and the good and bad among all of us.

In Maggie's interactions with Hattie, ethnic difference provides a source of conflict and argument, rather than interest and positive affect. Maggie is of Irish descent, Hattie is of Middle-Eastern descent. During the first few months after they moved into Fairhaven, Maggie and Hattie seemed to be "friends." They spent a lot of time together, walking and talking. Early on, however, there were also some conflicts between them. For example, one day an argument ensued between the two women about Hattie's intention to walk home. Hattie insisted she always went to her mother's and sisters' home at night. Maggie disagreed and said that Hattie, like Maggie, lives at Fairhaven. The argument became verbally violent, with each shouting that the other was a liar and was hallucinating. As Maggie's face grew redder and redder and Hattie began to make some physically threatening moves, Carol intervened and walked Hattie over to her house, where dinner was just being served.

While this immediate situation was defused, conflicts between Maggie and Hattie continued with an almost constant undertone of Hattie ignoring and making digs at Maggie, who was still trying to be friends. Maggie was quite aware of this and discussed it with Carol several times. After a while, staff began to try to keep these two women apart.

The reason for the conflict between Hattie and Maggie is not clear. Hattie has told Carol to stay away from Maggie because she "touches dead bodies" and "works for an undertaker." Much of the expression of their conflict, however, takes the form of ethnic slurs. Hattie usually begins by referring to Maggie as a lazy Irishman who also drinks too much. She then goes on to attribute the same characteristics to Maggie's deceased husband. Maggie frequently responds by shouting that her husband was Slovak, not Irish, and then calling Hattie a "dumb Hunky." Staff usually have to intervene to end these exchanges and to take Maggie to another part of the facility. It is not entirely clear how much this personal conflict and staff reaction to it has limited Maggie's choices at Fairhaven.

Facilitators and Barriers

A number of factors at Fairhaven appear to encourage demented individuals to continue with patterns of activity and interests developed prior to the onset of the disease, and thus to facilitate the continuation and expression of important social roles and of a sense of self. We have only identified some of these factors at this point in the study, while others remain as suggestive ideas to follow up in future research. Underlying each of these factors is the basic philosophy of Fairhaven, which emphasizes resident autonomy and choice and the avoidance of the use of restraints, both chemical and physical.

Of particular importance are those aspects of the facility's program and environment that encourage the formation of community and the active participation of residents in social interaction. A critical variable in this regard is the flexibility of the activities program and its ability to evolve and adapt to the changing needs of the facility's residents. In the early months after the opening of Fairhaven, large group activities with a strong expressive dimension seemed important for integration of new residents and for initial community building. Such activities, like parties, dances, picnics, or Olympic events, may also play an ongoing function of periodic ritual reinforcement of group solidarity and community membership. After a while, however, meaningful interactions began to occur in a greater diversity of contexts and in smaller group activities, both planned and unplanned. Some of these new activities appeared more effective in encouraging both close relationships and a higher level of functioning than the attempt to involve all residents in a common group. They may also allow more expression of individual social roles and perhaps the development or reinforcement of specialized skills. Some of these activities, such as "reminiscence sessions" led by a volunteer, may also provide opportunities to recall, recount, and reenact one's personal history.

Over the course of Fairhaven's history, there has been growing though uneven attention to the scheduling of a diversity of small-scale activities and the increased inclusion of both care attendants and volunteers in the organized activities program. Care attendants have thus been given more responsibility for running groups and for more consciously interacting with residents in informal activities. Volunteers have become part of an "eating out" program in which four to five residents have lunch with a volunteer on a regular weekly basis. This diversification of activities also draws in other staff, including the beautician, cooks, and housekeeping personnel, and includes special activities, such as visits by children and young adults, playing with pets, and the organization of field trips outside of the facility itself.

Also of special interest are the factors that encourage the formation and maintenance of ongoing personal relationships. For it is through such relationships that some residents act out diverse social roles and may also experience a greater continuity of self in relation to the other. Most residents in an Alzheimer's facility probably can't remember each other in terms of a mental picture, nor can they actively seek each other out. Yet, when they come together as part of daily activities, they may recognize and respond to affective dimensions of their personalities experienced in previous interactions. It may be that these connections are facilitated by the clustering of residents' rooms in houses with separate dining facilities, on the one hand, and, on the other, by the pattern of movement throughout the facility that is encouraged by participation in both formal and informal activities. Thus the spatial location of residents is structured in diverse ways throughout the day, which may encourage the development of ongoing but flexible relationships with distinct role behavior.

One major question is how large a part staff, volunteers, and researchers play in helping to facilitate social interactions that are crucial for role expression among demented residents. Our observations indicate that most residents have frequent, substantial, and positive interactions with staff. In many cases, there is a very active relationship between a resident and one or more care attendants, a relationship that often serves as the primary vehicle for a resident to talk about herself, her past history, and her present sense of self. At first it appeared as if staff or volunteers played a key role in facilitating resident-to-resident interaction as well. For example, care attendants or volunteers often had to start groups of people walking and even walk with them for this activity to proceed. Similarly, at first Carol often found herself "translating" from one resident to another because they didn't seem able to have a conversation without a go-between. This changed over time for many of the residents who developed an ability to initiate and carry out such activities more independently, including the sharing of personal history and social observations. However, the facilitating and translating role of care attendants and other staff becomes crucial again as residents experience a significant decline in their cognitive abilities.

The ability of staff to engage in or facilitate such interactions depends in great part on the conceptualization and organization of their own work. Unlike the highly specialized and hierarchical staffing patterns of most long term care facilities, staff at Fairhaven play multiple and intersecting roles that require more of a teamwork approach. Care attendants, the primary direct care staff, help residents accomplish daily personal care (e.g., eating, bathing, and toileting), perform a number of homemaking chores (e.g., serving food and doing laundry and dishes), monitor residents for medical problems, and participate in the organized activities program, even overseeing some planned activities themselves. The work of each care attendant is organized around a group of twelve residents who live together in one of the three areas referred to as a "house." There is a focus on relationships, rather than on specific tasks, with an expectation that care attendants will be responsive to the emotional and social as well as physical needs of the residents.

We have also noticed some barriers or constraints to role continuity and expression of self. Some of these result from aspects of the facility or program that can change; others arise from the nature of the disease and unavoidable institutional responses. One such barrier involves hostile or fearful interactions among residents. Both of these reactions militate against positive social relationships and also inhibit personal expression and the actualization of desired roles. Some residents actively dislike each other and frequently fight, verbally if not physically. Sometimes these conflicts arise when residents are competing to exert a dominant role, for example, over homemaking activities, in the same physical and social space. We have also observed residents express jealousy over personal relationships and argue about matters such as ethnicity or religion or even different choices in terms of the activities program. A few residents show more general patterns of aggression toward other residents as well as toward staff and visitors. In other cases, residents who are particularly impaired are shunned by others, especially if they are assertive in their social interactions. There is also the related experience of unsuccessful interactions between individuals of widely varying competencies, resulting in feelings of frustration and anger. Another aspect of this is the confusion generated by residents' distorted perceptions of each other, ranging from simple misunderstandings of verbal communications to fantasies and hallucinations about what others are doing and saying. While the level of conflict among Fairhaven residents is probably not significantly greater than that found in a typical city neighborhood, because of their impaired cognitive and perceptual functioning they cannot employ the usual social mechanisms, including avoidance, to handle the conflict and to allow people to "be themselves."

A second barrier to maintaining a personal identity and a secure sense of self involves actual or anticipated violations of privacy and personal space. This particularly happens when residents wander into others' rooms. We very often see people looking into, going into, or being in others' rooms, including their bathrooms [see Gubrium, this volume]. Closed doors do not necessarily deter residents from entering a room. Sometimes they move things around in or out of others' rooms, or lie down on and fall asleep in others' beds. Such behavior is very upsetting to some residents who sometimes accuse others of threatening to physically violate them or of stealing from them, and who then withdraw from positive interactions with the actual or suspected perpetrators. We need to consider whether there are environmental or program changes that could mitigate this problem. The other side of this, however, is the tendency of at least some residents to more clearly define and claim their own space and then to share it with others on their own terms. This clearly is an important aspect of self-expression and self-determination of roles. For example, Carol is frequently invited into the rooms of several residents who then show her things on their walls and other personal artifacts that represent significant happenings in their lives. The same kind of self-presentation happens, though less frequently, among residents themselves.

A third barrier or constraint to self-expression and the experience of role continuity is created by certain responses of staff and family members to the behavior of residents. Some of these involve institutional policies, such as discouraging residents from answering or making calls on the phones in the house kitchens. Others result from staff frustrations and impatience when responding to residents' repeated questions or when working with residents who attempt to "take over" daily housekeeping tasks. Sometimes staff burnout and exhaustion result in a decreased ability to follow the inclinations and desires of residents and a tendency to impose a staff-directed pattern of activity instead. A major arena of conflict between some residents and staff is around the issue of food and eating. Staff concern over providing nutritional and balanced meals often runs counter to residents inclinations to eat what they like and to favor desserts and other kinds of sweets. Family members also sometimes try to prevent a resident from doing what they want and find comfortable. A particular barrier is created when family members or staff are not sensitive to the new relationships among residents and discourage the development of a long-standing role, such as companion, friend, or parent, among residents themselves.

A final constraint results from tendencies in the formal programming or in patterns of daily care that limit residents' opportunities for full expression of self. For example, some care attendants have told Carol that they do not feel they have sufficient time to just talk with residents about their past experiences or present concerns and feelings. This is because of the overall organization of their work and their responsibility for several tasks, such as laundry and light housekeeping, in addition to the personal care of residents. Staff also report that as increasing numbers of residents experience a significant decline in their cognitive abilities, they must devote more of their efforts to physical care, leaving even less time for conversation and socializing. Our own observations corroborate these limitations, although we have also noted that such interactions still occur much more frequently at Fairhaven than in the traditional nursing home setting we are also observing. We also have some questions about the organized activities program in terms of the range of emotional expressions it encourages and discourages. In particular, we have noted that the tendency of organized activities to encourage residents to feel happy and positive may in turn militate against opportunities for expressing feelings of sadness and loss.

Yet, these more "negative" emotions are also an important part of one's identity and sense of self. We thus see that some of the very positive aspects of the Fairhaven program, such as integrated staff roles and a lively activity program, may themselves entail certain limitations in their ability to facilitate self-expression and continuity.

EMERGING ISSUES AND QUESTIONS

There are a number of issues or questions related to the matter of role continuity and expression of self that have emerged in the daily life of Fairhaven over the course of its first two and a half years of operation. One issue is how to maintain the degree of role continuity and expression of self as described above in light of the declining capacities of many residents. There are even questions about whether this is possible. This issue is particularly important given the projection that most residents will continue to steadily decline over the course of their stay at Fairhaven. Such a decline in cognitive capacities, especially among several residents at once, decreases their own abilities to function as a community and to maintain some kind of connection with their past lives and roles. It also leads to growing concerns among the staff about resident safety—for example, kitchen appliances and food in the refrigerators are periodically locked away while some care attendants feel that resident access to kitchen areas should be limited to times when staff are present. These concerns and subsequent restrictions may come into conflict with the program's commitment to resident involvement in daily activities and the encouragement of continued expression of domestic and occupational roles. Declining resident capacities likewise place growing demands on the staff, who must devote more time to the physical care of residents at the same time as they are increasingly needed to facilitate resident interactions and to address residents' emotional and social needs.

This leads to the more general question of resident versus staff needs. The issue posed is how to meet both sets of needs in an integrated and complementary way. There are ongoing questions of how to organize the work of staff so they remain in close contact with residents, encouraging their autonomy, self-expression, and social interaction, while at the same time being protected themselves from excessive stress, frustration, and burnout. This is an important question, since staff stress and frustration not only result in unhappy and dissatisfied workers but also tend to undercut the goals of Fairhaven for resident care as well. The quality of resident life, including the opportunity for residents to continue with patterns of activity and interests developed prior to the onset of dementia, is closely related to the quality of the work environment for caregiving staff. This requires that the two issues be dealt with together.

A final question concerns how long to keep severely declined residents at this specialized facility rather than transferring them to a more traditional nursing home. This issue focuses on the inability of Fairhaven, possibly due to licensing issues, to meet the needs of residents whose disease has significantly progressed. There are also ongoing discussions among staff and administration about whether certain residents are benefiting from the special nature of the Fairhaven program, including its opportunities for role expression and continuity. These concerns are cross-cut, however, by an awareness of a lack of appropriate alternative facilities for such residents. Severely demented residents may not be able to participate in and may even disrupt the community and social life of Fairhaven. At the same time, the general perception is that they are likely to lose whatever degree of personal dignity and sense of self they still retain if moved to another facility not especially designed to meet the needs of residents suffering from Alzheimer's. This dilemma is related to the larger picture of the changing needs of persons with Alzheimer's and the relative absence of programs and facilities to meet those needs. It places our study of Fairhaven in the general context of social policy and institutional practice regarding the long term care of the elderly, in particular those suffering from various forms of dementia.

CONCLUSIONS

This study illustrates that continuity in the life course occurs even among demented persons. Demented individuals do make decisions about what is useful and what they wish to continue in their lives, even within an institution where the options may be more reduced. However, discontinuities occur also, and it is sometimes difficult to determine the extent to which these are disease related or environmental-context related. Obviously, even in a facility as progressive in philosophy and environment as Fairhaven, there are inherent limitations in the extent to which the residents will be able to realize their inclinations to continue life-long interests or to express personal needs. This would be true even if their disease did not inhibit their ability to do so. Continuity was most discernible and most compatible with this setting in terms of the maintenance of common social roles, and less in the expression of more specific interests or specialized skills. This is partly explained by the more severe loss of functional capacity in these areas. It is also related to the fact that programs specifically oriented to these interests or skills have not yet been developed. Despite the attempt of the administration of Fairhaven to tailor their program and activities to the individual residents, the needs and personalities of 36 residents are quite diverse and may, in fact, not be able to be fully accommodated in an institutional setting. A problem also arises around the lack of compatibility between the needs of the staff and the needs of the residents. It would appear that circumstances creating tensions between residents and staff are likely to produce discontinuities rather than continuities in the life course. Of course, one such tension results from an inherent conflict between the efforts of staff to maximize the residents' potential for creative self-expression and the cruel and inevitable decline that is part of their disease.

This study also documents that it is possible to track life course continuities and discontinuities even among demented populations. It suggests that using a methodology that combines multiple methods, including participant observation and conversations with residents along with interviews with surrogates, provides an opportunity to assess the continuities and discontinuities in the life course. Of particular importance is our finding that use of an ethnographic approach can provide a more phenomenological perspective on the lives and experiences of persons with Alzheimer's disease. Through such a methodology, we come to more clearly understand not only what happens to such residents but their own perspectives on both major developments and everyday events.

Notes

CHAPTER 3

1. There is a preferred use of "resident" among nursing home staff. However, such labelling masks the reality of institutional care as it is typically practiced. A person who has a chart kept on him or her, whose time is regulated by institutional convenience, and whose privacy is compromised by "necessary" physical monitoring, such as vital signs, bowel habits, etc.—is a patient. Therefore, I use "patient" in an effort to convey the greater reality of institutional long term care.

CHAPTER 4

1. This research was supported by the Ohio Long-Term Care Project at the Scripps Gerontology Center, Miami University, Oxford, Ohio.

2. PASSPORT stands for Pre-Admission Screening System Providing Options and Resources Today. Established in 1984, this is a statewide system that seeks to link persons with long term care needs to the most appropriate services. It is intended to reduce Medicaid expenditures for nursing home care by preventing or delaying institutionalization. PASSPORT provides screening, case management, and an array of in-home long term care services for persons who are living in the community and who are at risk of institutionalization.

3. Working from a list of all nursing homes in this metropolitan area, I began by contacting homes that are located in neighborhoods with a sizable African-American population. Many administrators either refused to participate, claiming that they had no cognitively competent African-American residents, or did not

return my phone calls. Among the three institutions that participated, two have predominantly African-American residents; the other caters to a predominantly white clientele.

4. The other two nursing home residents did not fit these patterns. Their special cases illustrate the variety of reasons for African-Americans' nursing home placement; they belie the stereotypical notion that African-American elders invariably are embedded in large supportive networks of kin who are willing and able to provide long term care. One man, age 77, had taken refuge in the nursing home in his late fifties because he had no place to go. Placement in a group home would have been more appropriate for him. The second man, age 71, allegedly had alienated his children, his wife, and a series of choreworkers by sitting in an armchair for 10 years and refusing to move. When his wife no longer could take care of him, she had him admitted to the nursing home. According to staff members, he is a noncompliant person who is responsible for his present total dependence for all ADLs. Early mental health services might have averted his institutionalization.

CHAPTER 5

1. A shorter version of this article was presented at the 45th Annual Scientific Meeting of the Gerontological Society of America, November, 1992, Symposium on Qualitative Research in Nursing Homes. I am grateful to the following individuals for their continued support of my work and critical reviews of this chapter: Virginia Fraser, Colorado State Ombudsman; Enid Cox, Director, Gerontology Institute, Denver University; and Theresa Griffith, Volunteer Coordinator, Denver Regional Council of Governments.

CHAPTER 6

1. The material in this chapter is derived from an ongoing research project that is examining the culture of American nursing homes. The focus of the study is a series of geriatric institutions located in rural communities in upstate New York. The names of the nursing home and residents mentioned here are pseudonyms, but they refer to a real institution and real people with whom my students and I have worked. In the text, I have used the word "resident" rather than "patient" to refer to the people living at "Elmwood Grove" and other institutions. This usage reflects the terminology I found to be current at Elmwood Grove and other upstate New York facilities, and thus expresses the emic view of that local culture. A summary of the findings and recommendations which have come out of the larger study is given in Savishinsky (1991).

2. This phrase is derived from anthropologist Clifford Geertz (1973). He urged ethnographers to provide a "thick description" of the cultures in which they lived, including the details, conversations, and contexts of people's everyday experiences.

3. See, for example, the ideas and recommendations offered by Kayser-Jones (1981:121–133), Shield (1988:214–220), Savishinsky (1991:254–256), and Diamond (1992: 215–244).

CHAPTER 8

1. This research was funded by the Alzheimer's Association (Grant #11RG-92-076).

CHAPTER 10

1. The research on which this chapter is based was funded by a grant from the National Institute on Aging 1 R15 AGO8383-01. A RISM Landes Senior Fellowship award provided additional time off from teaching to complete the writing up of the material. A more detailed description of the nursing home studied, as well as an analysis of the full range of dilemmas that face nursing home aides, appears in Foner (1994a).

2. Most aides called each other by their last names. Usually, no title was used, either. Louise Tait was "Tait" to all the nursing staff, Winnifred Hill simply "Hill." "Ms." was added for a few older West Indian women, Ms. McKenzie, for example. Out of respect, I always added Ms. when addressing workers who went by their surnames. This is the form I generally use in this chapter, although of course all names are fictitious. Typically, patients were called by their last names as well, a pattern I also follow.

3. In a study of 42 female staff members (including 26 nursing aides) in an intermediate care facility, Duffy and her associates (n.d.) found that nearly three-quarters said that residents' families added to their stress.

CHAPTER 12

1. We want to acknowledge the financial support of the Vira and Howard Heinz Endowments and the Pittsburgh Foundation. We also appreciate comments on previous drafts and/or contributions of supplementary research data by Stefani Ledewitz, Judith Saxton, Annette Moulton, Edmund Ricci, Christopher Keane, Sue Smith, and Beth Deely. We thank Anna Marie Opalko for her indispensable secretarial services.

References

Agar, Michael. 1980. *The Professional Stranger: An Informal Introduction to Ethnography.* New York: Academic Press.
———. 1986. *Speaking of Ethnography.* Beverly Hills, CA: Sage Publications.
Altheide, David L., and J. M. Johnson. 1994. "Criteria for Assessing Interpretive Validity in Qualitative Research." In N. K. Denzin and Y. S. Lincoln (eds.). *Handbook of Qualitative Research.* Thousand Oaks, CA: Sage.
American Anthropological Association. 1990. "Statements on Ethics. Principles of Professional Responsibility." Washington, DC: American Anthropological Association.
Arras, John D. 1987. "A Philosopher's View: Risk and Notions of Competence." *Generations* 11:65–66.
Atchley, Robert C. 1989. "A Continuity Theory of Normal Aging." *Gerontologist* 29:183–90.
Atkinson, Paul. 1990. *The Ethnographic Imagination: Textual Constructions of Reality.* Routledge, London.
———. 1992. "The Ethnography of a Medical Setting: Reading, Writing and Rhetoric." *Qualitative Health Research* 2:451–474.
Beauvoir, Simone de. 1972. *The Coming of Age.* Trans. Patrick O'Brian. New York: G. P. Putnam's Sons.
Beck, Alan, and Aaron Katcher. 1984. "A New Look at Pet-Facilitated Therapy." *Journal of the American Veterinary Medicine Association* 184:414–21.
Beck, C. B., and P. Heacock. 1988. "Nursing Interventions for Patients With Alzheimer's Disease." *Nursing Clinics of North America* 23:95–124.

Becker, Gay. 1993. "Continuity After a Stroke: Implications of Life-Course Disruption in Old Age." *Gerontologist* 33:148–58.

Bell, Diane. 1993. "Introduction 1: The context." In Diane Bell, Pat Caplan, and Wazir Hahan Karim (eds.). *Gendered Fields: Women, Men and Ethnography*. London: Routledge.

Bergson, Henri. 1911. *Creative Evolution*. Trans. A. Mitchell. New York: Henry Holt.

Bernard, H. R. 1988. *Research Methods in Cultural Anthropology*. Newbury Park, CA: Sage.

Berry, J. T. 1990. "Information Memorandum AoA-IM-90-14: Report to Congress on Long-Term Care Ombudsman Activities for FY 1988." Washington, DC: Department of Health and Human Services, Administration on Aging.

Bogdan, Robert, and Steven Taylor. 1975. *Introduction to Qualitative Research Methods*. New York: Wiley.

Borden, W. 1991. "Stress, Coping, and Adaptation in Spouses of Older Adults With Chronic Dementia." *Social Work Research and Abstracts* 27:14–21.

Bott, Elizabeth. 1957. *Family and Social Networks*. Tavistock, London.

Bowers, Barbara. 1988. "Family Perceptions of Care in a Nursing Home." *The Gerontologist* 28:361–367.

Bowers, Barbara, and Marion Becker. 1992. "Nurses' Aides in Nursing Homes: The Relationship Between Organization and Quality." *The Gerontologist* 32:360–366.

Bowker, Lee H. 1982. *Humanizing Institutions for the Aged*. Lexington, MA: Lexington Books.

Brannen, J. 1985. "Suitable cases for treatment? Couples seeking help for marital difficulties." In J. A. Yoder (ed.). *Support Networks in a Caring Community*. Kluwer Academic Press, Lancaster.

Brewer, John, and Albert Hunter. 1989. *Multimethod Research: A Synthesis of Styles*. Newbury Park, CA: Sage.

Brock, Dan. 1991. "Trumping Advance Directives, in Practicing the PSDA, Special Supplement." *Hastings Center Report* 21:S5–S6.

Bruner, Edward M. 1993. "Introduction: The Ethnographic Self and the Personal Self." In Paul Benson (ed.). *Anthropology and Literature*. Urbana: University of Illinois Press.

Bruner, Jerome. 1986. *Actual Minds, Possible Worlds*. Cambridge, MA: Harvard University Press.

Burgener, S. C., M. Jirovec, L. Murrell, and D. Barton. 1992. "Caregiver and Environmental Variables Related to Difficult Behaviors in Institutionalized, Demented Elderly Persons." *Journal of Gerontology* 47:242–9.

Burgio, Louis, et al. 1994. "Studying Disruptive Vocalization and Contextual Factors in the Nursing Home Using Computer-Assisted Real-Time Observation." *Journal of Gerontology* 49:230–239.

Burgos-Debray, Elisabeth (ed.). 1984. *I, Rigoberta Menchu*. Verso, London.

Bustad, Leo. 1980. *Animals, Aging and the Aged*. University of Minnesota Press, Minneapolis, MN.

Butler, Robert. 1968. The "Life Review: An Interpretation of Reminiscence in the Aged." In *Middle Age and Aging*. Bernice Neugarten (ed.). Chicago: University of Chicago Press.

———. 1975. *Why Survive? Being Old in America*. New York: Harper and Row.

Clark, Margaret M. 1972. "Cultural Values and Dependency in Later Life." In Douglas O. Cowgill and Lowell Holmes (eds.). *Aging and Modernization*. New York: Appleton-Century-Crofts.

Clark, Patricia, and Ann Bowling. 1990. "Quality of Everyday Life in Long Stay Institutions for the Elderly. An Observational Study of Long Stay Hospital and Nursing Home Care." *Social Science and Medicine* 30:1201–10.

Clark, Phillip G. 1987. "Individual Autonomy, Cooperative Empowerment, and Planning for Long-Term Care Decision Making." *Journal of Aging Studies* 1:65–76.

Clifford, James. 1983. "On Ethnographic Authority." *Representations* 1:118–46.

———. 1986. "Introduction: Partial Truths." In James Clifford and George Marcus (eds.). *Writing Culture: The Poetics and Politics of Ethnography*. Berkeley: University of California Press.

Clifford, James, and George Marcus (eds.). 1986. *Writing Culture: The Poetics and Politics of Ethnography*. Berkeley: University of California Press.

Clough, Patricia T. 1992. *The End(s) of Ethnography: From Realism to Social Criticism*. Newbury Park, CA: Sage.

Cohen, Carl I., and J. Sokolovsky. 1989. *Old Men of the Bowery: Strategies for Survival Among the Homeless*. New York: Guilford.

Cohen, Donna, and Carl Eisdorfer. 1986. *The Loss of Self*. New York: Norton Press.

Cohen-Mansfield, J., P. Werner, and M. S. Marx. 1989. "An Observational Study of Agitation in Agitated Nursing Home Residents." *International Psychogeriatrics* 1:153–65.

Coleman, E. A., J. C. Barbaccia, and M. S. Croughan-Minihane. 1990. "Hospitalization Rates in Nursing Homes Residents With Dementia: A Pilot Study of the Impact of a Special Care Unit." *Journal of the American Geriatrics Society* 38:108–12.

Collopy, Bart J. 1988. "Autonomy in Long Term Care: Some Crucial Distinctions." *The Gerontologist* 28 (Supplement):10–17.

———. 1990. "Ethical Dimensions of Autonomy in Long-Term Care." *Generations* 14 (Supplement):9–12.

Collopy, B., P. Boyle, and B. Jennings. 1991. "New Directions in Nursing Home Ethics." *Hastings Center Report*, Special Supplement (March-April).

Colorado Ombudsman Program. 1989. *Training and Resource Manual*. Denver, Co: The Legal Center.

Conrad, Peter. 1990. "Qualitative Research on Chronic Illness: A Commentary on Method and Conceptual Development." *Social Science and Medicine* 30:1257–63.

Corson, Samuel, and Elizabeth Corson. 1980. "Pet Animals as Non-verbal Communication Mediators in Psychotherapy in Institutional Settings." In Samuel and Elizabeth Corson (eds.). *Ethology and Nonverbal Communication in Mental Health*. New York: Pergamon Press.

Cotrell, V., and R. Schulz. 1993. "The Perspective of the Patient with Alzheimer's Disease: A Neglected Dimension of Dementia Research." *The Gerontologist* 33:205–211.

Coulton, Claudia J., Ruth E. Dunkle, Julian C. Chow, Marie Haug, and David P. Vielhaber. 1988. "Dimensions of Post-Hospital Care Decision-Making: A Factor Analytic Study." *The Gerontologist* 28:218–223.

Coulton, Claudia J., Ruth E. Dunkle, Ruth Ann Goode, and Judith MacKintosh. 1982. "Discharge Planning and Decision Making." *Health and Social Work* 7:253–261.

Cox, E. O., and R. J. Parsons. 1994. *Empowerment-Oriented Social Work Practice With the Elderly*. Pacific Grove, CA: Brooks/Cole.

Crapanzano, Vincent. 1986. "Hermes' Dilemma: The Masking of Subversion in Ethnographic Description." In James Clifford and George E. Marcus (eds.). *Writing Culture: The Poetics and Politics of Ethnography*. Berkeley: University of California Press.

Curtin, Sharon. 1972. *Nobody Ever Died of Old Age*. Boston: Little, Brown and Co.

Cusack, Odeon, and Elaine Smith. 1984. *Pets and the Elderly*. New York: Haworth Press.

Davis, Dena S. 1991. "Rich Cases: The Ethics of Thick Description." *Hastings Center Report* 21:12–17.

Diamond, Timothy. 1986. "Social Policy and Everyday Life in Nursing Homes." *Social Science and Medicine* 23:1287–1295.

———. 1992. *Making Gray Gold: Narratives of Nursing Home Care*. Chicago: University of Chicago Press.

Dill, Ann E. P. 1987a. "The Case of George Sellers: A Safe Plan." *Generations* 11:48–53.

———. 1987b. "The Case of Rose Cepato: In Limbo on the Geriatric Ward." *Generations* 11:54–56.

Dubler, Nancy Neveloff. 1988. "Improving the Discharge Planning Process: Distinguishing between Coercion and Choice." *The Gerontologist* 28 (Supplement):76–81.

Duffy, JoAnn, Michael Duffy, Christopher Robinson, and Donald Barker. n.d. "Family Linkage to Stress Among Nursing Home Staff." Unpublished paper.

Duncan, Marie, and David Morgan. 1994. "Sharing the Caring: Family Caregivers' View of Their Relationships with Nursing Home Staff." *The Gerontologist* 34:235–244.

Eckert, J. Kevin. 1988. "Ethnographic Research on Aging." In Shulamit Reinharz and Graham Rowles (eds.). *Qualitative Gerontology*. New York: Springer.

Eley, Geoff. 1994. "Nations, Publics, and Political Cultures: Placing Habermas in the Nineteenth Century." In Nicholas B. Dirks, Geoff Eley, and Sherry B. Ortner (eds.). *Culture/Power/History: A Reader in Contemporary Social Theory*. Princeton: Princeton University Press.

Emerson, Robert M. 1983. *Contemporary Field Research*. Prospect Heights, IL: Waveland.

Estes, Carroll L., and Elizabeth A. Binney. 1989. "The Biomedicalization of Aging: Dangers and Dilemmas." *The Gerontologist* 29:597–605.

Estroff, Sue. 1981. *Making it Crazy: An Ethnography of Psychiatric Clients in an American Community*. Berkeley: University of California Press.

———. 1984. " 'Who Are You?' 'Why Are You Here?' Anthropology and Human Suffering." *Human Organization* 433:68–70.

Ewing, Katherine. 1990. "The Wholeness: Culture, Self and the Experience of Inconsistency." *Ethos* 18:251–279.

Fabrega, Jr., Horacio. 1974. *Disease and Social Behavior: An Interdisciplinary Perspective*. Cambridge, MA: MIT Press.

Faithorn, Elizabeth. 1986. "Gender Bias and Sex Bias: Removing Our Cultural Blinders in the Field." In Tony Larry Whitehead and Mary Ellen Conoway (eds.). *Self, Sex, and Gender in Cross-Cultural Fieldwork*. Urbana: University of Illinois Press.

Fielding, Nigel G., and Jane L. Fielding. 1986. *Linking Data*. Newbury Park, CA: Sage.

Filstead, William J. 1970. *Qualitative Methodology*. Chicago: Markham.

Fischer, Lucy Rose. 1994. Qualitative Research as Art and Science. In J. F. Gubrium and A. Sankar (eds.). *Qualitative Methods in Aging Research*. 3–14. Thousand Oaks, CA: Sage.

Foldes, S. 1990. "Life in an Institution: A Sociological and Anthropological View." In *Everyday Ethics: Resolving Dilemmas in Nursing Home Life*. R. A. Kane and A. L. Caplan (eds.). New York: Springer Publishing Company.

Folstein, Marshall F., Susan E. Folstein, and Paul R. McHugh. 1975. "Mini-Mental State: A Practical Method for Grading the Cognitive State of Patients for the Clinician." *Journal of Psychiatric Research* 12:189–98.

Foner, Nancy. 1973. *Status and Power in Rural Jamaica*. New York: Teachers College Press, Columbia University.

_____. 1978. *Jamaica Farewell: Jamaican Migrants in London*. Berkeley: University of California Press.

_____. 1987. "The Jamaicans: Race and Ethnicity among Migrants in New York City." In Nancy Foner (ed.). *New Immigrants in New York*. New York: Columbia University Press.

_____. 1994a. *The Caregiving Dilemma: Work in an American Nursing Home*. Berkeley: University of California Press.

_____. 1994b. "Nursing Home Aides: Saints or Monsters?" *The Gerontologist* 34:245–250.

Frank, G., and R. Vanderburgh. 1986. "Cross-Cultural Use of Life History Methods in Gerontology." In *New Methods for Old-Age Research*. C. Fry and J. Keith (eds.). South Hadley, MA: Bergin and Garvey Publishers.

Fraser, V. 1993. Colorado Ombudsman Program. Personal communication. Denver.

Freeman, Iris C. 1990. "Developing Systems that Promote Autonomy: Policy Considerations." In R. A. Kane and A. L. Caplan (eds.). *Everday Ethics: Resolving Dilemmas in Nursing Home Life*. New York: Springer.

Freidson, Eliot. 1973. *Professor of Medicine*. New York: Dodd, Mead and Company.

Freilich, Morris. 1970. *Marginal Natives*. New York: Harper and Row.

Garner, J. D., and S. O. Mercer. 1982. *Meeting the Needs of the Elderly: Home or Institutionalization?* Washington, D.C.: Health and Social Work National Association of Social Workers, Inc.

Gates, Henry Louis, Jr. 1994. "Authority, (White) Power and the (Black) Critic; It's All Greek to Me." In Nicholas B. Dirks, Geoff Eley, and Sherry B. Ortner (eds.). *Culture/Power/History: A Reader in Contemporary Social Theory*. Princeton: Princeton University Press.

Geertz, Clifford. 1988. *Works and Lives*. Stanford, CA: Stanford University Press.
——. 1973. *The Interpretation of Cultures*. New York: Basic Books.
George, Linda K., and Lisa P. Gwyther. 1986. "Caregiver Well-Being: A Multidimensional Examination of Family Caregivers of Demented Adults." *Gerontologist* 26:253–9.
Gerhardt, Uta. 1990. "Introductory Essay. Qualitative Research on Chronic Illness: The Issue and the Story." *Social Science and Medicine* 30:149–60.
Gibson, Rose C. 1991. "Race and the Self-Reported Health of Elderly Persons." *Journal of Gerontology* 46:S235–242.
Glaser, Barney, and Anselm Strauss. 1967. *The Discovery of Grounded Theory*. Chicago: Aldine.
Goffman, Erving. 1961. *Asylums: Essays on the Social Situation of Mental Patients and Other Inmates*. Garden City, NJ: Anchor Books.
Golant, Stephen M. 1992. *Housing America's Elderly: Many Possibilities/Few Choices*. Newbury Park, CA: Sage.
Gold, Raymond L. 1969. "Roles in Sociological Field Observations." In George J. McCall and J. L. Simmons (eds.). *Issues in Participant Observation*. Reading, MA: Addison-Wesley.
Greene, Vernon L., and Deborah Monahan. 1982. "The Impact of Visitation on Patient Well-Being in Nursing Homes." *The Gerontologist* 22:418–423.
Groger, Lisa. 1993. "African-American Elders' Trajectories to Long-Term Care Settings." Paper presented at the forty-sixth annual scientific meeting of the Gerontological Society of America, New Orleans.
——. 1994. "Decision as Process: A Conceptual Model of Black Elders' Nursing Home Placement." *Journal of Aging Studies* 8:77–94.
Guba, Egon G., and Y. S. Lincoln. 1981. *Effective Evaluation*. San Francisco: Jossey-Bass.
Gubrium, Jaber F. 1975. *Living and Dying at Murray Manor*. New York: St. Martin's Press.
——. 1988. "The Family as Project." *Sociological Review* 36:273–95.
——. 1991. *The Mosaic of Care*. New York: Springer.
——. 1992. *Out of Control: Family Therapy and Domestic Disorder*. Newbury Park, CA: Sage.
——. 1993. *Speaking of Life: Horizons of Meaning for Nursing Home Residents*. New York: Aldine.
Gubrium, Jaber F., and James A. Holstein. 1990. *What is Family?* Mayfield, CA: Mountain View.
——. 1992. "Phenomenology, Ethnomethodology and Family Discourse." In Pauline G. Boss, William J. Doherty, Ralph LaRossa, Walter R. Schuum, and Suzanne K. Steinmetz (eds.). *Sourcebook of Family Theories and Methods*. New York: Plenum Press.
Gubrium, Jaber F., James A. Holstein, and David R. Buckholdt. 1994. *Constructing the Life Course*. Dix Hills, NY: General Hall Press.
Gubrium, Jaber F., and Andrea Sankar (eds.). 1994. *Qualitative Methods in Aging Research*. Thousand Oaks, CA: Sage.
Gustafson, Elisabeth. 1972. "Dying: The Career of the Nursing Home Patient." *Journal of Health and Social Behavior* 13:226–35.

Hakmiller, K. L. 1966. "Threat as a determinant of downward comparison." *Journal of Experimental Social Psychology* 1 (Supplement):32–39.

Halibar, B. 1982. *Turnover among Nursing Personnel in Nursing Homes*. Ann Arbor, MI: Research Press, Hammersley, Martyn and Paul Atkinson.

_____. 1989. *Ethnography: Principles in Practice*. London: Tavistock.

Hall, E. 1966. *The Hidden Dimension*. New York: Doubleday.

Hammersley, M., and Atkinson, P. 1983. *Ethnography: Principles in Practice*. London: Tavistock.

Hanley, Raymond J., Lisa Maria B. Alecxih, Joshua M. Wiener, and David L. Kennell. 1990. "Predicting Elderly Nursing Home Admissions: Results from the 1982–1984 National Long-Term Care Survey." *Research on Aging* 12:199–228.

Harel, Zev, and Linda Noelker. 1982. "Social Integration, Health, and Choice: Their Impact on the Well-Being of Institutionalized Aged." *Research on Aging* 4:97–111.

Hastings Center. 1987. *Guidelines on the Termination of Life-Sustaining Treatment and the Care of the Dying*. Bloomington: Indiana University Press.

Hauerwas, S. 1979. "Reflections on Suffering, Death, and Medicine." *Ethics in Science and Medicine* 6:230.

Hazan, Haim. 1990. *The Paradoxical Community*. Greenwich, CT: JAI Press.

Henderson, J. Neil. 1979. *Chronic Life. An Anthropological View of an American Nursing Home*. Dissertation. University of Florida.

_____. 1981. "Nursing Home Housekeepers: Indigenous Agents of Psychosocial Support." *Human Organization* 40:300–305.

_____. 1987. "When a Professor Turns Nurse Aide." *Provider* 13:8–12.

_____. 1994a. "The Culture of Special Care Units: An Anthropological Perspective on Ethnographic Research in Nursing Home Settings." *Alzheimer's Disease and Associated Disorders* 8:S410–S416.

_____. 1994b. "Bed, Body, and Soul: The Job of the Nursing Home Aide." *Generations* 18:20–22.

Henry, Jules. 1963. *Culture Against Man*. New York: Random House.

_____. 1971. *Pathways to Madness*. New York: Random House.

Heritage, John. 1984. *Garfinkel and Ethnomethodology*. Cambridge, UK: Polity.

High, Dallas. 1988. "All in the Family: Extended Autonomy and Expectations in Surrogate Health Care Decision-Making." *The Gerontologist* 28 (Supplement):46–51.

Hing, Esther. 1989. *Nursing Home Utilization by Current Residents: United States, 1985*. Hyattsville, MD: National Center for Health Statistics.

Hochschild, Arlie. 1973. *The Unexpected Community*. Englewood Cliffs, NJ: Prentice-Hall.

Hofland, Brian F. 1988. "Autonomy in Long-Term Care: Background Issues and a Programmatic Response." *The Gerontologist* 28 (Supplement):3–9.

Holstein, James A. 1993. *Court-Ordered Insanity: Interpretive Practice and Involuntary Commitment*. Hawthorne, NY: Aldine de Gruyter.

Holstein, James A. and Jaber F. Gubrium. 1994a. "Constructing Family: Descriptive Practice and Domestic Order." In T. Sarbin and J. Kitsuse (eds.). *Constructing the Social*. London: Sage.

————. 1994b. "Phenomenology, Ethnomethodology and Interpretive Practice." In Norman Denzin and Yvonna Lincoln (eds.). *Handbook of Qualitative Research* 262–72. Newbury Park, CA: Sage.

————. 1995. *The Active Interview*. Thousand Oaks, CA: Sage.

Hooyman, Nancy, and Wendy Lustbader. 1986. *Taking Care: Supporting Older People and Their Families*. New York: Free Press.

Hornum, B. 1982. "Aspects of Aging in Planned Communities." In T. Wills (ed.). *Aging and Health Promotion*. Aspen Systems.

————. 1986. "Dependency Fears and Selection of Living Arrangements: A Study of One Life Care Community in America." In A. Sontz (ed.). *Compendium Series: Cultural Gerontology*. Jersey City, NJ: Brunswick Institute on Aging.

————. 1987. "The Elderly in British New Towns." In J. Sokolovsky (ed.). *Growing Old in Different Societies: Cross-Cultural Perspectives*. Littleton, MA: Copley.

Hornum, Barbara, and Anthony P. Glascock. 1989. "Whither Anthropological Gerontology?" In N. Osgood and A. Sontz (eds.). *The Science and Practice of Gerontology*.

Hostetler, John A. 1993. *Amish Society*. Baltimore, MD: Johns Hopkins University Press.

Hughes, Charles C. 1978. "Medical Care: Ethnomedicine." In Michael H. Logan and Edward E. Hunt, Jr. (eds.). *Health and the Human Condition: Perspectives on Medical Anthropology*. North Scituate, MA: Duxbury.

————. 1992. "Ethnography: What's in a Word—Process? Product? Promise?" *Qualitative Health Research* 2:439–450.

Hughes, C. P., L. Berg, W. L. Danziger, L. A. Coben, and R. L. Martin. 1982. "A New Clinical Scale for the Staging of Dementia." *British Journal of Psychiatry* 140:566–72.

Husserl, Edmund G. 1965. *Phenomenology and the Crisis of Philosophy*. New York: Harper and Row.

————. 1970. *The Crisis of European Sciences and Transcendental Phenomenology*. Evanston, IL: Northwestern University Press.

Hyman, Ruth, Wilma Bulkin, and Pierre Woog. 1993. "The Staff's Perception of a Skilled Nursing Facility." *Qualitative Health Research* 3:209–235.

Illich, Ivan. 1975. *Medical Nemisis: The Expropriation of Life*. London: Calder and Boyers.

Institute of Medicine. 1986. *Improving the Quality of Care in Nursing Homes*. Washington, D.C.: National Academy Press.

Jackson, James S. 1989. "Methodological Issues in Survey Research on Older Minority Adults." In M. P. Lawton and A. R. Herzog (eds.). *Special Research Methods for Gerontology*. Amityville, NY: Baywood.

Jameton, Andrew. 1988. "In the Borderlands of Autonomy: Responsibility in Long Term Care Facilities." *The Gerontologist* 28 (Supplement):18–23.

Jecker, Nancy S. 1990. "The Role of Intimate Others in Medical Decision Making." *The Gerontologist* 30:65–71.

Johnson, Allen, and Orna R. Johnson. 1990. "Quality into Quantity: On the Measurement Potential of Ethnographic Fieldnotes." In Roger Sanjek (ed.). *Fieldnotes: The Makings of Anthropology*. Ithaca: Cornell University Press.

Johnson, Colleen. 1987. *"The Institutional Segregation of the Aged."* In *The Elderly as Modern Pioneers*. Philip Silverman (ed.). Bloomington, IN: Indiana University Press.

Johnson, Colleen, and Leslie Grant. 1985. *The Nursing Home in American Society*. Baltimore: Johns Hopkins University Press.

Johnson, Sandra. 1991. "PSDA in the Nursing Home, in Practicing the PSDA, Special Supplement. *Hastings Center Report* 21:S3–S4.

Joint Commission on Accreditation of Healthcare Organizations. 1992. *Accreditation Manual for Hospitals*. Oakbrook Terrace.

Jonsen, Albert R. (ed.). 1993. "The Birth of Bioethics, Special Supplement. *Hastings Center Report* 23:S1–S4.

Kahana, Eva, Boaz Kahana, and Kathryn Riley. 1988. "Contextual Issues in Quantitative Studies of Institutional Settings for the Aged." In Shulamit Reinharz and Graham Rowles (eds.). *Qualitative Gerontology*. New York: Springer.

Kane, R. A, and A.L. Caplan (eds.). 1990. *Everyday Ethics: Resolving Dilemmas in Nursing Home Life*. New York: Springer.

Kane, R. A., A. L. Caplan, I. Freeman, et al. 1990. "Avenues To Appropriate Autonomy What Next?" In *Everyday Ethics: Resolving Dilemmas in Nursing Home Life*. R. A. Kane and A. L. Caplan (eds.). New York: Springer.

Kane, R. A., and Scott M. Geron. 1991. *Multidimensional Assessment in Case Management*. Minneapolis: University of Minnesota Long-Term Care DECISION Resource Center.

Kapp, Marshall B. 1991. "Health Care Decision Making by the Elderly: I Get By with a Little Help from My Family." *The Gerontologist* 31:619–523.

Kaufman, Sharon R. 1986. *The Ageless Self*. Madison, WI: University of Wisconsin Press.

Kayser-Jones, Jeanie S. 1981. *Old, Alone, and Neglected: Care of the Aged in Scotland and the U.S.* Berkeley: University of California Press.

———. 1990. "The Use of Nasogastric Feeding Tubes in Nursing Homes: Patient, Family and Health Care Provider Perspectives." *Gerontologist* 30:469–479.

Keith, Jennie. 1982. *Old People as People: Social and Cultural Influences on Aging and Old Age*. Boston: Little, Brown & Company.

———. 1986. "Participant Observation." In *New Methods for Old-Age Research*. C. Fry and Jennie Keith (eds.). Boston: Bergin and Garvey.

———. 1988. "Participant Observation." In Chris Fry and Jennie Keith (eds.). *New Methods for Old Age Research: Anthropological Alternatives*. Chicago: Loyola University of Chicago Center for Urban Policy.

Kennell, David L. 1990. "Predicting Elderly Nursing Home Admissions: Results from the 1982–1984 National Long-Term Care Survey." *Research on Aging* 12:199–228.

Kitwood, Tom, and Kathleen Bredin. 1992. "Towards a Theory of Dementia Care: Personhood and Well-Being." *Aging and Society* 12:269–288.

Kleinman, A. 1980. *Patients and Healers in the Context of Culture*. Berkeley: University of California Press.

———. 1988. *The Illness Narratives*. New York: Basic Books.

Kuypers, Joseph A., and Vern L. Bengston. 1984. Perspectives on the Older Family. In H. Quinn and G.A. Hughston (eds.). *Independent Aging*. Rockville, MD: Aspen.

Laird, Carobeth. 1979. *Limbo: A Memoir about Life in a Nursing Home by a Survivor*. Novato, CA: Chandler and Sharp.

Lawton, M. Powell, and A. Regula Herzog (eds.). 1989. *Special Research Methods for Gerontology*. Amityville, NY: Baywood.

Lederman, Rena. 1990. "Pretexts for Ethnography: On Reading Fieldnotes." In Roger Sanjek (ed.). *Fieldnotes: The Makings of Anthropology*. Ithaca: Cornell University Press.

Leininger, Madeleine. 1994. "Evaluation criteria and critique of qualitative research studies." In J.M. Morse (ed.). *Critical Issues in Qualitative Research Methods*. Thousand Oaks, CA: Sage.

Levinson, Boris. 1972. *Pets and Human Development*. Springfield, IL: Charles C. Thomas.

Lidz, C., L. Fischer, and R. M. Arnold. 1992. *The Erosion of Autonomy in Long-Term Care*. New York: Oxford University Press.

Liebow, Elliot. 1993. *Tell Them Who I Am: The Lives of Homeless Women*. New York: The Free Press.

Light, Jr., Donald. 1983. "Surface Data and Deep Structure: Observing the Organization of Professional Training." In John Van Maanen (ed.). *Qualitative Methodology*. Beverly Hills, CA: Sage.

Litwak, E. 1985. *Helping the Elderly: the Complementary Roles of Informal Networks and Formal Systems*. New York: Guilford Press.

Luborsky, Mark. 1994. "The Identification and Analysis of Themes and Patterns." In Jaber Gubrium and Andrea Sankar (eds.). *Qualitative Methods in Aging Research*. Thousand Oaks, CA: Sage.

Luborsky, Mark, and Andrea Sankar. 1993. "Extending the Critical Gerontology Perspective: Cultural Dimentions, Introduction." *Gerontologist* 33:440–444.

Lyman, Karen A. 1989. "Bringing the Social Back in: A Critique of the Biomedicalization of Dementia." *The Gerontologist* 29:597–605.

Malinowski, Bronislaw. 1961 [1922]. *Argonauts of the Western Pacific*. New York: Dutton Press.

Marcus, George E. 1986. "Contemporary Problems of Ethnography in the Modern World System." In James Clifford and George E. Marcus (eds.). *Writing Culture: The Poetics and Politics of Ethnography*. Berkeley: University of California Press.

Marcus, George, and Michael Fischer. 1986. *Anthropology as Cultural Critique*. Chicago: University of Chicago Press.

Markides, Kyriakos S., Jersey Liang, and James S. Jackson. 1990. "Race, Ethnicity, and Aging: Conceptual and Methodological Issues." In R. H. Binstock and L. K. George (eds.). *Handbook of Aging and the Social Sciences*, Third Edition. New York: Academic Press.

Marshall, Patricia A. 1992. "Anthropology and Bioethics." *Medical Anthropology Quarterly* 6:49–73.

McCall, George, and J. L. Simmons (eds.). 1969. *Issues in Participant Observation*. Reading, MA: Addison-Wesley.

McCracken, Grant. 1988. *The Long Interview*. Newbury Park, CA: Sage.

Mendelson, M.A. 1974. *Tender Loving Greed*. New York: Knopf.

Miller, Tracy, and Anna Maria Cugliari. 1990. "Withdrawing and Withholding Treatment: Policies in Long-Term Care Facilities." *Gerontologist* 30:462–468.

Mischler, Elliot. 1986. *Research Interviewing: Context and Narrative*. Cambridge, MA: Harvard University Press.

Monk, A., W. L. Kaye, and H. Litwin. 1984. *Resolving Grievances in the Nursing Home: A Study of the Ombudsman Program*. New York: Columbia University Press.

Moody, Harry R. 1987. "Ethical Dilemmas in Nursing Home Placement." *Generations* 11:16–23.

———. 1988. "From Informed Consent to Negotiated Consent." *The Gerontologist* 28 (Supplement):64–70.

———. 1992. *Ethics in an Aging Society*. Baltimore: Johns Hopkins University Press.

Moore, Sally, and Barbara Myerhoff (eds.). 1977. *Secular Ritual*. Amsterdam: Van Gorcum.

Morse, Janice. 1991. "Editorial. Subjects, Respondents, Informants and Participants?" *Qualitative Health Research* 1:4–3–406.

———. ed. 1992. *Qualitative Health Research*. Newbury Park, CA: Sage.

———. 1994. "Designing Funded Qualitative Research." In Norman K. Denzin and Yvonna S. Lincoln (eds.). *Handbook of Qualitative Research*. Thousand Oaks, CA: Sage.

Morycz, R. K. 1985. "Caregiving Strain and the Desire to Institutionalize Family Members With Alzheimer's Disease." *Research On Aging* 7:329–61.

Moss, F. E., and J. D. Val J. Halamandaris. 1977. *Too Old, Too Sick, Too Bad: Nursing Homes in America*. Germantown, MD: Aspen Systems Corporation.

Mullins, Larry C., Carnot E. Nelson, H. Busciglio, and H. Wenner. 1988. "Job Satisfaction among Nursing Home Personnel: The Impact of Organizational Structure and Supervisory Power." *Journal of Long-term Care Administration* 16:12–23.

Myerhoff, Barbara. 1974. *Peyote Hunt*. Ithaca: Cornell University Press.

———. 1978. *Number Our Days*. New York: Dutton Press.

National Association of State Units on Aging (NASUA). 1988. *Comprehensive Analysis of State Long-Term Care Ombudsman Offices*. Washington, DC: National Center for State Long Term Care Ombudsman Resources, Administration on Aging.

———. 1992a. *Comprehensive Curriculum—State Long Term Care Ombudsman Programs*. Washington, DC: National Center for State Long Term Care Ombudsman Resources, Administration on Aging.

National Citizens' Coalition for Nursing Home Reform. 1985. *A Consumer Perspective on Quality Care: The Residents' Point of View*. Washington, D.C.

Netting, F. E., R. N. Paton, and R. Huber. 1992. "The Long-Term Care Ombudsman Program: What Does the Complaint Reporting System Tell Us?" *The Gerontologist* 32:843–48

Neugarten, Bernice L. 1969. "Continuities and Discontinuities of Psychological Issues Into Adult Life." *Human Development* 12:121–30.

————. 1979. "Time, Age, and the Life Cycle." *American Journal of Psychiatry* 136:887–94.

Noblit, George, and Hohn Engel. 1991. "The Holistic Injunction: An Ideal and a Moral Imperative for Qualitative Research." *Qualitative Health Research* 1:123–130.

O'Brien, Mary. 1989. *Anatomy of a Nursing Home: A New View of Residential Life.* Owings Mills, MD: National Health Publishing.

Olson, Ellen, Eileen R. Chichin, Leslie S. Libow, Theresa Martico-Greenfield, Richard R. Neufeld, and Michael Mulvihill. 1993. "A Center on Ethics in Long-term Care." *Gerontologist* 33:269–274.

Omnibus Budget Reconciliation Act of 1987 (OBRA). 1987. Public Law 100–203, printed at *Congressional Record*, 133(205) Part III, December 24, 1987.

Orona, Celia.1990. "Temporality and Identity Loss Due to Alzheimer's Disease." *Social Science and Medicine* 30:1247–56.

Ortner, Sherry B. 1994. "Theory in Anthropology since the Sixties." In Nicholas B. Dirks, Geoff Eley, and Sherry B. Ortner (eds.). *Culture/Power/History: A Reader in Contemporary Social Theory.* Princeton: Princeton University Press.

Ory, M. G., and R. P. Ables (eds.). 1989. *Aging, Health and Behavior.* Baltimore: Johns Hopkins University Press.

Pelto, Pertti, and Gretel H. Pelto. 1970. *Anthropological Research: The Structure of Inquiry.* New York: Harper and Row.

————. 1978. *Anthropological Research: The Structure of Inquiry.* New York: Cambridge University Press.

Piven, Frances Fox, and Richard A. Cloward. 1993. *Regulating the Poor: The Functions of Public Welfare.* New York: Viking.

Powers, Bethel. 1988a. "Self-perceived health of elderly institutionalized people." *Journal of Cross-Cultural Gerontology* 3:299–321.

————. 1988b. "Social networks, social support, and elderly institutionalized people." *Advances in Nursing Science* 10:40–58.

————. 1991. "The meaning of nursing home friendships." *Advances in Nursing Science* 14:42–58.

————. 1992. "The roles staff play in the social networks of elderly institutionalized people." *Social Science & Medicine* 34:1335–1343.

Pratt, C. C., V. L. Schmall, S. Wright, and M. Cleland. 1985. "Burden and Coping Strategies of Caregivers to Alzheimer's Patients." *Family Relations* 34:230–9.

Quinlan, Alice. 1988. *Chronic Care Workers: Crisis Among Paid Caregivers of the Elderly.* Washington, D.C.: Older Woman's League.

Rabinow, Paul. 1977. *Reflections on Fieldwork in Morocco.* Berkeley: University of California Press.

Ramsey, Paul. 1970. *The Patient as Person.* New Haven: Yale University Press.

Reinardy, James R. 1992. "Decisional Control in Moving to a Nursing Home: Postadmission Adjustment to Well-Being." *The Gerontologist* 32:96–103.

Reinharz, Shulamit, and Graham D. Rowles (eds.). 1988. *Qualitative Gerontology.* New York: Springer.

Rhodes, Lorna. 1991. *Emptying Beds: The Work of an Emergency Psychiatric Unit.* Berkeley: University of California Press.

Robinson, I. 1990. "Personal Narratives, Social Careers and Medical Courses: Analyzing Life Trajectories in Autobiographies of People with Multiple Sclerosis." *Social Science and Medicine* 30:1173–86.

Rosenwald, G. C., and R. L. Ochberg. 1992. "Introduction: Life Stories, Cultural Politics and Self-Understanding." In G. C. Rosenwald and R. L. Ochberg (eds.). *Storied Lives: The Cultural Politics of Self-Understanding*. New Haven, CT: Yale University Press.

Roth, Julius. 1963. *Timetables: Structuring the Passage of Time in Hospital Treatment and Other Careers*. Indianapolis: Bobbs-Merrill.

Rothman, David J. 1991. *Strangers at the Bedside: A History of How Law and Bioethics Transformed Medical Decision Making*. New York: Basic Books.

Rowles, Graham D. 1978. *Prisoners of Space? Exploring the Geographic Experience of Older People*. Boulder, CO: Westview.

Rubin, Allen, and Guy Shuttlesworth. 1983. "Engaging Families as Support Resource in Nursing Home Care: Ambiguity in the Subdivision of Tasks." *The Gerontologist* 23:632–636.

Rubinstein, Robert L. 1986. *Singular Paths: Old Men Living Alone*. New York: Columbia University Press.

_____. 1988. "Stories Told: In-Depth Interviewing and the Structure of Its Insights." In Shulamit Reinharz and Graham Rowles (eds.). *Qualitative Gerontology*. New York: Springer.

_____. 1990. "Personal Identity and Environmental Meaning in Later Life." *Journal of Aging Studies* 4:131–47.

Rubinstein, Robert L., Janet C. Kilbride, and Sharon Nagy. 1992. *Elders Living Alone: Frailty and the Perception of Choice*. New York: Aldine.

Sabat, Steven, and Rom Harre. 1992. "The Construction and Deconstruction of Self in Alzheimer's Disease." *Ageing and Society* 12:443–461.

Sandelowski, Margarete. 1986. "The problem of rigor in qualitative research." *Advances in Nursing Science* 8:27–37.

Sanjek, Roger. 1990. "On Ethnographic Validity." In Roger Sanjek (ed.). *Fieldnotes: The Makings of Anthropology*. Ithaca: Cornell University Press.

Sarton, May. 1973. *As We Are Now*. New York: Norton.

Savishinsky, Joel. 1991. *The Ends of Time: Life and Work in a Nursing Home*. New York: Bergin and Garvey.

Schaie, K. W., R. T. Campbell, W. Meredith, and S. C. Rawlings (eds.). 1988. *Methodological Issues in Aging Research*. New York: Springer.

Schechner, Richard, and Willa Appel (eds.). 1990. *By Means of Performance: Intercultural Studies of Theatre and Ritual*. New York: Cambridge University Press.

Schechner, Richard, and Mady Schuman (eds.). 1976. *Ritual, Play and Performance: Readings in the Social Sciences/Theatre*. New York: Seabury.

Scheibe, Karl. 1989. "Memory, Identity, History and the Understanding of Dementia." In L. Eugene Thomas (ed.). *Research on Adulthood and Aging; the Human Science Approach*. Albany: State University of New York Press.

Schiman, C., and A. Lordeman. 1989. *A Study of the Use of Volunteers by Long-Term Care Ombudsman Programs: The Effectiveness of Recruitment*. Supervision, and Retention. Washington, DC: National Center for State Long Term

Care Ombudsman Resources, National Association for State Units on Aging.

Schmidt, M. G. 1990. *Negotiating a Good Old Age.* San Francisco: Jossey-Bass.

Schulz, R., and Rau, M. T. 1985. "Social Support Through the Life Course." In S. Cohen and S. L. Symes (eds.). *Social Support and Health.* Orlando, FL: Academic.

Schuttlesworth, G., A. Rubin, and M. Duffy. 1982. "Families versus Institutions: Incongruent Role Expectations in the Nursing Home." *The Gerontologist* 22:200–208.

Schwartz, Arthur N., and Mark E. Vogel. 1990. "Nursing Home Staff and Residents' Families' Role Expectations." *The Gerontologist* 30:49–53.

Schwartz, Howard, and Jerry Jacobs. 1979. *Qualitative Sociology.* New York: Free Press.

Shaffir, William, Robert Stebbins, and Allan Turowetz (eds.). 1980. *Fieldwork Experience.* New York: St. Martin's Press.

Shield, Renée. 1988. *Uneasy Endings: Daily Life in an American Nursing Home.* Ithaca: Cornell University Press.

———. 1990. "Liminality in an American Nursing Home: The Endless Transition." In *The Cultural Context of Aging: Worldwide Perspectives.* Jay Sokolovsky (ed.). New York: Bergin and Garvey.

———. 1993. "Forays into the Nursing Home: Different Approaches." *Journal of Cross-Cultural Gerontology* 8:473–481.

Silverman, David. 1993. *Interpreting Qualitative Data.* London: Sage.

Silverman, Phillip. 1988. "Research as Process: Exploring the Meaning of Widowhood." In Shulamit Reinharz and Graham Rowles (eds.). *Qualitative Gerontology.* New York: Springer Publishing Company.

Smerglia, Virginia L., Gary T. Deimling, and Charles M. Barresi. 1988. "Black/White Family Comparisons in Helping and Decision-Making Networks of Impaired Elderly." *Family Relations* July: 305–309.

Smith, Kristen, and Vern Bengston. 1979. "Positive Consequences of Institutionalization: Solidarity Between Elderly Parents and Their Middle-Aged Children." *The Gerontologist* 19:438–447.

Sokolovsky, Jay. 1980. "Interactional dimensions of the aged: Social network mapping." In C. Fry and J. Keith (eds.). *New Methods for Old Age Research.* Chicago: Center for Urban Policy.

Sokolovsky, Jay, and C. Cohen. 1983. "Networks as adaptation: The cultural meaning of being a 'loner' among the inner-city elderly." In J. Sokolovsky (ed.). *Growing Old in Different Societies.* Belmont, CA: Wadsworth.

Spencer, J. 1989. "Anthropology as a Kind of Writing." *Man* 24:145–64.

Spindler, George, and L. Spindler. 1982. "Roger Harker and Schonhausen: From familiar to strange and back again." In G. Spindler (ed.). *Doing the Ethnography of Schooling.* Prospect Heights, IL: Waveland.

Spradley, James P. 1979. *The Ethnographic Interview.* New York: Holt, Rinehart and Winston.

———. 1980. *Participant Observation.* Fort Worth: Harcourt Brace Jovanovich.

Stannard, Charles I. 1973. "Old Folks and Dirty Work: The Social Conditions for Patient Abuse in a Nursing Home." *Social Problems* 20:329–42.

Stein, Howard. 1991. *American Medicine as Culture.* Boulder, CO: Westview Press.

Stephens, Mary A. P., Jennifer M. Kinney, and Paula K. Ogrocki. 1991. "Stressors and Well-Being Among Caregivers to Older Adults With Dementia: The In-Home Versus Nursing Home Experience." *Gerontologist* 31:217–23.

Strahan, Genevieve. 1987. "Nursing Home Characteristics, Preliminary Data from 1985 National Nursing Home Survey." *Advance From Vital and Health Statistics*. Hyattsville, MD: National Center for Health Statistics.

Strathern, Marilyn. 1987. "Out of Context: The Persuasive Fiction of Anthropology." *Current Anthropology* 28:251–81.

Strauss, Anselm, and Juliet Corbin. 1990. *Basics of Qualitative Research: Grounded Theory Procedures and Techniques*. Newbury Park, CA: Sage.

Stryuker, R. 1982. "The Effect of Managerial Interventions on High Personnel Turnover in Nursing Homes." *Journal of Long-Term Care Administration* 10:21–34.

Tisdale, S. 1987. *Harvest Moon: Portrait of a Nursing Home*. New York: Henry Holt & Company.

Tourigny, Sylvie. 1994. "Integrating Ethics with Symbolic Interactionism: The Case of Oncology." *Qualitative Health Research* 4:163–185.

Turnbull, Colin. 1983. *The Human Cycle*. New York, NY: Simon and Schuster.

Turner, Victor. 1969. *The Ritual Process: Structure and Anti-Structure*. Chicago: Aldine.

———. 1974. *Dramas, Fields and Metaphors*. Ithaca: Cornell University Press.

———. 1987. *The Anthropology of Performance*. New York: PAJ Publications.

Turner, Victor W., and E. M. Bruner (eds.). 1986. *The Anthropology of Experience*. Chicago: University of Illinois Press.

Van Gennep, Arnold. 1960. *The Rites of Passage*. London: Routledge and Kegan Paul.

Van Maanen, John. 1988. *Tales of the Field: On Writing Ethnography*. Chicago: University of Chicago Press.

Van Manen, Max. 1990. *Researching Lived Experience: Human Science for an Action Sensitive Pedagogy*. London: University of Western Ontario.

Vesperi, Maria D. 1985. *City of Green Benches: Growing Old in a New Downtown*. Ithaca: Cornell University Press.

———. 1987. "The Reluctant Consumer: Nursing Home Residents in the Post-Bergman Era." In Jay Sokolovsky (ed.). *Growing Old in Different Societies: Cross-Cultural Perspectives*. Littleton, MA: Copley.

———. 1994. "Perspectives on Aging in Print Journalism." In Dena Shenk and W. Andrew Achenbaum (eds.). *Changing Perceptions of Aging and the Aged*. New York: Springer.

Vladeck, B. C. 1980. *Unloving Care: The Nursing Home Tragedy*. New York: Basic Books.

Watson, Wilbur, and Robert Maxwell. 1977. "Social Interaction in a Home for the Black Elderly." In Wilbur Watson and Robert Maxwell (eds.). *Human Aging and Dying*. New York: St. Martin's Press.

Wax, Rosalie (ed.). 1971. *Doing Fieldwork*. Chicago: University of Chicago Press.

Waxman, Howard M., Erwin A. Carner, and Gale Berkenstock. 1984. "Job Turnover and Job Satisfaction among Nursing Home Aides." *The Gerontologist* 24:503–509.

Webb, E., D. T. Campbell, R. D. Schwartz, and L. Sechrest. 1966. *Unobtrusive Measures: Nonreactive Research in the Social Sciences*. Chicago: Rand McNally and Company.

Wenger, G. Clare. 1987. "Dependence, Independence, and Reciprocity after 80." *Journal of Ageing Studies* 1:355–377.

———. 1989. "Support networks in old age: Constructing a typology." In M. Jefferys (ed.). *Growing Old in the Twentieth Century*. London: Routledge.

Werner, O., and G. M. Schoepfle. 1987. *Systematic Fieldwork*. Vol. 1 *Foundations of Ethnography and Interviewing*. Vol. 2 *Ethnographic Analysis and Data Management*. Newbury Park, CA: Sage.

Whitehead, Tony Larry, and Mary Ellen Conoway (eds.). 1986. *Self, Sex, and Gender in Cross-Cultural Fieldwork*. Urbana: University of Illinois Press.

Wideman, John Edgar. 1985. *Brothers and Keepers*. New York: Penguin.

Wiener, Joshua M., Raymond J. Hanley, Robert Clark, and Joan F. Van Nostrand. 1990. "Measuring the Activities of Daily Living: Comparisons Across National Surveys." *Journal of Gerontology* 45:S229–237.

Willcocks, Dianne, Sheila Peace, and Leoni Kellaher. 1987. *Private Lives in Public Places: A Research-Based Critique of Residential Life in Old People's Homes*. London: Tavistock.

Wills, Thomas Ashby. 1981. "Downward comparison principles in social psychology." *Psychological Bulletin* 90:245–271.

Wilson, Cindy, and F. Ellen Netting. 1983. "Companion Animals and the Elderly: A State-of-the-Art Summary." *Journal of the American Veterinary Medicine Association* 183:1425–29.

Wolcott, Harry F. 1985. "On ethnographic intent." *Education Administration Quarterly* 21:187–203.

Wolf, Margery. 1992. *A Thrice-Told Tale*. Stanford: Stanford University Press.

Woodward, Kathleen. 1991. *Aging and Its Discontents: Freud and Other Fictions*. Bloomington: Indiana University Press.

Index

About the Contributors

NANCY FONER is a Professor of Anthropology at the State University of New York, Purchase. She is author of *The Caregiving Dilemma: Work in an American Nursing Home* (1994), *Ages in Conflict: A Cross-Cultural Perspective on Inequality Between Old and Young* (1984), *Jamaica Farewell: Jamaican Migrants in London* (1978), and editor of the volume *New Immigrants in New York* (1987).

LISA GROGER is an Associate Professor in the Department of Sociology and Anthropology and a Fellow of the Scripps Gerontology Center at Miami University in Oxford, Ohio. She received her Ph.D. in Anthropology from Columbia University.

JABER F. GUBRIUM, Professor of Sociology at the University of Florida in Gainesville, has conducted research on the social organization of care in diverse treatment settings, from nursing homes and physical rehabilitation to counseling centers and family therapy. Gubrium is editor of the *Journal of Aging Studies* and author of *Living and Dying at Murray Manor* (1975), *Describing Care* (1982), *Oldtimers and Alzheimer's* (1986), *Out of Control* (1992), *Speaking of Life* (1993), and co-editor with Andrea Sankar of *Qualitative Methods in Aging Research* (1994).

J. NEIL HENDERSON is an Associate Professor of Psychiatry at the Suncoast Gerontology Center, College of Medicine, and the Department of Community and Family Health, College of Public Health, University of South Florida Health Sciences Center. He is editor of the *Journal of Cross-Cultural Gerontology*.

BARBARA HORNUM is an Associate Professor of Anthropology at Drexel University in Philadelphia. Her publications include *Employment in the Retirement Years: A Survey of Older Americans at Work* (1991).

LYNN D. MASON is Assistant Dean of the Graduate School and an Assistant Professor in the Department of Biometrics and Preventive Medicine at the University of Colorado Health Sciences Center in Denver.

CAROL MCALLISTER is a Research Assistant Professor of Health Services Administration and Anthropology at the University of Pittsburgh. Her original ethnographic research in Malaysia has resulted in several published articles. In addition to her research on aging, her interests include ethnographic approaches to program evaluation, gender and economic change, and cultural forms of resistance.

ATHENA MCLEAN has been a Research Anthropologist at the Philadelphia Geriatric Center and an Adjunct Professor of Anthropology at Temple University. She has studied western medical institutions and their dehumanizing tendencies.

MARGARET PERKINSON is a Research Anthropologist at the Polisher Research Institute of the Philadelphia Geriatric Center. She has directed a four-year program project studying the impact of caregiving on 800 adult daughters and daughters-in-law of single, impaired parents, and is collaborating on a book about this research. She currently directs a study investigating the expressing of emotions among dementia patients in a nursing home.

BETHEL ANN POWERS is an Associate Professor at the University of Rochester School of Nursing in Rochester, New York. She conducts research in the area of long term care, with particular emphasis on issues of nursing home life. She is co-author, with Thomas Knapp, of *A Dictionary of Nursing Theory and Research* (second edition, 1995).

JOEL SAVISHINSKY is a Professor and Chairperson of Anthropology at Ithaca College. He has done research in Turkey, England, the Bahamas, the Canadian North, and rural America. He is the author of *The Trail of the Hare: Environment and Stress in a Sub-Arctic Community* (1994), and *The Ends of*

Time: Life and Work in a Nursing Home (1991), which won the Gerontological Society of America's Kalish Award for Innovative Publishing.

RENÉE ROSE SHIELD is a Clinical Assistant Professor of Community Health at Brown University where she teaches in the Medical School. She is the author of *Uneasy Endings: Daily Life in an American Nursing Home* (1988).

MYRNA SILVERMAN, an Associate Professor of Public Health and Anthropology at the University of Pittsburgh and Director of the Alzheimer's Disease Research Center's Training and Information Core, has conducted research in the fields of aging and long term care for over ten years.

MARIA D. VESPERI is an Associate Professor of Anthropology in the Division of Social Sciences at New College, the honors campus of the Florida State University System. She is author of *City of Green Benches: Growing Old in a New Downtown* (1985).

ISBN 0-89789-422-7

EAN

9 780897 894227

HARDCOVER BAR CODE